Frontiers of Risk Management

Frontiers of Risk Management

Key Issues and Solutions

Volume I

Edited by
Dennis Cox

BEP BUSINESS EXPERT PRESS

Frontiers of Risk Management: Key Issues and Solutions, Volume I

Copyright © Business Expert Press, LLC, 2018.

First published in 2018 by
Business Expert Press, LLC
222 East 46th Street, New York, NY 10017
www.businessexpertpress.com

ISBN-13: 978-1-94709-846-6 (paperback)
ISBN-13: 978-1-94709-847-3 (e-book)

Business Expert Press Finance and Financial Management Collection

Collection ISSN: 2331-0049 (print)
Collection ISSN: 2331-0057 (electronic)

Cover and interior design by Exeter Premedia Services Private Ltd., Chennai, India

First edition: 2018

10 9 8 7 6 5 4 3 2 1

Printed in the United States of America.

Abstract

Frontiers of Risk Management was developed as a text to look at how risk management would develop in the light of Basel II. With an objective of being 10 years ahead of its time, the contributors have actually had even greater foresight. What is clear is that risk management still faces the same challenges as it did 10 years ago. With a series of experts considering financial services risk management in each of its key areas, this book enables the reader to appreciate a practitioner's view of the challenges that are faced in practice identifying where appropriate suitable opportunities. As editor, I have only made changes in the interests of changing regulations but generally have enabled the original text to remain unaltered since it remains as valid today as when originally published.

Keywords

Basel II, credit risk, enterprise risk management, insurance risk, loss data, market risk, operational risk, outsourcing, risk appetite, risk management

Contents

Foreword

The importance of proper risk management, and the consequences of failure to have it in place, have never been greater. Where failure occurs, not just firms but also individuals may face consequences. The FSA's Director of Enforcement, Margaret Cole, said in 2006 that "Failure to manage risks properly is now, more than ever, likely to result in disciplinary action being brought against individuals as well as firms." The FSA has power to censure publicly, fine and even ban individuals from working in the financial services, where there are serious contraventions of the FSA rules.

The Frontiers of Risk Management therefore was initially developed to meet an important need and was well timed. The book was comprehensive in its scope, seeking to cover the entire range of financial services risk management. But that is surely appropriate when firms face so many increasing kinds of risk, not least geopolitical risks and the consequences of climate change. Many of the chapters are extremely topical in terms of current regulatory concern, for example, senior management responsibility (see Chapter 2—Strategic Risk: bringing the discussion into the boardroom), hedge funds (see Chapter 7—The risks within the hedge fund industry), and stress testing (see Chapter 17—Stress testing and risk management) are all areas on which the FSA has focused recently.

As the regulator was moving toward an increasingly principles-based approach, there was a greater expectation on firms to work out for themselves how to satisfy their regulatory obligations, and that they would have less certainty that they are doing so. Good risk management can help to reduce the uncertainty, and provide a road map for senior management on the key areas that require greater attention (as well as helpful documentary evidence and an audit trail for the regulator). Firms that do this well will enjoy a regulatory dividend—less attention and scrutiny from the regulators. Those that have poor risk management will endure more intrusive regulatory examination. However, as Tom Fitzgerald points out in his chapter (Chapter 1—The cultural frontiers of total risk management), risk management is not just about satisfying minimum regulatory compliance but is also at the heart of more effective and efficient business management.

Sometimes risk managers are viewed (perhaps not always unfairly) as a specialist breed, inhabiting the dark spaces between compliance and internal audit. This book demonstrates why risk management should be viewed as a core discipline, at the center of an organization. It deserves to be read by a broad audience.

Originally published in 2007 this reissue is after a 10 year period since the original text is now out of print. The original material is largely republished as first issued with minor changes where necessary. With an original objective of being five years ahead of the market, what perhaps is most surprising is that the material remains at the cutting edge of risk management and accordingly of interest to the current risk market.

Dennis Cox
London May 2018

Introduction

Frontiers of Risk Management was always a bold title for any book to try to live up to. Our objective was simple: to consider the entire spectrum of financial services risk management and to identify the best writers we could who would be able to both appreciate current problems and predict future issues and solutions. We did this in 2007and it is that text which is largely reproduced here. Authors are shown with the positions they held at that time since they wrote based upon their experiences at that time.

While this is an easy objective to write, it is a difficult one for the authors to achieve. Finding authors that really understand the issues, techniques, and practice in the current environment is hard enough. The challenge that we set of asking the authors to go boldly into the future makes this a stimulating and interesting book. I am sure you will agree that all of our authors, each from their own perspective, have risen to achieve these ideals. What is perhaps surprising is that they not only looked to future, but the future they foresaw is still some years away. They were not just a few years ahead, in many cases they were 15 years ahead. When you now read these papers it will be clear to you that people did see the problems that were coming, it was just that firms were not yet acting. In these two volumes of reprint we look at these issues in detail.

Some of the chapters look at mathematical issues, while avoiding detailed discussion of mathematical techniques, while others focus on the practical and qualitative approaches. Some authors were asked to look at risk management from a horizontal industry perspective corporate finance, for example—while others were asked to look at it from a risk perspective for example, the impact of credit ratings. Taken together, they represent a complete current view of thought within the financial services risk-management industry.

The Nature of Change

The financial services risk-management industry is going through a period of unprecedented change. This is driven in part by the guidance issued by the Bank for International Settlements (BIS) and the so-called Basel Accord, which has changed the way that banks will in future calculate regulatory capital. But the Accord goes much further than that and requires management involvement in risk management together with the development of a series of new techniques for new challenges. Some of these have been the subjects of new, specific papers from the BIS; stress testing and liquidity risk management, for example.

What these chapters highlight is that risk management is pervasive throughout a firm, from the chairman to the security guard. While a few may be involved directly with market, credit, or strategic risk, all will be involved with reputational and operational risk. Perhaps the most important issue coming out of the Accord is that operational risk requires a regulatory capital charge and is therefore elevated in importance within the risk-management framework.

The Accord now requires regulatory capital to be set aside for market risk, credit risk, and operational risk, but not in Pillar 1 for strategic risk, reputational risk, or liquidity risk. These are all dealt with in Pillar 2, which means there is no explicit calculation and the capital levels will be effectively set by the local regulator. The main reason for this is that the BIS considers these risks to be difficult to model.

When a board considers risk management within a financial institution, it is for the board to consider all of the risks that may befall a company. There would be little point in having excellent controls over credit, market, and operational risk, only to be wiped out by liquidity risk impacting reputational risk, for example. Then there is the issue of insurance and the extent to which it can protect an institution. Again, there are problems with firms not purchasing insurance for every potential loss situation, but rather for reasonably plausible but painful situations. What would be the point of buying insurance for a loss that is greater than the capital value of the firm? The institution would fail because of the event and the receiver would claim on the insurance!

Of course, it would be nice to be able to say that regulation was the result of deep, meaningful, considered thought developed from academic research through the technical skills of industry professionals. What we actually see is regulation often resulting from public failures that are of such magnitude that the regulators have been required to take action. Sarbanes-Oxley in the United States is perhaps the most obvious recent example of this—the US response to Enron—but it is by no means unique. While regulation developed in haste is repented at leisure, there can be no doubt that these public failures have elevated the science of risk management to a much higher plane.

The Problems with Risk Measurement

Boards need to look at risk holistically, considering all of the risks to which the institution is subject all at the same time. This is easy to say, but difficult to achieve. At the heart of this issue is the problem with measurement of risk, for you cannot have risk management without some form of risk measurement.

We are accustomed to measuring market risk and are generally moving to a mark-to-market basis, with a few exceptions—an approach that effectively looks at current value. Credit risk is different. Here the measurement is primarily based on historic experience judging a current portfolio based on historic accounting principles. Operational risk measurement is a developing skill but makes use of a series of building blocks, including control and risk self-assessment and internal and external loss data. There are no common techniques yet for measuring reputational, strategic, or even liquidity risk, or the BIS would have implemented Pillar 1 rules. To make matters even worse, the BIS rules lead to calculating capital based on differing parts of the risk curve. We shall see this explained in more detail within the various chapters.

So what is the result of all of this? Clearly the modeling approaches are all inconsistent, so it is difficult for a board to take the results of the credit, market, and operational risk measurement systems and come up with a total risk for the institution for these three risks, let alone deal with the others that are not currently modeled.

We recognize this to be one of the greatest challenges to the industry going forward—to deal with the entire spectrum of risks on a consistent basis so that boards, regulators, and other stakeholders can actually have confidence in the stability of these institutions.

What Is the Purpose of Capital?

At the heart of this discussion is the issue of regulatory capital itself. The key question is what is it for? It is one opinion that regulatory capital is not very good at protecting the customer. When things go wrong all of an institution's capital tends to disappear and the depositors still lose out. Clearly the best way for a customer to be protected is either a deposit protection scheme or insurance. Can capital protect an investor? It is hard to argue that it can—the capital is actually part of what the investor is paying for when purchasing an investment. If the capital is dissipated through an unlikely risk event occurring, then their investments will also fall away in value.

There are then only two stakeholders that could be protected by the regulatory capital the market and the regulator. Yet these two stakeholders have opposite objectives. For a market to operate effectively it clearly needs effective and efficient regulation, yet one man's regulation is another's competitive advantage. There is no benefit to a regulator in reducing regulatory capital. When an institution fails as a result of some unlikely event, there will be criticism aimed at the regulator for their failure to regulate adequately the institution and to ensure that the institution had capital adequate to cover this unlikely eventuality that somehow seems more likely in retrospect.

The problem is that banks do fail, for a variety of reasons. History is full of old names of institutions where an event caused their demise, with Barings being only one of the most recent examples. Banks will fail and no amount of regulatory capital or supervisory attention can ever act as a total insurance against this. We can clearly see the tension between the regulators wanting higher capital and the market wanting flexibility operating in the creation of the current regulatory regime.

The Challenge of Regulatory Capital

Thus, if we follow the proposition that regulatory capital is designed to protect the regulators and the market, then it must be that it should be mostly concerned with what might be called unlikely nongoal correlated events—or, in plain English, things we do not expect to happen. That is why we welcome the increased emphasis on both stress testing and scenario modeling.

What financial institutions need to increasingly focus on are these low-incidence, high-impact events that might plausibly occur, but have not occurred to date.

The challenge to the regulators is, therefore, to come up with a basis which will enable them to isolate this part of the risk spectrum from expected risks that are better dealt with through budgeting and product pricing within financial control. The challenge for management is to consider the impact on certainty and planning from such unexpected events.

Of course, no book can be completed without the assistance of a number of people. Our thanks must primarily go to the authors who have all dealt with what was a difficult brief. My thanks also go to Saketh Kaveripatnam of Citigroup who acted as Associate Editor and provided invaluable assistance in the identification of suitable authors combined with constructive criticisms and creative suggestions for this publication; and to Lisette Mermod from Risk Reward Limited for her assistance throughout this process.

Risk management is a discipline that is always dealing with change. An event will occur somewhere that immediately makes you question what you have done to date. Perhaps it is a change to the volatility of an instrument that impacts upon your assumptions within a model; perhaps, instead, it is the occurrence of an operational risk event that you had previously considered impossible. It may, of course, be some form of new legislation or regulation implemented either locally or globally. Whatever the change, one thing that can be said with certainty is that risk management is a developing discipline that will continue to evolve over future months and years.

The Following Decade

It is ten years since this work was first produced and this was just prior to the financial crisis. The expectations included within this text were not fulfilled and indeed it is the current regulatory requirements that are now driving their implementation. Indeed perhaps the failure of the market to recognize the importance of risk management as key to the success of a firm probably was a major contributor to the crisis occurring. Now we have moved on from Basel 2 to Basel 3 and its revisions, but has risk management improved? In another work I have set out in a nutshell the practical steps a firm should take. Indeed Risk Management in a Nutshell can be taken as a text that underpins much of what is here.

In this revised edition in two parts I have sought to be faithful to the original text from 2007 and have only made changes where they were clearly necessary. I am sure that any reader will gain something from some of the material here and identify common themes. For me the continued failure of some firms to recognize that the currency of their firm is risk with results being a consequence of the calculated taking of risk remains a disappointment. Too many firms still have failed to appreciate how risk management should be embedded and what they need to do in practice. Risk management is a driver to the success of any firm and this text seeks to provide some pointers. Written by industry professionals who were at the leading edge of the development of this subject I hope you find this revised text of interest.

Dennis Cox
London, 2018.

Dennis Cox
Risk Reward Limited

PART I

Total Risk Management

CHAPTER 1

The Cultural Frontiers of Total Risk Management

Dennis Cox

Risk Reward Ltd

Introduction

Peter Bernstein's *Against the Gods*[1] illustrates how the remarkable story of risk has been an ever-evolving one, where the frontiers of risk have continually been pushed back with new breakthroughs in our understanding of risk and consequently in our improved ability to identify, measure, and manage risk. Best practices in risk management continue to be designed, defined, and refined by industry participants and their stakeholders. Indeed, there are libraries of books, reams of research papers, and years of discussion dedicated to the continual improvements that are being made in risk identification, measurement, and management. This will remain a perpetual frontier of risk management. However, rather than revisiting these best practices, I would like to focus on some of the other challenges faced by risk managers today. For many, one of the key frontiers is not to design or define new best practices—it is to embed established best practices in the management of their firms. In facing this frontier, the challenge is neither conceptual nor computational, it is in fact cultural.

Risk managers face many challenges today in supporting their businesses. These include the increasing demands on our industry by regulators, investors, and legislators. Regulators have redefined the minimum

---

[1] Peter, B. 1996. *Against the Gods—The Remarkable Story of Risk*. New York, NY: Wiley.

capital adequacy standards for the industry via Basel II and its successors. Rating agencies and investors are increasingly demanding about the standards of risk disclosures by firms. Legislators, via the Sarbanes-Oxley Act and similar papers, are increasingly holding management boards personally responsible for the corporate governance of their firms. Management boards, in turn, are consequently becoming more demanding of their own risk functions. This is a very heavy change agenda for risk managers and one which often meets with significant cultural challenges in many firms—particularly in more traditional firms. We will now review some of the cultural challenges faced by risk managers.

Beyond Minimum Compliance

Of the multifarious challenges faced by risk managers today, the increasing regulation of our industry has understandably attracted much focus. Despite the heavy regulatory burden, we need to remain mindful not to focus solely on minimum regulatory compliance. In an era of increasing regulatory demands, where compliance fatigue is a common industry ailment, it is easy to forget our primary purpose; that of more effective and efficient business management for our shareholders. The danger is that firms develop a culture of minimum compliance. Of course, regulatory compliance can often be compatible with better enterprise risk management. For example, the development of internal rating models is not just a means to achieving regulatory compliance. Rating models are merely decision tools that must be utilized better to manage risk and extract business benefits. For example, the development of Basel-compliant models, which are externally validated by regulators, will open up new opportunities to mitigate risk in portfolios, which previously could not easily be traded due to difficulties of consistently measuring different risks in different firms. The emphasis on model use is a common and necessary theme throughout the Basel II use test requirements.

Improved Risk Communication

As a result of the increasing regulation and complexity of our business, there are growing requirements for better risk communication with all stakeholders. Internal stakeholders need to understand the more complex regulatory capital impacts on their businesses and how their firms need to respond strategically. Risk managers must proactively engage the business generators in their firms by communicating the strategic context of the change agenda and facilitating their firms in responding strategically to those changes. Business generators, who have their own market-driven priorities, also need to engage with and support risk managers. Without such a partnership approach, neither will achieve their strategic objectives from the heavy change agenda.

Risk management itself is ever evolving. In the same way that risk managers utilize the tools of modern portfolio management theory and value-at-risk methodologies, they must also utilize the communication skills within their toolboxes. In doing so, they must move away from the boilerplate language, with its often specialist jargon, and engage stakeholders on their terms. This is both a cultural challenge and an opportunity for risk managers to be more centrally involved in the management of their firms.

Enterprise Risk Management

With management board members now personally responsible for the corporate governance of their firms, they are rightly more demanding of their risk functions in terms of risk comprehension and risk assurance. Management boards are responsible for the economic health of the entire business and are consequently more interested in an integrated view of all risks and how these risks might change and interact in response to various scenarios. This is often termed an enterprise risk management (ERM) approach which encompasses credit, market, operational, and other material risks[2] for the enterprise as a whole. An ERM approach is very different to the traditional "silo-based" approach to risk management where different risk components are managed in separate silos (e.g., credit risk vs. market risk) with little interaction between silos. An ERM approach to risk management seeks to create the ability to integrate risks

---

[2] Other risks include business risk, structural balance-sheet risks, reputational risks, pension risks, and so on.

and report them at consolidated levels while recognizing potential diversification benefits both within and across risks. The Risk Management Association (RMA) defines ERM as:

> a holistic approach to measuring and managing major risk types based on their simultaneous consideration (and inter-relationships where appropriate), thus allowing an institution to understand and adjust its risk exposures in an overall risk-reward framework.[3]

There is already much literature available on what an ERM approach entails. Suffice to say, management boards need to refocus on an integrated view of risks across their enterprises and accordingly will seek risk assurances in a similar vein. However, introducing an ERM approach is a major undertaking for any firm and poses significant cultural challenges.

Integration of Risk Silos

These cultural challenges arise as many firms still manage their risks quite strictly within risk silos. This silo-based approach often pervades the entire risk infrastructure of a firm, including its systems, processes, and people. Risk information systems are often designed specifically for one risk type and can impede integration or aggregation with other risk types. In addition to the difficulties in integrating risk information across risk silos, risk information can sometimes be difficult to integrate with other related information (such as earnings), thereby making it more difficult to evaluate risk—reward trade-offs either within or across risk types. Decision-making processes also tend to have different risk committees and risk personnel who evaluate different risks based on different evaluation criteria.

For example, while a VaR[4] approach to market risk is well accepted in many firms, there is no reason why a credit VaR approach could not equally be employed in the same firms. Aside from the obvious but

---

[3] RMA Survey 2003. *Negotiating the Risk Mosaic*, conducted by First Manhattan Consulting Group.

[4] Value-at-Risk (VaR).

surmountable data constraints, why is it acceptable for a quantitative portfolio management approach to be adopted for one risk type (i.e., market risk) and not for another (i.e., credit risk) within the same firm? Even where different risks are not easily aggregated, we need to begin to speak the same language—for example, economic capital—and develop nomenclature across risk categories if we are to have an integrated view of enterprise risks.

However, while changing the systems and processes in a firm is one thing, changing the embedded staff culture of a firm is another entirely. Herein lies the real cultural challenge for any enterprise in seeking to adopt a more integrated approach to risk management. In many firms, risk professionals tend to operate in one silo (e.g., credit risk) with little interaction with other silos (e.g., market risk) and consequently tend to have little understanding of, or perhaps interest in, other risks. Moreover, professional progression and reward is often based on technical expertise within one silo and consequently those who succeed in becoming senior risk officers tend to have the majority of their experience in only one risk silo. Where this happens, risk managers do not receive the best preparation for understanding or managing enterprise-wide risks.

Staff Development

The divisions between risk silos are in many ways cultural divisions. To break down these cultural divisions, firms must invest in extensive training and development of their staff so that they can take a more integrated view of enterprise risks. They must encourage and promote job rotation across risk types in order to break down the artificial barriers between different risk silos. Job rotation between risk functions and the business also need to be encouraged so that the symbiotic nature of their relationship is recognized by all. Equally, staff must be willing, and incentivized if necessary, to become more risk-literate and consequently more quantitatively literate. Unless this is done, an ERM approach will remain an aspirational objective in many firms.

In addition to the training and development of staff, many firms may also need to look to the skills balance of staff across risk functions. In many traditional firms today, the majority of risk professionals remain focused on credit risks such that the cost of credit risk management is often a multiple of the actual expected loss for a portfolio. This is despite increasing evidence that the major killer risks faced by firms are increasingly of a nontraditional or operational risk nature. While credit risk probably remains the primary risk source for many firms, is the high concentration of risk staff in credit risk functions justifiable when this is the area of risk in which firms have developed the most experience and expertise over many years? This is sometimes exacerbated by the type of risk analysis undertaken where credit risk professionals are focused on transaction-by-transaction credit approval rather than on overall portfolio management.

Proactive Portfolio Management

While financial firms are in the business of actively taking on risks, once assumed these risks must also be proactively managed while simultaneously recognizing their contribution to portfolio dynamics. However, this does not always occur, particularly where there is no trading-book discipline. Even firms which have developed sophisticated performance measurement models for loan origination purposes are sometimes guilty of poor portfolio management thereafter. For example, many firms calculate the RAROC[5] or EVA[6] of every transaction at origination, which takes into account complex economic capital calculations and transactional optionalities. However, once these loans are underwritten, little portfolio management may then be evident. While one can confidently assert that such transactions add shareholder value at the "point in time" of origination, one cannot be as confident as these assets season or as their risk profiles inevitably fluctuate over time. This demonstrates the limitations of any point-in-time metrics, no matter how sophisticated. Portfolios need to be proactively re-evaluated and managed over time; not just at origination or default.

Proactive portfolio management does not end with ongoing risk evaluation. Risk managers also need to go further and ask the fundamental

---

[5] Risk-Adjusted Return on Capital (RAROC).
[6] Economic Value Added (EVA).

question—so what? It is insufficient to determine whether a portfolio is value-enhancing or not. Portfolios must also be proactively managed using various risk management and mitigation techniques. For example, where a portfolio is outperforming expectations due to a tightening of market spreads, this is not necessarily the time to rest in the knowledge of a good investment decision. Indeed, good portfolio management may dictate that the embedded value of these assets be realized rather than waiting for market spreads to widen again. Alternatively, we may believe spreads will continue to narrow and increase our position. This is proactive portfolio management, which is rarely passive.

While most firms have made significant progress in developing their risk measurement capabilities, many firms have further to go in implementing proactive portfolio management models. Such portfolio management requires significant cultural change from the traditional banking model where lenders sometimes feel personal ownership over "their assets." It requires the functional separation of loan origination and portfolio management. This is a critical step in moving away from the transaction-by-transaction approach to risk so favored by the traditionalists. It allows a firm to optimize its overall shareholder return and to minimize nasty surprises. Without a portfolio management view of risk, how can a firm identify risk concentrations or diversification benefits? How can it provide incentives to increase portfolio diversification or disincentives to the build-up of any undue concentration risks in a portfolio? Such objectives are very difficult to achieve without a portfolio management view of risks. Loan originators can continue to underwrite business on a case-by-case basis but risk managers must manage risk at the portfolio level.

Raising the Bar

This illustrates that cultural change is not driven solely by regulation and is also a prerequisite for good business management, which must remain our primary objective. Indeed, most of the Pillar 1 requirements of Basel II were already being fulfilled by the advanced firms in our industry. Indeed even the Basel III requirements focus on capital as being the answer with liquidity to any problems. It is these advanced firms that are continuing to push back the frontiers of risk management with regulators by seeking more independence to utilize their own more sophisticated and risk-sensitive risk methodologies rather than the prescriptive regulatory rules in Basel II/III. This interaction with regulators and policy makers will inevitably lead to better regulation for the entire industry by raising the bar for all.

Despite this, Basel II/III will not necessarily lead to a leveling of the risk management playing field. Whereas many firms are struggling with the regulatory compliance challenges, the more advanced firms are already moving on and will always continue to develop more sophisticated risk management infrastructures. Later iterations of the Basel Accord should reward this increasing sophistication and raise the bar further for the entire industry. This increasing sophistication also needs to be recognized by stakeholders other than regulators; however, such recognition will not happen by right. It is also behoven upon risk managers to demonstrate and communicate their superior risk management capabilities. This, too, is a cultural challenge.

Improved Risk Disclosure Standards

Improved communication with stakeholders will become a critical requirement if firms are to achieve the benefit of their improved risk management capabilities. Moody's Investor Services recently produced a damning commentary on the *Risk Disclosures of Banks and Financial Firms*.[7] Its main findings are summarized as follows:

> Moody's overall opinion is that the current risk disclosures of banks and security firms fail to inform on the full scope and nature of risk exposures and risk mitigation efforts of these firms. The following are our top level observations:
>
> • Disclosures tend to be limited to measures such as VaR, which give an incomplete picture of risk and use mostly boilerplate language.

[7] *Risk Disclosures of Banks & Financial Firms*, Moody's Investor Services, May 2006.

- Contextual and qualitative elements necessary to understand the real magnitude of exposures and risks typically lack depth.
- There is no standardized format across firms surveyed: risk disclosures are uneven in size and quality, and they are scattered across annual reports.
- Finally, risk disclosures basically lack the minimum reliability requirements for relevant and consistent comparisons across firms.

The Moody's report did not suggest that surveyed firms did not have sophisticated risk management capabilities: rather that their disclosure practices were lacking. Across the industry, however, we can certainly expect some causal link between the sophistication of risk infrastructures and the quality of risk disclosures. Indeed, the quality of risk disclosures represents a potential area for firms to achieve a competitive advantage over their peers and to achieve an additional investment return from their risk infrastructures. Rating agencies and other stakeholders obviously take the quality and sophistication of risk management practices into account in evaluating firms. It is, therefore, imperative for firms not only to have best-in-class risk management practices but also to be able to communicate such practices to stakeholders.

Investor Relations

It is inevitable that the wider investment community will also require similar improvements in disclosure standards in order to identify those firms with superior risk management capabilities. Banks and financial firms are unlike other entities in that they actively seek out risk-taking opportunities. As a result, investors cannot realistically be expected to distinguish between different financial firms based solely on traditional performance multiples without reference to the amount, type, and volatility of risks a firm undertakes (its risk profile) and how it manages and mitigates those risks (its risk strategy). How long then before investment brokers also begin to really challenge firm's vis-à-vis the quality of their risk disclosures?

If a bank already has a comprehensive and effective risk management infrastructure, such disclosures will already be utilized in managing the firm and can easily be reproduced with different emphases for different external audiences. A superior risk management capability should lead to more sustainable economic performance and fewer nasty surprises for investors, particularly when the economic environment is less favorable. Such a capability should also lead to competitive advantages in terms of capital requirements, external ratings and, consequently, investment efficiency and performance. Needless to say, this will only happen when the quality of risk disclosures improves significantly beyond current standards. In the interim, investors will continue to judge the quality of firms' risk infrastructures by the quality of their financial performances and by comparing the content, frequency, and timeliness of their various risk disclosures.

Regulatory Relations

Regulators are also moving in this direction as is evident from Pillars 2 and 3 of the Basel II Accord. Whereas Pillar 3 will formally address some of the public disclosure requirements, Pillar 2 will require firms to describe and explain to regulators the process by which they ensure their capital adequacy. Significantly, there is no distinction in these later pillars between standardized and advanced status. The regulatory prescriptions around capital adequacy and public disclosures will apply equally to all firms. In fact, Pillar 2 is probably the most challenging component of Basel II, requiring, as it does for the first time, a more holistic risk assessment across the entire firm. As a result, it is Pillar 2, rather than Pillar 1, that will transform the frontiers of risk management.

The internal capital adequacy assessment process (ICAAP) of Pillar 2 requires firms to identify and assess all material risks, to describe how these risks are managed and how internal capital is adequately attributed to these risks. This process must be consistent with a firm's current risk profile and must be embedded into the business strategy and decision making of the firm. As a result, the requirements of Pillar 2 are consistent with an ERM approach to business management and should result in a much-changed relationship between firms and their supervisors.

Supervisory Outsourcing

Significantly, supervisors are not being overly prescriptive about how firms ensure capital adequacy. The lack of prescriptive detail is both an opportunity and a challenge for firms. It is an opportunity for firms to design their own bespoke ICAAP that is intimately tied to their own risk profile, business strategies, and environment. It allows firms to focus on business benefits while at the same time achieving regulatory compliance. More significantly, supervisors are effectively outsourcing to firms the supervisory modeling that they traditionally undertook themselves at an industry level. This supervisory outsourcing is most apparent in the nonprescriptive nature of the ICAAP and in the stress-testing requirements in particular. Firms need to have a rigorous and comprehensive stress-testing program in place which is meaningful to the portfolio characteristics of each individual firm. This is a significant and welcome change of emphasis by regulators and will allow firms to use their own scenario analysis capabilities for regulatory stress testing.

There are significant sanctions for firms who have an inadequate ICAAP, particularly considering the lack of distinction between advanced and standardized approaches. Where firms can demonstrate, however, that they have a rigorous and well-understood ICAAP, they should benefit from a more favorable capital treatment. That is, if supervisors are to promote more sophisticated risk management practices, they must also provide a positive correlation between the capital required to adequately address a firm's risks and the strength of its risk infrastructure. Of course, a superior risk management capability is not just about capital efficiency, it is also a sine qua non for good business management, which is our primary objective. Moreover, a well-defined and rigorous ICAAP will also meet many of the disclosure requirements of external stakeholders discussed earlier. As the Basel II Accord and the Moody's disclosure report demonstrate, however, inadequate risk disclosures will no longer be tolerated by external stakeholders. Neither should inadequate risk reporting be tolerated by management boards.

Cultural Challenges

Overall, great progress is being made by all firms in developing more sophisticated risk management infrastructures. This progress is being made at a time of unprecedented regulatory, legislative, and market demands. Some of the major challenges faced by many risk managers are not regulatory, legislative, or market-driven, however; they are, in fact, internal cultural challenges. More importantly, without cultural change, many firms may continue to manage their businesses suboptimally.

Occasionally at risk conferences, bankers can be heard openly discussing the issues of the day. A number of themes are common. First, risk managers not only speak passionately about the capability and potential of their improved risk management infrastructures, but they also talk about the project fatigue from regulatory compliance and the difficulties in embedding change in firms. Second, lenders discuss their difficulties in achieving RAROC hurdles when credit spreads tighten, as they have done in many markets over the last few years. Are these lenders' views invariant to market risks? Do they consider a business line is no longer viable at current margins and exit this market? Alternatively, do they believe the market spreads have overshot and do they continue to underwrite business, in order to maintain market share, even though they think it may be destroying shareholder value? By underwriting such business, are they merely contributing to the (real or perceived) overshooting of the risk—reward relationship? What is the tolerance for such behavior within the firm? What would they do if they thought of the conundrum as a shareholder instead of as an employee? How aware, if at all, are shareholders of this regular conundrum?

These questions are, in many ways, queries about the risk culture of the firm. If a firm has a strong risk culture such questions are readily understood and addressed. Developing such a risk culture, however, is not easily achieved as it must permeate all levels of an organization. The management board may define the risk culture and set the "tone from the top" but it is often behoven upon the risk management function to embed this risk culture throughout the organization. A risk culture does not merely come about top-down: it has to be nurtured, developed, and embedded in an organization.

This is a major challenge for most firms and one that falls heavily on the shoulders of risk functions in these firms. Risk managers cannot, however, effect cultural change on their own. They need to bring their colleagues with them on a journey. To do this, risk managers must also be willing to change. Moreover, they must be supported and championed by their own management boards. Only then will shareholders realize the full business benefits of the huge investments being made in risk infrastructures. This is in many ways one of the real frontiers of risk management today. *Plus Áa change, plus c'est la même chose.*

CHAPTER 2

Strategic Risk: Bringing the Discussion into the Boardroom

Craig Cohon

The Next Practice

Financial institutions and their leaders are very comfortable discussing market risks in terms of equity and fixed income risk, derivatives, treasury, asset and liability risks, and hedge-fund risks. In addition, a large proportion of time is spent on developing models, processes and systems to look at credit risk. With Basel II and Sarbanes-Oxley, operational risk management and the importance and quality of internal processes and controls are self-evident. This is a comfortable way to look at strategic risk.

A more holistic approach, is the well thought-through strategic risk models put together by Adrian J. Slywotzky and John Drzik of Mercer Management that look at industry, technology, brand, customer, competitor, project, and stagnation risks.

Strategic risk, however, should challenge and explore the very basis of the firm and the business model. These two approaches miss a key component.

Strategic risk is not only about reputation. It is about the long-term survival of business as we know it. It is about building additional sustainable value into your business. Many leaders tend to think about this in terms of more active and strategic government, communications, or external relations. It is not.

This chapter will provide answers to two important topic areas and articulate an initial plan to better understand and evaluate this strategic risk:

- How can you bring strategic risk into the boardroom and make it a robust and relevant discussion?
- Is strategic risk the same in developed and emerging markets? What are the key components of this strategic risk?

Strategic Risk as a Boardroom Responsibility

Often, integrated strategic risk never makes it into a boardroom discussion. This is looking at multiple risks and ensuring that leadership evaluates risks that viewed together could have a very different profile for the firm. Boards are often left to make decisions based on what might be only gut instinct and high-level summary. Why?

Different components of overall risk usually get buried in operating units within the firm. For instance, industry risk, which includes risks such as margin squeeze, rising R&D/capital expenditure costs, overcapacity, commoditization of products, deregulation, and extreme business-cycle volatility, is often vetted by the CFO.

Technology risk and shifts in technology, patent expiry, outsourcing, and process improvements often stop at a lower level in the IT department.

Brand risks, social legitimacy and CSR (Corporate Social Responsibility) risks rest with corporate affairs or a committee of the board.

Strategy departments often look at competitive risk and analyze emerging global rivals, consumer trends, gradual market-share gainers, and one-off competitors in local markets.

Shifting customer priorities, increasing customer power, "me-too product" development and over-reliance on chasing the same few corporate or high net-worth customers fall on the shoulders of the product development teams.

Summarizing and synthesizing all these risks can lead to a very different conclusion and forward strategy. Bringing it together allows the board to look at new and innovative ways to manage the risk and take advantage of trends in the industry. Two examples outlined as follows highlight the issue.

The first concerns not seeing the industry convergence between the banking and telecom sector. If the retail banking sector had synthesized risk categories and looked beyond the traditional industry players might have pre-empted this rapidly growing competitive threat.

• For instance, cell-phone technology coupled with remittances of more than US$12bn in the Philippines led to the
creation of an innovative telecom banking solution. SMART
phone continues to threaten established banks in the region.
SMART money is the ultimate in cashless convenience.
A consumer simply transfers cash through the cell phone
to pay bills, shop and reload "pay as you go" time.

The second example concerns not spotting consumer trends and calculating forward risk in a large merger in the media/Internet arena. Furthermore, if boards had integrated consumer trends thinking and long-term value creation, they might have spotted the high-level risk in the AOL/Time Warner merger in 2000.

• A merger gone wrong—the AOL/Time Warner merger was
driven by the convergence of media and the rapid rise of the
Internet. Fuelled by emotion and senior management egos
and the desire to be bigger and bolder, this merger missed the
key consumer insight. Consumers were becoming unwilling
to pay for e-mail and content access. Customers converted to
free services in the thousands and have fled the AOL brand.
The write-down of the AOL assets continues to be significant.

These examples demonstrate the need for a simple and highly efficient integrated strategic risk process. There is a simple four-step plan to bring the discussion into the boardroom and ensure value is created for the firm.

Step One—Change the Language Throughout the Organization

It is the responsibility of senior management to reframe the language asso-ciated with strategic risk. The language should focus on three elements:

- Continue to ask for risk analysis that highlights important issues;
- Request leadership not only to develop risk mitigation plans but create the necessary innovation to reduce the risk; and
- Once the innovation is highlighted, articulate the strategy to implement the innovation.

This simple reframing will help move the organization from a negative and often defensive frame to a positive solution-driven mode.

Step Two—Develop Systems for the Siloed Risk Analysis to Be Shared Across the Group

The individual risks are seldom shared across divisions or business units. Therefore, when the risks become aggregated the overall impact on the organization is only seen too late in the process. Leaders should develop a risk, innovation and strategy quarterly review with the most senior managers in the firm. The rigorous implementation of this process is critical. This step allows the top leadership team to understand deeply the different risks and begin to have a common view on a total, strategic risk profile for the firm.

Step Three—Synthesize the Risks, Articulate the Necessary Innovation and Develop a Strategic Way Forward

This is the most difficult step. It is often left to the CEO to integrate all the thinking and determine the best way forward. Organizations are great at analysis and often poor at synthesis. It should be the responsibility of the senior leadership team to take the time and develop the capability to scan across and innovate. They will have to think very strategically about the firm. Together, they should create the capacity to understand deeply the entire risk and opportunity space.

Step Four—Engage the Board in a Yearly Strategic Workshop

Engaging the board is the final, critical step. We often "dumb down" board meetings and make them highly orchestrated review sessions.

Boards should be thought of as strategic support as well as external oversight. Most board members only use a small amount of their total skills and intellect during board meetings. Develop a yearly workshop that allows the board to really understand all risks across the firm and help develop the strategic way forward.

This four-step process has the following benefits.

- It enables mitigation of the total risks and makes sense to protect company stability.
- It develops tools and systems for thinking systematically about the future and identifying opportunities.
- It turns strategic threats into growth opportunities.
- Capital can be better utilized and its costs reduced.
- Organizing systems and processes will increase the Risk-Adjusted Return on Capital (RAROC) of the firm.
- Corporate reputation is protected.
- It helps companies to fend off additional regulatory and legislative assaults on how they run their businesses.
- It helps corporate executives to defend themselves against lawsuits of the sort that have been filed against former Enron, Tyco, and WorldCom executives.

Strategic risk as a board responsibility will allow better thinking and strategic development for the firm. The other key strategic risk is outlined in the next part of this chapter.

- Is strategic risk the same in developed and emerging markets? What are the key components of this strategic risk?

The Developing World and Strategic Risk

Financial services organizations have felt the renewed strategic risk of a significantly increased regulatory environment and highly aware public. There has been the failure of the unregulated Enron and many of the financial titans of Wall Street have been put on notice a number of times through heavy financial fines. From Japan to London, the industry is under the lens of not just a watchdog but also of an aggressive pack of regulatory and civil society wolves.

Some companies and highly experienced CEOs see the risks coming and understand them. They then plan for this change and create the right systems, culture, processes, and measurement to reduce the risk. Others miss out.

Furthermore, leaders and their companies that do not deeply understand the risks of operating in emerging markets may take short cuts and get into trouble. Get it wrong here and disaster can strike.

The Western public's understanding that the highest global standards should be imposed on corporations has further accelerated the risk of losing social legitimacy. Most leaders in the financial services industry have understood this risk and have actively put policies and procedures in place to deal with the developing world.

PR and policy implementation, however, is different from a fundamental change to one's business model. The board-level discussions that occur when financial institutions are faced with a new form of risk in a developed market must occur for developing markets, just as would be the case for any other risk.

The Emerging Consumer—Not What You Think

These new potential consumers in emerging markets are very diverse in habits, attitudes and behavior. They may be very local but have immense aspirations. Income may come from a variety of sources including traditional work, highly entrepreneurial local activity, and even remittances from family within and across national borders.

Despite this, most financial institutions are not innovating to identify new types of customers. Not actively investing in this option has a significant strategic risk that could reduce shareholder value over time and destroy future brand value. Why does this happen?

Types of Missed Opportunity

There are three types of strategic opportunity risk that will be explored:

- Opting out of new growth opportunities;
- Not recognizing possibilities for innovation; and
- Missing the new competitive threat.

Opting out of new growth opportunities. The largest national and multinational corporate clients will also be on every financial institution's target list. Just providing the same services as the competition is unlikely to be a successful strategy. In the developed markets and emerging markets with this segmentation frame, the battle continues to be fought with ever-increasing competition for a growing but limited pie. While the total available capital pool is increasing, the cost of customer acquisition and retention is also increasing and the pace of that growth is often dependent on international and national macroeconomic factors.

The risk here is of opting out of increasing the revenue pie and building deeper and more profound lasting relationships with a whole new consumer segment.

Not recognizing possibilities for innovation. If you do not think a market exists, then it is difficult to create a business to service that market. Even if a market has been identified, often credit procedures, distribution models, product and service solutions, marketing and HR practices are within a similar corporate framework. Indeed, the regulations driven by the BIS require this to be the case. The conclusion that this cost structure cannot support this market is often therefore right; little innovation takes place, the business does not get leadership attention and does not expand. Actually, it is often killed. Even so, the opportunity to innovate with these consumers will be throughout every part of the business model.

There is a basic need for innovation in product and service solutions for credit, savings, equity and insurance. New credit and deposit systems and procedures need to be put in place. Interesting and innovative, low-cost distribution models are required to increase access that can be leveraged with the help of technology, especially cell-phone banking.

There is the risk that new entrants will figure out how to develop financial products and services for an emerging consumer segment, develop a profitable business model, create grassroots social legitimacy and build a compelling long-term business proposition.

Missing the new competitive threat. If you believe that a market does not exist, then you will not enter it. If you do not innovate, then you will not be in a position to see the emerging consumer as an opportunity, but someone else will. They will develop a new business model. They will get the cost structure down to a point where the business is run on a primarily variable cost basis. They will take the license to operate in this consumer space away from the established players. They will be entrepreneurial and agile. They will experiment relentlessly and they will create value.

Commercial and investment banks, insurance companies and certain private equity and financial advisory firms are all vulnerable. These new financial service companies will potentially become experts on innovation with emerging consumers and use their capability to build relevant business models to disrupt traditional banking sectors.

These new market entrants are potentially able to give similar value and service at lower costs with greater product and service innovation. It is happening today and is a trend that will accelerate.

Financial institutions should undertake a fundamental risk-reduction assessment. Furthermore, a structure and plan should be developed to capture the opportunity and challenge the very basis of the firm and its business model. The final section of this chapter lays out the initial roadmap.

To reduce the risk, one must start by asking different questions. The strategic risk assessment should include some of the following questions.

- The opportunity—do I see an opportunity with the emerging consumer? What is the opportunity? Is it part of my strategic plan? If not, why not? What is preventing my organization from capturing this market opportunity?
- Organizational readiness—how do I think about the market? What are the best areas for us to commit resources? Can I pilot a new business model without the system killing it? Will it take energy and focus away from our core operations? What am I missing?
- Outside support—do I have the skills and knowledge, mental attitudes and beliefs on the inside of the firm to capture this opportunity? Will the politics and technocrats get in the way? Do I need an outside catalyst?

Once these questions have been answered, then you can move to testing this market space.

Here are the four key guidelines to follow:

• Set up an independent team;
• Deeply understand the emerging consumer;
• Create constrained innovation and develop the business model from the ground up; and
• Learn before investing.

Set up an independent team. Find a highly entrepreneurial team of young professionals and give them the space to innovate in one market. Watch out for the five traps.

• *The team recruitment trap.* The wrong people are recruited for the team. This type of work calls for an entrepreneurial skill and knowledge base. This is often hard to find in large companies. Setting up a typical corporate team on this will not get you the breakthrough concept development. The teams are often too risk-averse and think of success in corporate terms versus entrepreneurial terms. The killer instinct and passion is often lacking.
• *Company inertia kills the innovation before it can develop.* The company, not the individuals, often acts as the devil's advocate. This means that the internal inertia, company policies, politics and overall skepticism of the organization kills the innovation and does not listen to the insights before they have the chance to be developed into a new business concept.
• *Leadership control—typical governance.* Corporate leaders like to be in control. "Updates, review sessions, pre-reads . . . leadership must be in the details or they don't get the job done." This space is about the art of letting go as a leader. The team creates upward dependency on the leadership to have the answer and never fully develops its own unique thinking and business idea.
• *Death by PowerPoint.* The business never actually gets built. You get a PowerPoint presentation at the end of six months (a business concept on paper). This often happens because

the default setting is to push away any model that does not fit with the existing proven successful structure. Taking on the existing business model and creating something that bumps up against this is threatening to the organization. The Power-Point deck dies and never turns into a pilot business model.

- *You don't know what you don't know.* This is the highest risk. Companies and most individuals in them do not know how to work in this new area. The data are not easily available. Therefore, the team does not ask the right questions or put the process in place to discover the deep insights that can create the breakthrough. Once the team is in place, however, it is critical to understand the new consumer.

Deeply understand the new consumer. The traditional approach in this space is to look at income as the surrogate for defining the market opportunity. However, this only scratches the surface.

Creating a scalable business in an entirely new market demands the development of consumer insights, value propositions, product design criteria and market analytics (including data sources) from the bottom up. Methodologies and frameworks, databases and algorithms, and embedded assumptions and conclusions that are applied by companies in mature market settings generally do not apply in these new markets—and often impede the definition of a realizable growth opportunity.

- New consumers may not operate according to mature market consumer expectations and patterns.
- Existing consumer practices and product uses are very heterogeneous, even within local and micro-markets.
- Reliable, statistically valid data are scarce—or simply does not exist in the private sector.
- Companies only superficially understand user requirements and values, and the untested assumptions of managers have not been challenged in the market.

To understand the new consumer, begin to take the following three steps.

- Get close: develop an immersion program where you can have direct, intensive exposure to the lives of the new consumers and their user/market environment.
- Do the analysis: implement a research phase in which the company develops the data, methodological and analytical foundation in the following areas: (i) deep, qualitative consumer insights and ethnographic research; (ii) market sizing and segmentation; (iii) existing product price-performance analysis; (iv) product solution evaluation; (v) local route to market benchmarking; and (vi) environmental analysis.
- Validate and integrate: use the previous analysis to develop and statistically validate consumer hypotheses and value propositions, design criteria and the conditions for the new business model.

Create constrained innovation and develop the business model from the ground up. There should be four conditions imposed:

- The innovation must result in a product or service of world-class quality.
- The innovation must achieve a significant price reduction— at least 90 percent off the cost of a comparable produce or service.
- The innovation must be scalable: it must be able to be produced, marketed and used in many locales and circumstances.
- The innovation must be affordable.

Learn before investing. Think big, start small and scale fast—before a global business case is developed, learn how to create a business with new consumers in three phases.

Prototype—get the business model right. Work with consumers to develop product and service offering, test new route-to-market opportunities with existing infrastructure. Get the right team in place to lead this business.

Pilot—begin to put some capital into the business idea and see if the model can pay out. Start to understand the global standards necessary (IT infrastructure, brand, governance, etc.) from the local nuanced and relevant consumer opportunities (product and route-to-market innovation).

Scale—slowly develop the ability to scale and conservatively put additional capital to go deeper within a market or begin operations across markets.

CHAPTER 3

Risk Management and Corporate Finance

Frank Moxon

Evolution Securities Limited

Introduction

It is tempting in today's heavily regulated securities industry to think that risk is something to be eliminated or avoided in order both to achieve full regulatory compliance and maximize profitability. All business activities, however, involve some degree of risk and most entrepreneurial managers, at least, acknowledge that risks often need to be taken in order to gain a competitive advantage or to secure higher financial returns. Among the issues, therefore, facing senior management in any business enterprise are:

- the identification of key risks within the business;
- the establishment of an effective risk management and reporting system to record the actual incidence of risk and ensure that it is mitigated quickly and efficiently; and
- the review, maintenance, and upgrading of those systems from time to time.

While senior management may not fully understand certain business activities under their control, as was clearly demonstrated in the Nick Leeson affair at Barings Bank, a well thought-out operational risk management system should enable them to control and mitigate risks in these areas.

There is a wide range of risks faced by any investment bank but those in corporate finance tend to be specific to that particular discipline. In contrast, many of the risks faced by staff trading in equities, bonds, and currencies or advising or acting as an agent for private, institutional or other investors are identical or at least fairly similar in nature. To this end, it is essential that in establishing an effective operational risk management system for a corporate finance business the experience and expertise of a firm's central management team is optimized by the flexible application of the professional expertise of the firm's senior corporate finance practitioners. If handled properly, this in itself can be an educational and performance-enhancing experience in its own right. In the words of General George Patton, "Don't tell people how to do something. Tell them what to do and let them surprise you with their ingenuity."

Other chapters in this book cover the main concepts behind the need for and the effective management and measurement of risk management procedures in general. During the remainder of this chapter, I intend, mainly, to restrict the subject to the issues faced by corporate financiers in particular.

Overall Risk Environment

There is often a tendency among corporate financiers to consider themselves to be in a far less-risky environment than their trading counterparts. After all, corporate finance is a profession governed by financial services laws and regulations, market rulebooks, and internal procedures manuals. The corporate financier is often aided by legal and other professional advisers and can usually count on his compliance department to act as an additional resource in times of doubt. As much as regulators might operate, often retrospectively, as policemen, they can also act as helpful consultants or interlocutors, for example, the UKLA readers involved in some Official List transactions.

To this fortuitous mix of "how to" guides and help on hand can be added other resources and structures provided by the corporate financier's own firm. Staff have been selected using rigorous recruitment procedures and, as their time is served, acquire years of relevant transaction experience and other necessary life skills. They are then organized into transaction teams or other structures designed to maximize efficiency and skills coverage. They are regularly trained and attend continuing professional development courses. Senior members of the firm vet new transactions and the head of corporate finance maintains regular contact with corporate finance directors and their teams to ensure that all problems arising and the risks they bring with them are recognized and dealt with on an efficient and timely basis. As if this were not enough, engagement letters with corporate clients often contain sweeping indemnities in favor of the corporate financier's firm. So, what could possibly go wrong?

Sadly, life is not so simple. Regardless of all these aids and benefits, corporate finance business involves a number of risks. At an internal staff level alone, these can present a number of issues for senior management to consider when formulating operational risk management systems. At one extreme is the rogue employee. He presents the, hopefully unlikely, scenario of an individual who overrides systems, either willfully or through incompetence, resulting in damage to the firm and its clients. This risk should be mitigated through careful selection procedures and internal transaction monitoring. At the other extreme is the scenario of the truly conscientious employee who is faced with a difficult professional decision within the bounds of his own operational competence and authority but who makes a wrong judgment call. This risk should be mitigated by internal transaction monitoring systems, adequate training, a clearly understood company policy on acceptable risk levels and a work environment in which consultation and risk reporting are considered by all to be an available benefit.

Nevertheless, both these extremes along a particular operational risk curve remain potential threats regardless of the preventative measures a firm may put in place. The US diplomat, Edward J. Phelps, reminds us, "The man who makes no mistakes does not usually make anything." Risk can be mitigated but can rarely be eliminated altogether.

General Risk Areas

There are a number of risks facing the dealing and trading areas of broking firms or banks that do not necessarily affect directly their corporate finance counterparts such as currency risk, hedging risk or, *per se*, systematic risk. Nevertheless, other macro risks are relevant, including:

- *Market risk*. Significant market movements or, more often, general market sentiment can adversely affect corporate finance business if they result in timetable delays or an inability to secure investors in sufficient numbers to fund transactions.
- *Credit risk*. Brokers and bankers often deduct fees from funds remitted to their clients and therefore suffer little or no credit risk once a transaction has been successfully completed. Some transactions, however, involve raising funds for companies that are, without such new funds, an effective credit risk and there is always the potential for a dispute with a client resulting in nonpayment of fees.
- *Financial risk*. Other than nonpayment of fees and loss of fees due to adverse market conditions terminating transactions, this has other relevant forms such as underwriting risk and, in rare cases, events such as the incurring of additional legal fees outside of those normally covered by the client.
- *Regulatory risk*. There is always a risk that the rules themselves are infringed on a transaction but other important regulatory risks can be overlooked. These would include, for example, the risk that transaction files have not been properly maintained, perhaps even with vital documents missing.
- *Litigation risk*. This tends to be a rarity and, sadly, when it does occur is often when least expected. From a risk management point of view, this can be difficult to detect or prevent as there is always the possibility that the litigation can be very successfully defended (that is, it should never have arisen).
- *Reputational risk*. This can usually be avoided, if adequate due diligence procedures are maintained, but is sometimes embraced as part of the acceptable risks of a particular transaction. Risk management systems should be designed to cope with both scenarios.

- *Operational risk.* This covers most other identifiable risks from staff errors and inadequacies to the risks inherent in any particular transaction. For example, in the financing of natural resource transactions, country risk, political risk, and legal title risk are key considerations on many transactions.

These are the sorts of risk that need to be taken into account in the macro sense when creating risk management systems for corporate finance departments. Next, some of the micro risk considerations are considered.

Specific Risk Areas

It is useful to start by reflecting on some fairly basic questions before responding to a request by the compliance department, the risk management department or senior management to assist with the development or refining of risk management systems and their application to corporate finance. It can be difficult for corporate financiers to wrestle with the fact that there are inherent risks to their business. In a peculiar way, precisely because corporate financiers are often by nature either control freaks or risk-takers, or an interesting combination of both, they can, in conceptualizing appropriate risk management systems, be their own worst enemies.

To this end, the sort of questions that should be framed before sitting down to design any corporate finance-related risk management system might include:

- *Can the risks be identified?* What sort of risks are they? Can they be easily recognized or categorized? Can they be prioritized or graded in some way? It is also important to consider what sorts of liabilities are involved. This might be a turnover or balance-sheet issue or it could have a nonmonetary impact, reputational for example.
- *What sort of timetables are involved?* Some risks are relatively instant in their occurrence such as the discovery of fraud or a failure picked up as part of a due diligence process. Other risks may be contingent or otherwise involve a longer time frame

such as a financing transaction for a client whose financial survival is dependent upon the success of the fundraising.

- *Are staff adequately qualified, trained, and experienced?* This question can be extended in a number of different directions and, where weaknesses are identified, teams can be assembled with a view to covering all necessary skills and degrees of experience. At a basic compliance level, it is also important to ensure that employees are actually familiar with relevant internal codes such as the department's procedures manual and the firm's own ethos and approach to risk. On another level, consideration needs to be given to mitigating risk in situations where regardless of the skill and experience of those involved the transaction is unique, the first of its kind or where factors involved in executing the transaction have not been encountered before.

- *On a related issue, are staff properly incentivized?* An incentivization policy centered purely on revenue generation may, without adequate safeguards, expose the firm to an unacceptable level of risk. At the same time, employees are often encouraged to take risks or make executive decisions to address risk as part of their mandate procurement and transaction execution responsibilities and need to be incentivized accordingly. The key issue is to ensure that the financial and other interests of both employer and employee are aligned at a level of business risk acceptable to the firm.

- *Does the firm have an adequately disclosed culture or policy in respect of risk?* Clearly, whether written or oral, it is important that these things are readily accessible to and understood by staff. Apart from internal regulations and compliance manuals, the tools for inculcating such values and implementing successful risk controls may include, for example, committees to screen new business proposals and authorize the entering into of underwriting and other financial risks.

- *Are conflicts of interest adequately identified and resolved?* This applies not only to conflicts of interest within the firm but also those applicable to individuals such as personal account dealings and nonexecutive directorships held.

- *Are transactions adequately monitored internally?* Risk manage-ment systems need to cope with a range of different scenarios here. Some transactions may involve a degree of contingent risk that needs to be monitored until resolved. In other situ-ations, a material adverse change may occur during a trans-action and need to be resolved. It is important not only that the system can identify and monitor risks but also that staff operate in a culture where risks, adverse circumstances and even mistakes can be readily reported and discussed without fear of retribution.

- *Are due diligence, documentation, and other transaction-processing and reporting procedures adequate?* On the one hand, too much bureaucracy and form-filling can stifle deal flow and general effectiveness. On the other, risk management procedures must be able to identify failings in the system, whether human or systematic, that could expose either the firm or its corporate clients to unnecessary levels of commercial or regulatory risk.

- *Is the firm winning or losing clients?* Most firms can expect a reasonable degree of client and indeed staff turnover as part of the ordinary course of business. Even if the firm is gaining clients on a net basis, it is important to monitor leavers and understand their reasons for doing so. There are times when a firm is simply experiencing a bad period. Most likely, there is an underlying trend, identification of which might prevent undetected client management issues from manifesting themselves as material commercial or regulatory problems.

- *Does the firm learn from its mistakes?* This is not simply a question of accepting that a risk has transposed itself into a problem but also of amending procedures both at the oper-ational level as well as the risk-management level in order to benefit from the experience. In a business that involves a high degree of risk as a matter of course, recognizing honest mistakes and learning from them is sometimes more import-ant than identifying scapegoats.

This is not an exhaustive list, if indeed such a thing exists. There is a slightly nebulous aspect to this general scoping process in that manifestations of risk in the form of problems or other negative outcomes are often quantitative. The damage can be measured in terms of a financial cost or loss. However, identifying and grading the sort of risks that a risk management system should manage has a qualitative aspect. It requires judgments to be made, often subjectively, on the potential issues involved.

Selecting Appropriate Key Risk Indicators (KRIs)

Having established what sort of risks are involved in a corporate finance business, at both a macro and a micro level, senior management must come up with a risk management system which is realistically operable while adequately fulfilling its key purpose. This is often an optimizing rather than a maximizing process. Some simplification is also required at times in order to ensure that objectives are met. Too much detail can confuse both operational and risk management personnel if it results in the means becoming an end in itself.

On the one hand is the detail. By their very nature, risk management systems need to cater for the "impossible" and "unlikely" scenarios. Do not be afraid therefore to think the unthinkable. "The reason the mainstream is referred to as a stream is because of its shallowness" (George Carlin). Yet, if the systems are designed in the first instance to identify risk at a very precise level of detail, there is a danger of inventing thousands of key risk indicators, none of which is ever likely to arise let alone be recorded. A broad category such as "due diligence failure" may make a better KRI than a more specific derivative such as "due diligence failure: person A did not accurately fill in form B."

KRIs are the basic reporting units on which a risk management system is based. Across most departments in a financial services group, there are some common areas for KRIs such as bad debts and counterparty risk (in its more general sense). Most of these can have either a large number of readily identifiable forms or a small number of less likely manifestations. Corporate finance can present problems for those attempting to design an appropriate risk management module for it with prior knowledge of only similar modules for trading and dealing departments. There are hundreds of ways, I suspect, in which a trade can be badly executed but thousands in which a corporate finance transaction can go awry.

For this reason, it makes for a more manageable system if KRIs can be few in number but broad in scope. Consider that in an optimally functioning risk management system, KRIs serve not only as a reporting requirement but also as a management tool.

Examples of useful corporate finance KRIs include:

- Breaches of any terms set by the committees authorizing the entering into of new transaction mandates or underwriting commitments;
- Breaches of the corporate finance procedures manual or relevant industry regulations;
- Termination of live transactions;
- Complaints from or loss of corporate clients;
- Loss of potential transactions (e.g., either due to a competitive tender process or due to advice given or alleged personality clashes);
- Bad debts or nonpayment of fees; and
- Regulatory enquiries (whether the regulator is making enquiries regarding the conduct of the corporate financier or of his corporate client).

Again, this list is not exhaustive. It is important not only that all key areas of risk are covered by KRIs but also that the reporting system allows for, and that staff involved in the process are aware of, the provision of further information in respect of the incident that has necessitated the reporting of a KRI event. If a KRI report is issued because a corporate client has resigned, the reporter should provide details as to why the client has resigned.

As with all corporate finance-related issues, the designers of the risk management system also need to take into account the fact that corporate finance sits on the secret side of the Chinese Wall. Access to the detail contained within the risk reporting and monitoring system may need to be made available to staff on two or more levels of restricted access, depending upon the compliance department's view on appropriate access to unpublished price sensitive or otherwise privileged information.

Further Points on Setting and Interpreting KRIs

In designing and effectively operating a risk management system in corporate finance, it is well to remember that each of us is, after all, only human. The design, commissioning, and operation of such a system are not always an infallible process and further adjustments will inevitably need to be made throughout the life of the system. The useful interpretation of the data collated by the system is also subject to human error. These failings include such things as self-deception, probability calibration issues, cognitive dissonance, and hindsight bias.

Self-deception is the trait that makes us think something will never happen because it has never happened before. This can manifest itself in a number of ways. Probability calibration issues arise where something is forecast not to happen. Unfortunately for us, a study by Kahneman and Riepe[1] showed that only two professions showed good probability calibration skills. Neither one was financial-services related. The theory of cognitive dissonance[2] is based on an observed tendency for humans to ignore facts contrary to their own beliefs and even to seek evidence on a selective basis in order to confirm the original, unscientific view. Clearly, these types of failings can make it difficult either to frame the right sort of KRIs or to interpret them properly and therefore learn from the data collected in order to prevent repetitions of the same problem.

Hindsight bias acts in a similar manner. It is too easy either to blame someone in a situation where the risk was actually unavoidable or, on the other hand, to overlook or waive concerns about a risk because it is considered that the next manifestation of it is likely to be detected earlier. An associated failing is a tendency to only prepare for or seek to identify those risks that are perceived as more likely to occur, simply because they are related to the most frequently occurring problems in our recent experience. As an old Chinese proverb says, "A man who has been bitten by a snake is afraid of a piece of rope."

---

[1]   Kahneman, D., and M. Riepe. 1998. *Journal of Port Management*, summer.
[2]   Festinger, L. 1957. *A Theory of Cognitive Dissonance.* Stanford, CA: Stanford University Press.

Conclusion

Although corporate finance often embraces risk and despite the skill of its practitioners and the fact that they have recourse to all manner of professional advice and other assistance, it does still require a degree of risk management monitoring, over and above that normally performed by, say, the compliance department.

Risk management in corporate finance is based on the same principles as any other financial services risk management system. However, the specifics are necessarily different to those of trading and dealing departments and require careful thought not just to identify key risks but also to ensure that the system is not undermined either by too much detail in the level of KRI reporting or an excessive degree of generality.

Planners of such systems therefore need to utilize the skills of those they seek to police. The thought processes required by corporate financiers in order to participate in the task are, in my experience, a useful educational tool and likely to ensure the overall success of the system both as a reporting function and as an effective management program.

Finally, in implementing a risk management system, real success depends upon more than simply creating a well-designed, beautifully crafted mechanical system. The system comprises not just a few thousand carefully considered words and a bespoke ORM computer program but also the people who use it and maximize its performance. There is another old Chinese proverb that advises: "If you are planning for one year, plant rice. If you are planning for 10 years, plant trees. If you are planning for 100 years, educate people."

A Securities and Investment Institute Master Class on Behavioural Finance by Mark Tapley of the London Business School contributed significantly to the ideas presented here on some of the pitfalls of setting and interpreting KRIs. I am also indebted to a number of my colleagues at Evolution Securities, in particular Zoe Hine, Ngaire Stone, Mitchell Gibb, and Laurence Blake who patiently reviewed this chapter and also provided helpful comments and advice.

CHAPTER 4

The Risk Management of Asset Management

Dennis Cox

Risk Reward

Introduction

Within asset management, risk management has always been a well-established discipline, even if it has not been seen in that light. With performance being king and the need to show good results, asset managers have needed to be aware of the risks that they are running and to convert these into superior reported statements.

In this chapter, all of the key elements of risk within an asset manager will be addressed and future developments that are likely to impact the industry will be considered.

The key risks within fund management are:

- Market risk;
- Credit risk;
- Operational risk;
- Strategic risk;
- Reputational risk; and
- Liquidity risk.

In this, asset managers are no different from other financial service companies. It is the nature of the relationship with their clients that makes a difference to the approach.

With performance at all counts being of such importance, for most asset managers risk management was synonymous with management of the market risk within client portfolios. Other risks were generally not considered—as a consequence other risks could easily be taken on that actually had the impact of undermining performance.

Risk departments in fund managers rarely existed—there were performance measurement teams looking at specific market-based performance risks, but little else. Operational risk was within operations, credit risk was rarely considered and other risks hardly modeled. All of this has changed with the Basel Accord, which has encouraged asset managers also to implement a higher level of control.

Market Risk

Market risk within an asset manager is different from other financial institutions in that it is normally taken on for the benefit of investors. The depositors in an asset manager provide funds for the asset manager to invest for the benefit of the depositor. If the assets go up in value then the client's portfolio increases in value. Likewise, if the investment decreases then the client's portfolio also decreases.

Most of the market risk is not maintained by the fund manager, so what is the market risk that they continue to maintain? Within asset management, the relationship with the client is specified within a client agreement. This sets out the parameters within which the fund will be managed going forward, including the benchmarks against which performance will be measured, perhaps the FTSE 100 index, for example.

If a fund manager manages within the requirements of the client agreement then it will pass all of the market risk on to the client. It will then receive a fee for the management of the client assets based on the terms of the agreement. This normally provides a fee in two parts, one being the service element and the other being a performance element.

So long as the agreement is complied with, the client picks up gains and losses, so there is no market risk as such with the fund manager. If the fund is not managed in accordance with the agreement, however, this position changes. Then the fund manager has a potential risk that the client will come back to them and state that the losses should be made good.

Effectively, there is a moral risk to manage the fund in accordance with the client agreement that the fund manager has failed to comply with.

Thus, it is important for the risk management function within an asset manager to ensure that the fund is managed in accordance with the agreement with the client. This is done as follows:

- By measuring the performance of the fund against the benchmark, and calculating the tracking error caused by the fund not having the same constituents as the benchmark itself.
- By hard-coding into the system a series of parameters that cannot be broken, for example, reflecting that a fund has a prohibition on investing in a certain type of asset.

By measuring and modeling tracking error and evaluating the difference between the client's portfolio and the benchmark, the fund manager is able to ascertain the level of risk of over-or underperformance that it is actually running. Increasingly narrow allowances for tracking error are now being implemented which could change a fund into one that effectively works little better than a tracker. The risk of failure being so much greater than the reward for success within the industry further contributes to this natural risk aversion.

Investment Styles

Fund managers will state that they have a particular investment style. Excluding hedge funds, which are dealt with elsewhere in this book, the main styles are:

- Value;
- Growth;
- Passive; and
- Lethargic.

A value house looks to identify individual stocks that are underpriced relative to the market and the firm's models. These will then be acquired and it is hoped that performance will ensue. Actually, value principles normally lead the market when the market is in decline, but can lag behind in a growing market.

A growth fund, rather than looking at such pricing inefficiencies, is actually looking for companies that are growing in the market and will seek to invest in them. This tends to work very well in a rising market, but can be a problem in a falling market.

Both of these styles will suggest a level of tracking error if a fund is to be measured against a benchmark, the FTSE 100, for example. There is, of course, the problem with the selection of the benchmark. A client may want a fund to follow a growth or value path, yet also wish to compare performance against the FTSE 100 benchmark. The FTSE 100 will include growth and value stocks along with declining and lagging stocks, so this is a difficult comparison to make.

The consequence of this is that the fund manager will temper their stance to take account of the level of risk aversion of the client. As a result, they may become either passive or, at worst, lethargic in their approach.

The passive manager follows the market whereas the lethargic manager only plays at the edge of the fund and holds positions for much longer than would be the case for the value or growth manager.

The risk manager will continually review the tracking error and will seek to involve the investor in the decisions to be taken on the fund. If there is an investment bubble of some form in progress that contradicts the style of the house, an involvement of the investor in the decision-making process will ensure that the moral risk does not become an actual risk.

Asset Pricing

Another aspect of the market risk in a fund is in the pricing of the underlying assets. Clearly, if there is a liquid market for the assets that are held, then the price at a point in time is clear and will reflect the price quoted in the market. This price is readily available and can easily be reflected in the portfolio valuation. But what about illiquid stocks or other investments where there is no clear price?

The risk manager will be seeking to ensure that the valuation of the investment was fully considered when the asset was acquired and that an independent price is available. In the case of venture or private capital deals, this may involve an independent third party coming up with a valuation. For derivatives, the problem requires the risk management function actually to perform a recalculation of the price. In the case of property, while there are indexes available that are becoming of increasing quality, there is still a problem with independent valuation. Yet, it is these asset classes that can often provide a fund with outperformance.

Performance Attribution

The regulations make it clear to any Board that it is now inappropriate to reward excessive risk taking. Indeed, any performance measure which runs contrarian to effective risk management should probably be rewarded. With bonuses now being either deferred or being capable of being repaid much change is afoot.

For a risk manager in asset management performance attribution is fraught with danger. As a fund manager takes on greater volatility they increase the risk of negative performance and increase tracking error. Clearly fund managers should not be rewarded for achieving benchmark returns—that is what they are expected to achieve. Likewise, any returns that they do achieve should be discounted if they have taken on excessive tracking error as a measure of volatility. However, I know from bitter experience that this is a minefield foe a risk manager. Front office professionals fail to buy into this proposition and consider that they should be rewarded for all gains but not penalized for failure.

To be successful in this area the risk manager needs the Board to really buy into what we are seeking to achieve and to develop a complete set of risk based performance metrics which have been properly explained to the investment professionals, gaining their support to the fairness of the approach adopted. A great objective but hard to achieve in practice.

Model Risk

Where models are used to provide valuations, this creates additional problems. The risk management function needs to be able to both understand and recalculate the asset calculation, understanding the assumptions that are inherent in the primary model and replacing them with an independent model. This needs to take data feeds for pricing that are as independent of that of the primary model as possible.

The question is whether the risk management functions possess the skills necessary to undertake this work. In many cases, I doubt that this is the case. Similarly, such skills are unlikely to be available within either an internal or external audit. The requirement is for an advanced risk management team that fully understands such valuation principles. Such people will have the skills possessed by the front office dealing personnel supplemented with a detailed understanding of risk, perhaps a long shot.

Without this risk management back-up there is inappropriate model reliance. Models are only as good as their underlying assumptions. If these assumptions, for example, liquidity or volatility, are invalid, then the output from the model will be at best unreliable. Generally, we would expect any report on a model to include a statement of key assumptions to be assessed.

Credit Risk

Just as funds do not take direct market risk, nor do they take direct credit risk. The issue is rather different here, however. Generally, funds do not take on credit risk with the intention of making money from taking this risk. It emerges as a consequence of the investment process through settlement risk and through placement of excess funds in the market. It also arises in the case of derivatives—mark-to-market positions and collateral.

Funds are increasingly building credit rating-based limit monitoring systems to address the risks that arise from counterparty credit risk and also to comply with the requirements of the client agreements. This requires fundamental credit analysis to be undertaken prior to a fund manager utilizing a financial institution for business.

In practice, however, many of the institutions are less than forthcoming with the information required by a fund manager to complete this activity. In the case of derivatives, collateral limits are placed to reduce the exposure to the counterparty and any consequent risk, but this then requires collateral management and collateral mark-to-market to be conducted.

Using credit limits for limit setting is helpful and allows a system to be implemented promptly, but it must be recognized that credit ratings by their nature are more likely to follow a market than to lead.

The risk management function is increasingly leading in all of these areas and providing assurance to the fund manager that there will be no moral losses arising from counterparty credit risk.

Operational Risk

Operational risk encompasses operations risk, together with people, legal and compliance risks. As such, historically it was not considered separately from the normal operations risks that a firm would run. This has now changed and operational risk is seen correctly as a discipline in its own right.

All of the key elements of operational risk should be undertaken within a fund manager:

- Risk appetite calculation;
- Development of a risk register;
- Modeling of business processes;
- Identification of key controls that add value to the institution;
- Development of an internal loss database;
- Utilization of external loss event data;
- Development of key risk indicators;
- Exception-based reporting;
- Implementation of control and risk self-assessment;
- Development of sensitivity analysis;
- Development of stress testing and scenario modeling; and
- Development of business continuity plans for both normal and severe events.

In this way, fund management operations are no different to other financial institutions and similar systems and controls can be implemented.

One area of difference is within security lending. This is an activity where assets held by a fund manager are lent out to a third party to meet obligations that they might have. Within the industry, this is an area where higher levels of vigilance are required. A single security lending loss can easily wipe out a year's profits from a relationship and this is unlikely to be capable of being passed on to the client. Times when this is higher risk includes the lending of securities around corporate events, for example, a reorganization. The risk management function needs to keep such areas under close observation.

Strategic Risk

In common with other types of business, strategic risk within the fund management industry is still not modeled on a coordinated basis with other risks. Key strategic risks arise in the course of corporate activity, product development and sectoral stances taken by the firm. Yet, in practice such decisions are often made independently of a consideration of other types of risk.

The consequence can be that sectoral or industry stances may undermine the ability of a fund manager to really make a difference through asset selection. The risk management function should seek to evaluate the impact of such decisions and to report this to senior management, such that they are able to understand the levels of risk that they are running.

Reputational Risk

Is reputation a separate risk or is it just a consequence of other risks that the fund undertakes? While the Basel Accord does not explicitly require capital to be put aside for reputational risk, this neither means that there is no capital put aside, nor that management should not take the risk seriously.

Reputational risk within the fund management industry is paramount. Fund management companies offer similar services with reputation, size, and performance being the key determinants of differentials. The consequence of this is that the reputation of the firm must be maintained at all costs. Yet reputational risk is often seen as being the responsibility of compliance or the chief executive, rather than being within the remit of the risk management function.

Clearly, if you are to look at the totality of risk that a fund manager incurs, then reputational risk would be part of this equation. It is, therefore, imperative for the risk management team to ensure that the risk is properly considered and that the appropriate policies and procedures are implemented. Not having Basel-explicit capital calculation does not mean that there is no risk to be managed, indeed quite the contrary.

Boards do tend to consider reputational risk as one of the key risks that they are concerned about, yet we do not tend to see significant modeling, perhaps due to the absence of risk management input. So how should it be managed? Clearly, reputational risk is only incurred if a suboptimal event becomes public knowledge. If a firm incurs a loss of £1m and nobody hears about it, then the loss to the firm is just £1m. If the event becomes public, this then increases to a multiple of the loss, depending on the market's view of the quality of management and whether the institution appears to have become accident-prone. It is, therefore, quite realistic to model reputational risk as follows:

- Identify the likelihood of suboptimal events occurring;
- Identify the loss that would result directly from the suboptimal event;
- Evaluate the likelihood that the event would become public;
- Assess the financial impact that would result from such disclosure; and
- Reduce the overall liability by the controls that can be implemented to mitigate this loss.

At present, however, this is not generally undertaken within the fund management industry.

Liquidity Risk

Liquidity and asset and liability management are crucial to a fund manager. Public cases have identified the problems that can occur. To obtain superior performance, fund managers are increasingly seeking alternative asset classes, including:

- Property;
- The use of derivatives;
- Private equity;

- Venture capital;
- Unlisted securities;
- Commodities; and
- Credit derivatives

Each of these carries its own risk. What they all tend to have in common is that they are not easy to liquidate in a hurry. If a fund has a substantial level of unlisted securities and the investors request their funds to be returned, then the fund manager has a problem. It is unable to get a quality price for the assets due to the absence of a liquid market in the securities. Accordingly, the fund manager tends to transfer the assets from the fund to their own account, or to reimburse the fund for consequent losses resulting from the failure to realize the assets promptly.

Accordingly, it is imperative for the risk management function to consider the likelihood of customer withdrawals from a fund and to ensure that the fund managers have maintained liquidity adequate to meet these obligations.

That being said, full asset and liability management at a fund level is not generally undertaken. Perhaps this is because most of the funds do maintain adequate liquidity for normal purposes. Risk management is not, however, restricted to normal market conditions. Rather, it is intended to deal with stress and under stress liquidity declines exponentially.

Again, it is not difficult for the risk management function to implement a series of metrics and controls in this area, yet this is again often overlooked. We still have too many risk management functions within funds management restricting their attention to market and operational risk.

The Future of Risk Management

There can be little doubt that risk management practices within funds management are undergoing a sea change. The Basel Accord has been the catalyst for many funds to implement risk management, but many still have a long way to go. Mistakes are being made, mostly through what might be considered a lack of vision.

The objective of risk management is to provide management with the assurance that they require that business is being conducted in accordance with the risk framework that they have approved and the risk appetite that drives the process. As such, a series of policies, procedures, controls and, importantly, metrics can be implemented to ensure that the executive management is fully aware of the risks that they are currently running.

Working from the total view of risk, including liquidity, strategic and reputational risk, it is possible to build a consistent structure to ensure that all risks are evaluated consistently. The best way to do this is to use some form of risk-probability approach, akin to the loss-distribution approach within operational risk. It is clear, however, that loss is not a simple proxy for risk, rather the future expectation of impact would be a better measure.

The absence of quality software is one of the main issues that we currently see. The consequence is that the executive committee receives information that has been designed for income-generative purposes (i.e., tactical data) rather than the information that it requires (strategic data). Too often, the wrong information is provided to the wrong people at the wrong time.

In the future, fund managers will maintain risk databases that consider the totality of risk and evaluate future loss expectation using a series of realistic distributions. Risk management will address all of the plausible scenarios which can be foreseen—and we will be talking about Basel V rather than Basel II.

All of this is quite possible to implement now and some of the more enlightened institutions are making moves toward this approach. The win is clear—management adequately appreciates the totality of its risk and the results of the firm therefore become increasingly predictable and certain. What is also clear is that risk management within the fund management industry will continue to grow in the coming years, both in terms of its size and also the quality of the analysis conducted.

PART II
Market Risk

CHAPTER 5

Asset Liability Management in Major Banks

Asif Ahmed

Citigroup

Those who triumph compute at their headquarters a great number of factors prior to a challenge. Little computation brings defeat. How much more so with no computation at all!
—Sun Tzu, c.490 BC, Chinese military strategist

Introduction

Basel II has been a catalyst for many banks to revisit their market and credit risk management. Flattening yield curves and consolidation in the banking market has meant that the treasury functions within a bank are often asked to help with the formulation of strategy. Risk budgeting based on return on economic capital has become a key platform for capital allocation decisions.

This chapter will describe some of the ways the treasury assists in this strategy-setting process. Two case studies are used to illustrate the concepts. The remainder of the chapter will focus on some of the challenges banks face in implementing this approach in a uniform and consistent manner.

The chapter deliberately avoids elaborating on liquidity, interest rate, and credit risk management. It is assumed that the reader is already familiar with the relevant terminologies (such as gap analysis, sensitivity testing using simulations, transfer pricing, and economic capital) and the underlying complexity involved in managing in a dynamic environment.

Asset Liability Management Dynamics

Charting alternative futures lies at the heart of strategic planning. Understanding the interaction between interest rate, prepayment, liquidity, and credit is similar to understanding the interaction between the current, wind speed and any submerged obstacles in navigating a ship. Net interest income (NII) and market value of equity (MVE) are key elements to judge the robustness of any planned route. A focus on MVE ensures that the short-term accounting returns, captured by NII, are not emphasized at the expense of longer-term economic sense. Any scenario charted, therefore, must be seen in light of these two metrics. Other measures such as return on assets, return on risk-adjusted assets, return on economic capital and return on equity can be seen as variants of these two measures.

This chapter starts by looking at how a balance sheet generates the income and expense statement.

Proper coordination of the aforementioned in the asset liability management (ALM) process can be simplified through six policy objectives:

- Spread management: this involves both the yield curve gap as well as the margin.[1] In a dynamic environment the spread from any given product is dependent on the business cycle, which in turn is correlated to interest rates. The same applies to prepayment speed.
- Loan quality: this is a function of interest rate levels, existing bad loan assessment processes and default experience per product.
- Fee income and service charge: this invariably is a function of the products that can be reliably managed by the existing infrastructure of the bank, including personnel. The underlying risks of the products will range from interest rates, credit, foreign exchange, equity, and commodities.

---

[1] The treasury is strictly not responsible for the margin particular business units make for a product. However, the process of transfer pricing ensures treasury involvement. The spread earned on a product must be incorporated in the RoEC calculation.

Asset	Liability
• Loans growing faster than deposits	• Depositors' becoming more price–sensitive
• AFS portfolio yields have too much negative carry	• Wholesale market more demanding on risk disclosure
• Impact of complex investment products on the whole bank not transparent	• Core capital ratio more volatile

Exhibit 5.1 *The business of managing the balance sheet is a tough balancing act*

Source: Author's own.

- Control of noninterest operating expenses: for instance, additional customer service cost required to increase or maintain the core depositor base.
- Tax management.
- Capital adequacy: this is where the indirect impact of interest and credit management becomes evident.

In a dynamic analysis, changing any one or a combination of these internal or external variables will have an impact on the NII and MVE. The role of the ALM is to allow management to present the options in an intuitive and quantifiable form.

Implementing a Robust ALM Framework

Risk needs to be captured consistently across all the risk factors and reported uniformly across all the business lines (see Exhibit 5.3). Monte Carlo simulation offers a flexible and intuitive methodology to achieve this objective. Joint simulations of all the risk factors allow us to control the inputs, stress test the assumptions, incorporate jump-like behavior (fat tails) and combine management expectations of business growth and

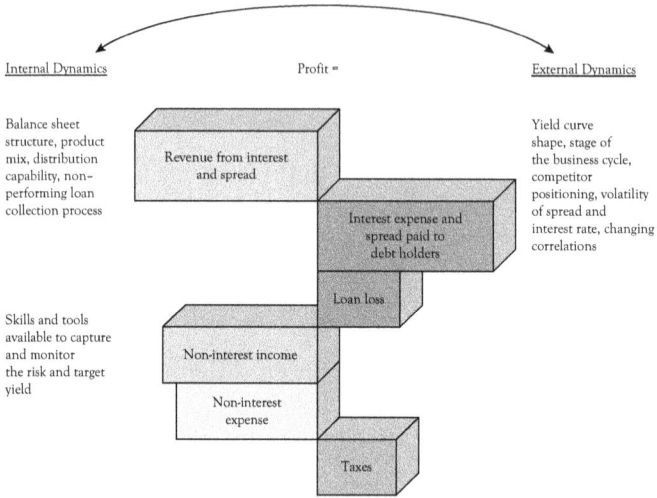

Exhibit 5.2 The ALM dynamics

Source: Author's own.

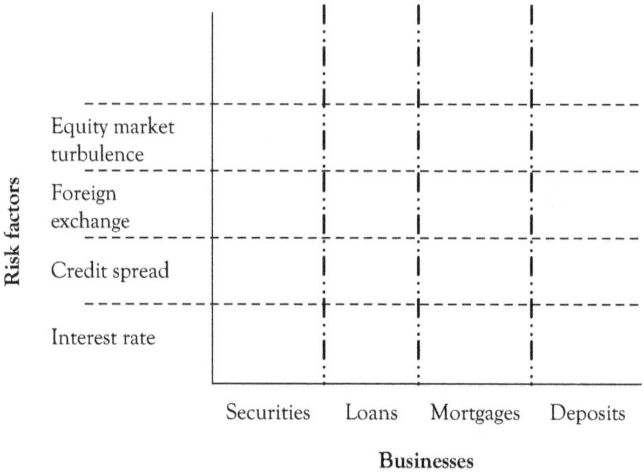

Exhibit 5.3 Different facets of risk

Source: Author's own.

spread trends (see Exhibit 5.4). The transparency and flexibility this offers also helps to check the model's robustness.[2]

_____

[2] A common method of validating a model is to ensure robustness—that means the model must produce consistent results for a wide range of reasonable initial parameters. Initial parameters for our purposes will be correlations, volatilities and various management assumptions on spread trends.

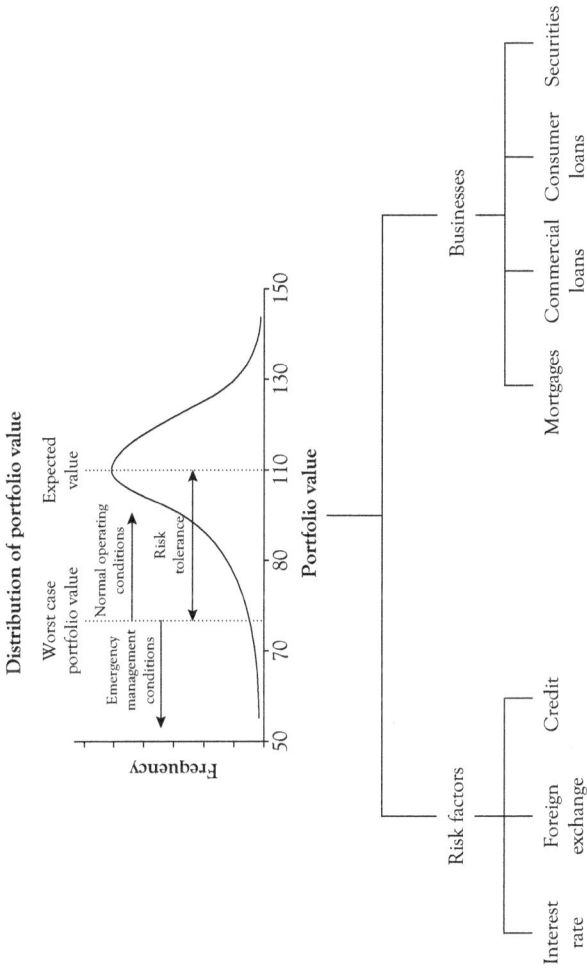

Exhibit 5.4 Model risk consistently

Source: Author's own.

Case Study: Regional Bank with Falling NII

This is a case study of a medium-sized regional bank focused on its core activity of lending to local clientele. In the last two years, it has faced falling NII due to:

- Rising cost of retaining the core deposit base.
- Rising default rate in a cooling housing market.
- Legacy of fixed-rate mortgages that had not been swapped to floating. In a flat/inverted yield curve environment, this had added to the spread compression.
- A portfolio of trading securities invested mainly in medium-term, fixed-rate government bonds. Again, in a flat/inverted yield curve situation, this negative carry had played a major part in compressing the NII.

Although the positive gap position had been considerably reduced in the quarter since results were published, the core problem of falling NII remained. Citigroup performed a top-level ALM analysis to first quantify the magnitude of the issues and then elaborate a given number of practical solutions for the bank's Asset and Liability Committee (ALCO) to consider.

The following charts (see Exhibits 5.5 and 5.6), which has been rebased to disguise the identity of the bank, shows the top-level diagnostics, their implication and the impact of the solutions pursued. A standard definition of economic capital is used, being expected MVE in one year's time less 2.5 percent tail-end MVE.

The risk cones of NII and MVE belie a given initial set of parameters—in this case, a base-case scenario of management projections, asset correlations and volatilities. We see that the MVE is really on a steady upward trend with only a 2.5 percent chance that in two years' time the current structure could lead to any serious trouble. In practice, management focuses mainly on the MVE in one year's time and that is seen to be pretty much the same as today. Thus, the rest of the investigation will focus on the causes of a flat/falling NII and ways to improve this situation.

More granular analysis of the underlying risks revealed that most of the risks were concentrated in consumer and commercial loans (see

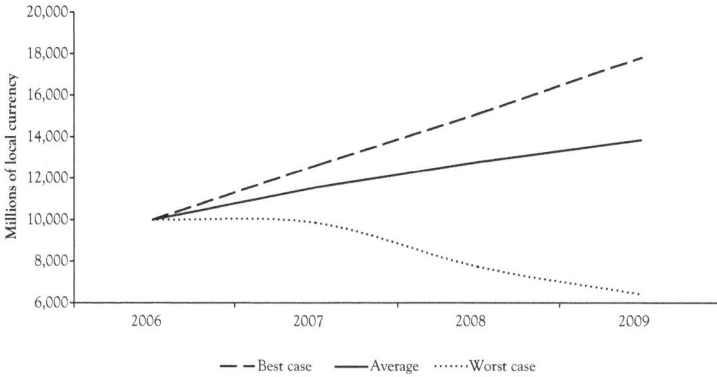

Exhibit 5.5 Best case, mean, worst case MVE

Source: Author's own.

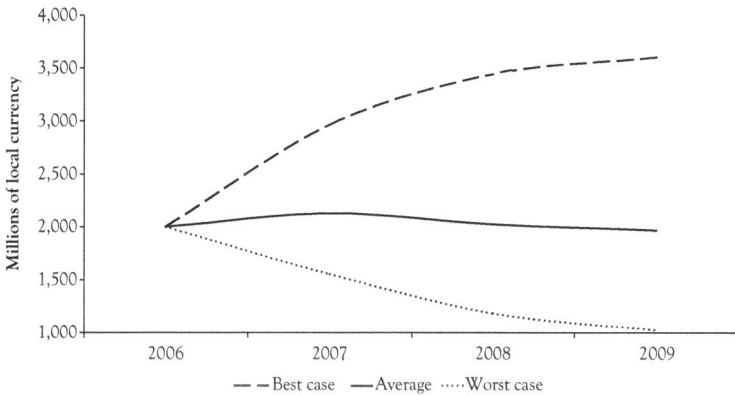

Exhibit 5.6 Best case, mean, worst case NII

Source: Author's own.

Exhibit 5.8). Investigation revealed that these two areas offered particularly lucrative margins and were also areas where existing mortgage customers wanted to utilize their unsecured lines. Although a fast way to grow the balance sheet, the bank had frequently lent 110 percent of the value of the underlying asset. While such practices can be averted in the future by modifying the products, in the short term these changes would not have had much impact on the NII.

The next step of the analysis is to combine the internal dynamics and market-related variables with management projections of what they expect

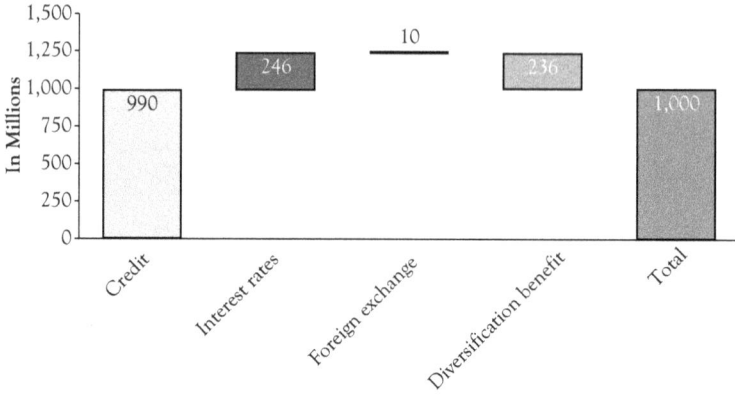

Exhibit 5.7 Risk factor breakdown

Source: Author's own.

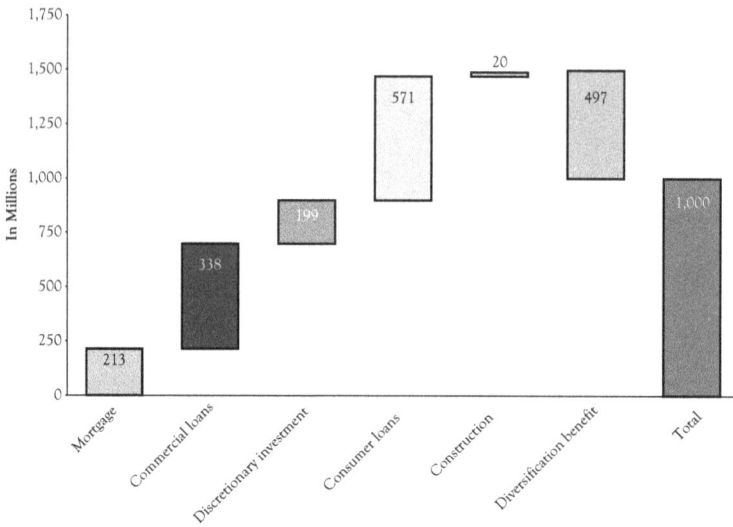

Exhibit 5.8 Risk breakdown by business lines

Source: Author's own.

spread to do going forward in their particular market. Exhibit 5.9 shows expected return on the Y axis and risk represented by 2.5 percent worst-case MVE on the X axis. The sizes of each of the respective businesses are represented by the diameter of the circles.

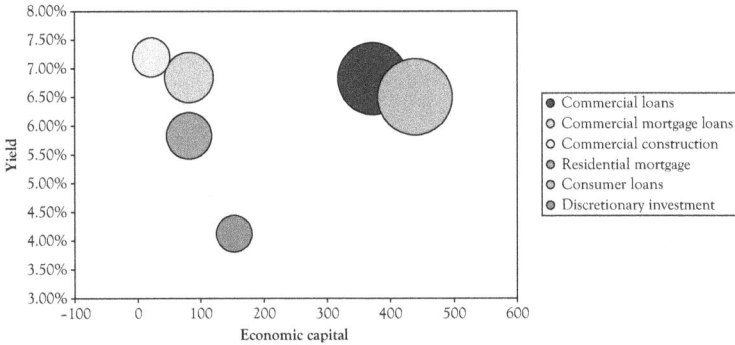

Exhibit 5.9 Risk return by business size—current

Source: Author's own.

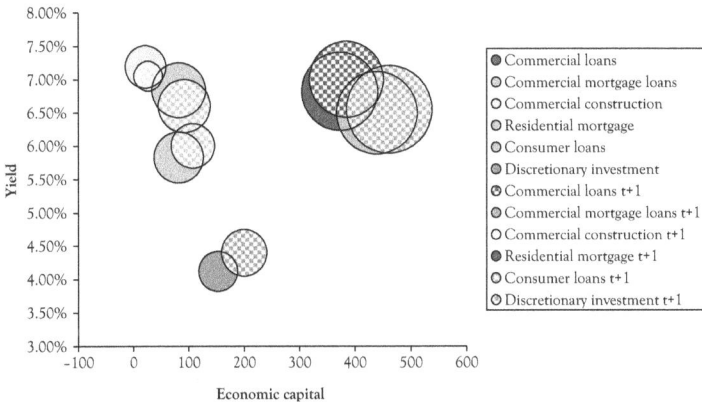

Exhibit 5.10 Risk return by business size—projected

Source: Author's own.

We can see that commercial construction loans yield the best risk-adjusted return, followed closely by commercial mortgages. Commercial unsecured loans form a big part of the business with the same return as that achieved in respect of secured loans, but with more risk.

Exhibit 5.10 overlays management expectation of spread as well as the business's forecast of asset growth. The patterned colored circles are the projections, with the solid colors being the current situation.

We see that both commercial and consumer loans increase in risk for a small increase in return and construction and commercial mortgage fall

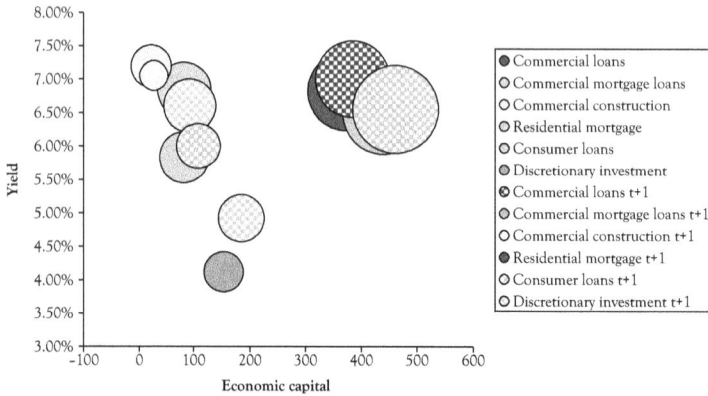

Exhibit 5.10a Risk return by business size—solution 1

Source: Author's own.

in size and yield. Indeed, securities and mortgages are the only business lines to exceed their risk-adjusted returns.

The investigation following the analysis mentioned earlier revealed the following trends:

- The bank's risks are highly correlated with the local economy. As of August 2006, the economy is experiencing reduced growth and this is evident in the increase in risk in both types of unsecured loans. Due to technical inertia, however, (e.g., lines have already been given for a year), it was not possible for the bank to reduce the size of its exposure to these two core sectors.

- The most lucrative businesses in the portfolio, construction and commercial mortgage, are even more cyclical than loans. As such, both of these may experience a downturn. Furthermore, there is a natural constraint in how much business can be done locally in these two niche sectors. Nevertheless, management may consider investing more in building relationships in this niche for future growth.

- Securities and residential mortgages both experience greater risk-adjusted return for virtually the same size. Management may consider investing more in these for the next year.

Solution 1

The initial analysis suggests that the bank should try to find an investment that is less correlated to the existing asset portfolio. Citigroup suggested a combination of hybrid assets and structured credits based on a collateral pool of foreign banks. Correlation analysis showed that the hybrid asset solution was the more effective route.

The initial parameters for this scenario were then changed to reflect an LCU2bn reduction in the securities portfolio, which was substituted with the Citigroup Hybrid Index. The impact of the hybrid solution can be seen in the two MVE distributions—the worst case has improved as well as the portfolio return by year three (see Exhibit 5.11).

On the risk-return graph, this has the net impact of increasing return on a risk-adjusted basis. The improved risk-adjusted return is also apparent in the MVE cone, which shows a higher trend for slightly reduced risk.

Solution 2

Credit risk is one of the key components of overall economic risk capital. Of this, commercial loans form a major part. Management expects that in the coming year the losses from this book will increase.

The following chart shows the loss distribution function in a normal scenario and in an increased loss stress-case scenario for the commercial loans book.

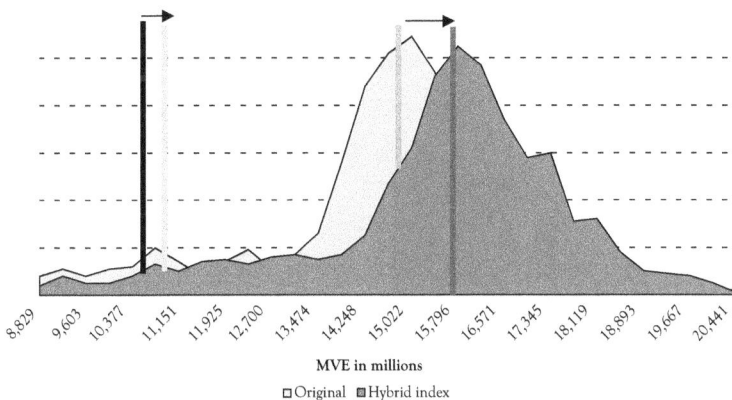

MVE in millions
□ Original ■ Hybrid index

Exhibit 5.11 Benefit from diversifying assets

Source: Author's own.

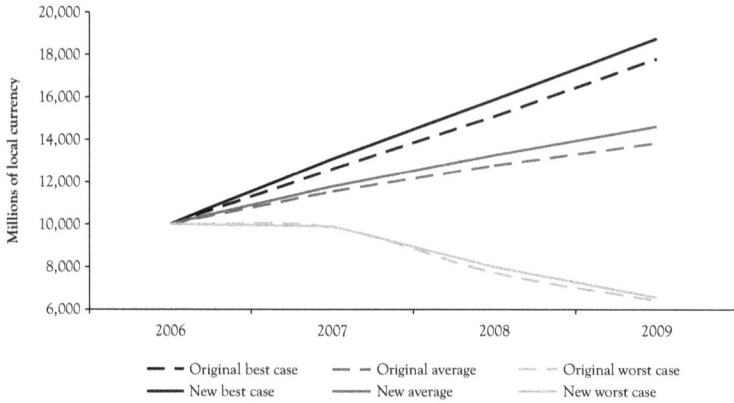

Exhibit 5.12 Best case, mean, worst case MVE

Source: Author's own.

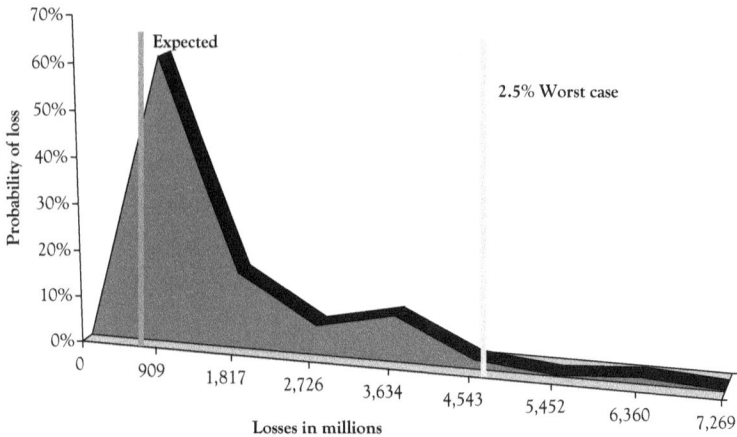

Exhibit 5.13 Loss distribution function—stress scenario

Source: Author's own

More granular analysis identified a subset of names that were contributing to the excess default events or fat tail (see Exhibit 5.15). These were ranked by their impact on economic capital losses. Citigroup's correlation desk was able to sell protection on most of these names, thereby reducing the overall default exposure of the commercial loans book.

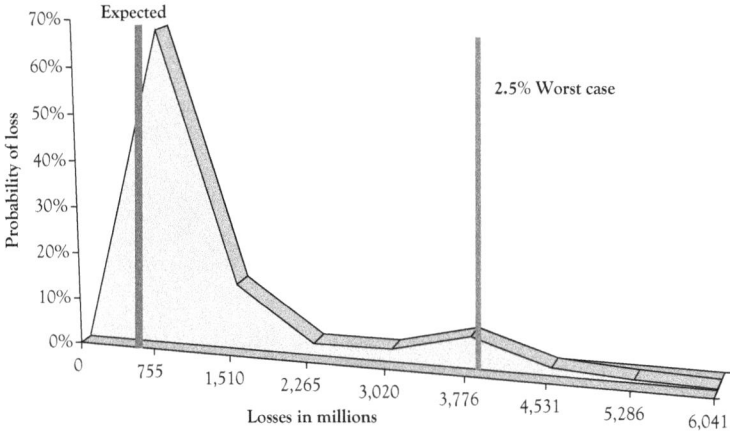

Exhibit 5.14 Loss distribution function—normal scenario

Source: Author's own.

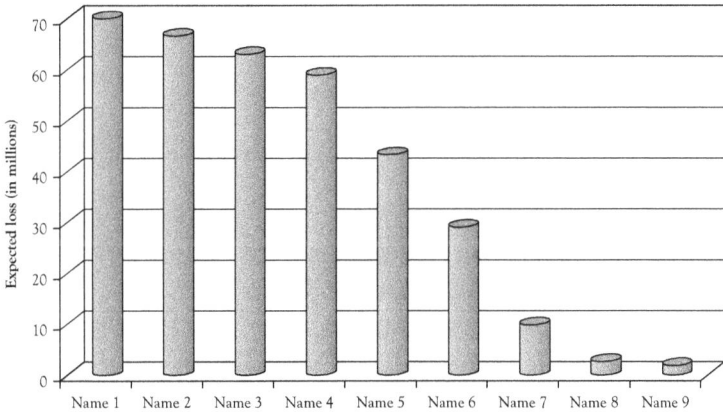

Exhibit 5.15 Loss concentration by names

Source: Author's own.

Implementation Issues

The difficulty for most banks lies in the legacy systems they have inherited. Credit risk assessments are often performed on a name-by-name basis using fundamental analysis with risk limits set per sector/region. Portfolio analysis in this case is not the norm. Market risk, on the other hand, is performed at a bank level. Combining the two, often different,

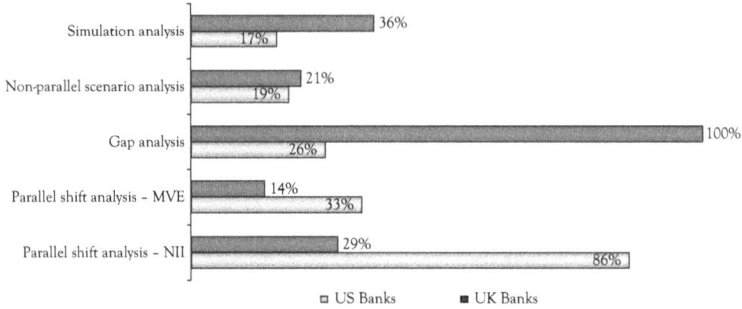

Exhibit 5.16 *Type of market risk analysis disclosed by US regional banks and UK banks*

Source: Company Annual Reports.

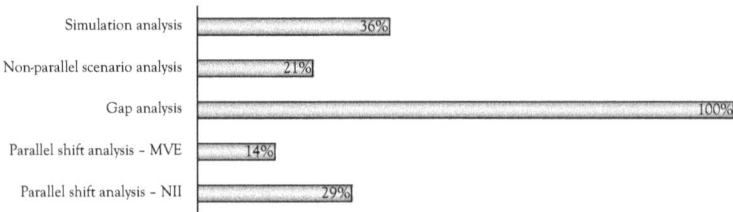

Exhibit 5.17 *Type of market risk analysis disclosed by mid-tier UK banks and building societies*

Source: Author's own.

departments can prove to be a daunting task. Most off-the-shelf software packages are robust in one aspect (e.g., market risk) and weak in the other. Moreover, these packages are designed for reporting purposes and do not facilitate scenario-building—an essential component for strategy-setting. Add to this the shortage of qualified personnel to handle these types of projects and we soon see why most mid-sized banks have resorted to compromise solutions.

A survey of 42 US regional banks shows that most still concentrate on the sensitivity of their NII to parallel shifts of the yield curve. Compare this to UK banks where the FSA requires repricing gap analysis. These risk measures mainly capture the short-term risks. While this is a reasonable measure for a balance sheet that is relatively neutral or has a short duration gap, it can potentially hide structural imbalances embedded in the businesses, for example, any inherent options—whether financial or contractual.

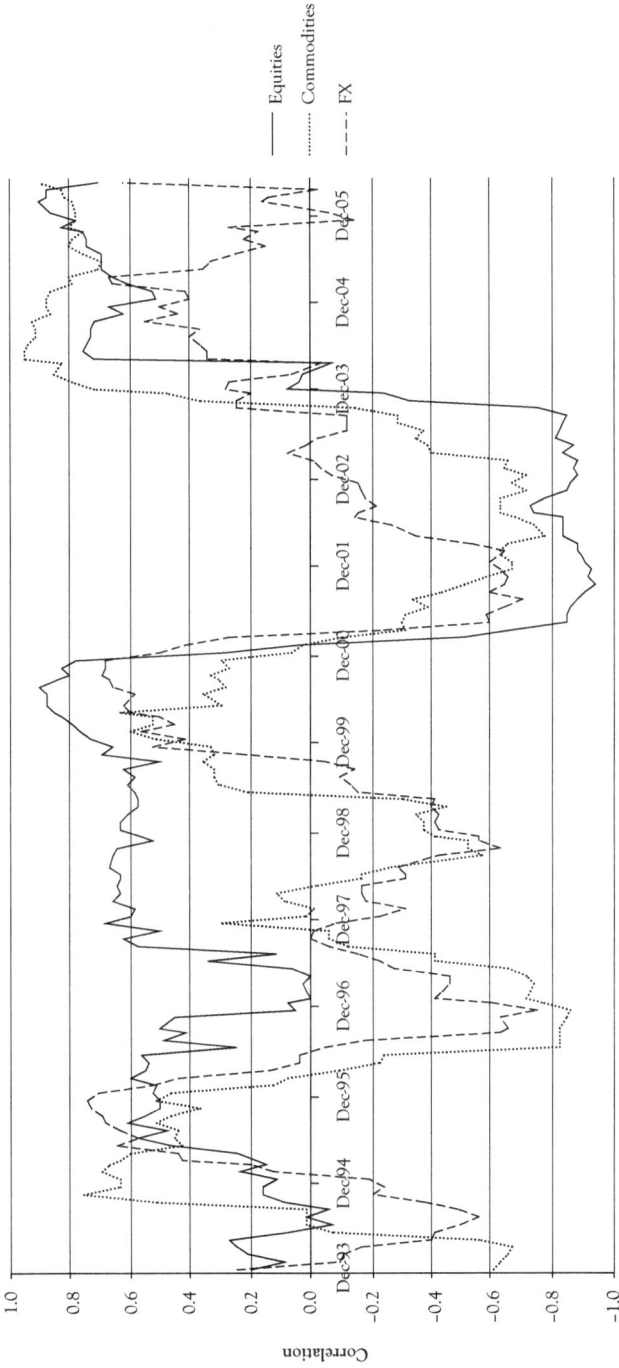

Exhibit 5.18 Underlying asset classes correlation with CHI

Source: Author's own.

Analyzing portfolio credit risk poses numerous practical constraints, the major one being reliable data. Default experiences per product lines and locality are not widely available. As such, internal estimations of worst-case losses and correlation to business cycles have to be incorporated into a bank-wide analytical framework.

Conclusion

The potential for using real-time RoEC is already being realized: banks have released capital by comparing their regulatory capital to economic capital; correctly priced loans have been made, where previously the line would have been declined; trends in growing businesses have been spotted earlier, enabling greater focus in those areas; and risk-return hurdle rates are guiding securities investment decisions. Asset liability management is encouraged throughout the bank as a core discipline underlying all capital allocation decisions of its managers. The bar is being raised across the industry to generate greater return for each unit of risk capital the bank has and a bank-wide ALM methodology is imperative for this goal.

CHAPTER 6

Treasury and Asset/Liability Management

Thomas Day

SunGard BancWare

Introduction

The demand of today's marketplace requires a more proactive and integrated view of balance sheet risks and returns. Given the market's relentless pursuit for the most efficient and productive use of capital, measuring the efficiency of capital utilization subject to a firm's consolidated risk and return appetite remains of utmost importance for banks of all sizes. This drive toward improved enterprise risk measurement and governance is not happening in isolation, nor is it merely a response to government policy or compliance mandates. Markets are becoming more liquid, and portfolios, positions and the idiosyncratic attributes of portfolios are becoming more tradable. Components of risk that historically have not been "actionable" are being made increasingly liquid through the use of advanced financial engineering and structuring tools, broader acceptance of new financial models and methods, enhanced communication and technology and improved data analysis capabilities. As markets continue to provide richer sets of risk management tools, such as structured investment vehicles, credit derivatives[1] and loan and

---

[1] Just a few years ago (1995), the US credit derivatives market was only US$2bn in notional, as reported by James Allen in *American Banker*. As of 2005, this number ranges from US$5.8tn (source: OCC and based on insured US commercial banks) to more than US$17.3tn (source: ISDA). This remarkable rate of growth reflects not only risk management within the dealer community, but is also indicative of growing acceptance and use within the end-user community.

credit risk trading mechanisms and markets,[2] the requirement that internal risk measurement and pricing systems be consistent with market-based pricing mechanisms will only increase.

To keep pace with these changes, large financial institutions are embracing the principles of advanced risk management as advocated under emerging policy regimes, such as the Basel II Capital Accord. While opinions are numerous and varied as to the efficacy and appropriateness of Basel II's somewhat prescriptive set of rules, it is clear that market and financial professionals understand the importance of enhanced governance around risk-based pricing and economic value creation, considering the risk-based capital attributed to deals as well as costs and returns. Slowly, the financial firm is moving from a "buy, fund and hold" mentality (a "warehouse" for risk) to "buy, decision and act" (a "weigh station" for risk). In support of this evolution, quantitative risk measurement, data analysis, and reporting tools—which have been traditionally used to drive transaction-level decisions—increasingly inform strategic enterprise-wide decisions.

At center stage of this change sits the treasury and asset/liability (A/L) management group. It is within the treasury division that decisions revolve around portfolios, risks, and markets. Treasury is ideally situated to help the organization navigate the transition from reaction-oriented risk measurement to action-oriented risk management. Positioned between the internal origination channels and the external distribution channels, treasury has good understanding of the internal volume and risk-generation capabilities of the bank, on both sides of the balance sheet, and the price of risk in the primary and secondary markets. It can execute trades, buy and sell portfolios and represent portfolio attributes, risks, and opportunities to the market. For these reasons, treasury can often play a critical role in "activating" modern portfolio strategies and tactics across an organization and the organization's balance sheet.

---

[2] In the future, it is likely that firms will also be able to buy and sell derivatives tied to catastrophic operational risk losses. The analogy would be catastrophe bonds currently being used by the insurance and reinsurance business to lay off second-loss pieces in the event of some natural disaster, such as hurricane exposure.

This chapter will discuss the importance of balance sheet management and the role of the treasury division in creating more enterprise value for the financial services firm. It will discuss the common practices and responsibilities of this group. Finally, it will provide an introduction to the key risk measurement objectives of financial organizations, the most common risk modeling methods and some of the more fundamental assumptions used within these models.

The Nature of the Balance Sheet

One of the most important artifacts created by a financial services organization is its balance sheet. The balance sheet is the engine that drives earnings power, risk and capital requirements. It can be a measure of strength or—depending on its embedded risks—it can be a measure of actual or potential weakness. The balance sheet is often considered a mysterious creation of accounting rules and is far too often thought of in a vacuum, a relatively static entity with no heartbeat; merely the amalgamation of numerous journal entries by accounting and finance staff. This is a poor, albeit far too common, conceptualization.

A more accurate analogy positions the balance sheet as a living, breathing entity with its own personality, character flaws, and strengths; it moves, alters course and sometimes surprises, although "surprise minimization" should be an implicit, if not explicit, goal of treasury. Given that the balance sheet is complex and changing, managing its personality, complexion, and direction is absolutely critical to the safety and soundness of a financial organization.

Covering all aspects of balance sheet risk is a monumental task, especially given the volume of activity represented by a typical bank's balance sheet and the complexity and diversity of risks implied by its composition. Often, the balance sheet is the result of millions of underlying transactions, with a taxonomy of risk attributes that is truly staggering, including: loans with irregular payment schedules; leases with peculiar features; commercial loans with embedded rate collars; mortgages with interest-only lock-in/float periods and other hybrid characteristics; deposits with embedded options; periodic caps; periodic floors; negative amortization features; servicing rights—and the list goes on and on. Capturing these transactions and their contribution to enterprise risk is a challenging, albeit necessary, task. Moreover, given that the balance sheet changes dramatically over time, it is crucial that this "position change" is somehow captured, measured, and assessed.

Fundamentally, it is the role of the treasury group to understand the balance sheet and the diverse organizational activities that cause it to change over time. Treasury must be in a position to explain these changes and, where necessary, act to mitigate, offset or control assumed and anticipated risks. Thinking of the balance sheet in this context is a powerful analogy as it helps explain some fundamental truths about treasury and A/L management.

Responsibilities of the Treasury Division

In performing its core function—to influence the strategic direction of the balance sheet—the treasury group weighs and measures activities, influences, and sometime re-orients the direction of business. It should be skeptical of inflated performance plans and should challenge business strategies where necessary. Of key importance, the group ensures that new business is priced relative to its risk and maintains an unflinching eye on the "market price" for equivalent portfolios of risk. Across the balance sheet, the treasury group must always evaluate whether the best use of capital is for originating risk and holding, or "buying in," transferring or offsetting risk due to irrational pricing or product structuring.

To enable it to perform accurately so many different activities requires a diverse staff with deep knowledge and skill across a wide variety of risk disciplines including credit, market, liquidity, operational, legal and reputational risks. A treasurer's activity centers on the balance sheet and on creating the appropriate governance structures, reporting mechanisms and the agility necessary to monitor and control balance sheet utilization. This often includes, but is not necessarily limited to, activities listed in Exhibit 6.1.

Of all of these responsibilities, perhaps the most important is developing an intuition as to how the bank's business, departmental activity and market movements will influence earnings, both today and over an appropriate forecast horizon. In this regard, the treasury division should

Direct responsibilities	Indirect responsibilities
• Economic and market analysis • Establishing and executing proper A/L, portfolio, liquidity and balance sheet management policies and procedures • A/L modelling, management and committee reporting • Income forecasting, risk analysis and reporting • Inculcating a risk-sensitive pricing mechanism and/or culture into the balance sheet management process (usually by ownership of funds transfer pricing (FTP) methodologies) • Investment portfolio modelling and management (i.e. the 'discretionary' books; often the available for sale (AFS) and held to maturity (HTM) investment portfolios) • Off-balance sheet modelling, conduit management and reporting • Structural derivative positions • Wholesale liquidity and liquidity risk management, including all shelf registrations and associated overhead • Capital management products (e.g. TPS, subordinated debt, mandatory convertible debt and other hybrid capital instruments/programmes) • Various wire-transfer activity related to portfolio operations • AFS and HTM portfolio operations • Portions or sometimes complete ownership of cash management operations. In many large banks, this will be housed in a separate division • Bank owned life insurance (BOLI) programme(s) • Holding company liquidity, funding and portfolio management operations • Discretionary strategy analysis • Investment banker relations and strategy assessment(s)	• Understand and influence risk pricing across the organization • Administered rate deposit pricing and repricing (sometimes directly influenced) • Campaign management (new business; treasury must be indirectly involved) • New product creation • Mergers and acquisitions • Shareholder relations • Capital planning and risk-based capital scenario analysis (sometime owned directly by treasury) • Budgeting and planning (sometimes integrated with treasury A/L systems, but often owned by the controller or finance division) • FTP processes and exception reporting • Credit spread pricing and other loan pricing • Client derivatives activities (sometimes owned directly by treasury) • Mortgage servicing rights valuation, accounting, analysis and reporting (sometimes owned directly) • Mortgage pipeline and portfolio hedging • IAS 39 and/or FAS 133 (United States) accounting, effectiveness testing and reporting (sometimes directly owned by treasury; depends on jurisdiction) • Credit portfolio stress testing and risk analysis • Accounting for (1) leases, (2) discretionary portfolio (i.e. AFS and HTM), (3) fees, (4) Special purpose entities/vehicles (SPE/SPVs), (5) currency translation, (6) employee stock options, (7) business combinations, (8) segment reporting, (9) fair value reporting • Model validation and risk control

Exhibit 6.1 Direct and indirect responsibilities of treasury and A/L management

Source: Author's own.

be focused not only on routine operational duties and roles as described previously, but instead should also seek to understand the firm's balance sheet risk exposures in as detailed and analytical manner as practical. Over time, the treasury group will be expected to evolve into a much more active balance sheet management function charged with instilling active risk management strategies across the traditional asset/liability, liquidity, and credit risk groups.

As products such as credit derivatives become more mature and risk factors are more easily exchanged across counterparties, organizations will need to monitor and react to market opportunities as well as understand and mitigate balance sheet exposures quickly and efficiently. This represents a tremendous opportunity for treasury to inform forecasting and risk, capital management and enterprise asset/liability allocation, as well as acting as the cultural champion for enhanced risk understanding and process improvement.

Given that the aggregate composition and changing nature of the balance sheet is so fundamental to a bank's long-term success and financial health, it is critical that the treasury division is well supported and equipped. Without the proper tools, techniques, organizational stature and structure, the group can become overwhelmed with tactical activity, permanently impairing its ability to influence the strategic direction of the balance sheet. Without proper board and senior management oversight, technical understanding and support, treasury will not be effective in its goal of ensuring that the earnings power of the financial firm is sustainable and repeatable over time.

Risks Managed by Treasury

There are five principal risks managed by the treasury division:

- Accrual book market risk (.interest rate risk.);
- Funding liquidity risk;
- Investment and derivatives portfolio[3] risks;

---

[3] The treasury division often manages the derivative hedge book, which is used to offset repricing mismatches or adjust duration exposures.

- Counterparty credit risks; and
- Certain elements of capital risk.
- We shall consider each in turn.

Accrual book market risk. One of the most important risks managed by the treasury division is the risk embedded in the structural balance sheet. This risk is managed by applying a variety of models, economic scenarios, and stress tests to the structural balance sheet position in an effort to understand exposure to embedded interest rate risk types and sensitivity to budget and forecast business volumes. Interest rate risk is composed of four main types of risk (see Exhibit 6.2). Proper risk management within treasury means that the firm has a process to model these risk types and understands the earnings and value impact of exposure to these risk factors.

Risk Type	Definition
Repricing mismatch risk	The most commonly discussed and well-understood form of interest rate risk, repricing risk is the measure of risk related to timing mismatches associated with repricing events. Banks intentionally accept mismatch risk in order to improve earnings. Repricing mismatch risk is often, but not always, reflected in a bank's current earnings performance; however, a bank may be creating repricing imbalances that will not be manifested in earnings until sometime in the future. For example: a bank uses a 10-year no-call 2-year funding vehicle to leverage a 10-year bullet-bond purchase. Repricing risk is minimal in years 0 through 2, but exposed for years 3 through 10. A bank that focuses only on short-term repricing gaps may be induced to take on increased interest rate risk by extending maturities to improve yield. When evaluating repricing mismatch risk, therefore, it is essential that the bank consider not only near-term gaps but also long-term repricing gaps. It should also be noted that repricing mismatch can be a cause of hedge ineffectiveness when attempting to apply FAS 133 and IAS 39.
Yield curve risk	Yield curve risk – often confused with basis risk – addresses changes in the relationship between interest rates of different maturities of the same index or market (e.g. a three-month treasury versus a five-year treasury). These relationships change when the slope of the yield curve for a given market flattens, steepens or becomes inverted (i.e. negatively sloped) during an interest rate cycle, which can create significant behavioural incentives across the bank's product market. For example: when long-term and short-term rates are relatively equivalent, the

(Continued)

	volume of adjustable rate lending may be reduced and long-term fixed rate lending may increase, as the costs are relatively equal. However, when differences emerge, the incentives can shift, creating important behavioural patterns that should be modelled and captured in the bank's A/L risk management process. Many banks assume scenarios that simply address parallel or proportional curve shift and thus do not effectively measure yield curve risk. The extent to which a bank is mismatched along the term structure will increase its exposure to yield curve risks. Certain complex investments can be particularly vulnerable to changes in the shape of the yield curve, including structured products such as dual index notes.
Basis risk	Basis risk arises from the non-parallel responses in the adjustment of interest rates among two or more rate indices, or 'bases'. For example: the index of a variable rate loan that re prices monthly may be based on a 'prime', which changes infrequently, and funded by 30-day certificates of deposit that are based on a LIBOR index, and changes quite frequently. As the loans are based on the 'prime' index and the CDs on the LIBOR index, even though maturity is matched, there is still a potential basis risk exposure. Another common form of basis risk is the relationship between non-maturity deposit rates and market rates. The manner in which these deposit basis risks are captured should clearly show the range of exposure to error related to model assumptions made around this risk factor. Many industry practitioners view basis risk as the most significant type of interest rate risk, likely due to the basis risks embedded with non-maturity accounts.
Option risk	Option risk arises when a bank or a bank's customer has the right (not the obligation) to alter the level and timing of the cash flows of an asset, liability or other instrument. An option gives the option owner the right to buy (call option) or sell (put option) a financial instrument at a specified price (strike price) over a specified period of time. For the seller (or writer) of an option, there is an obligation to perform if the option holder exercises the option. The option owner's ability to choose whether to exercise the option creates an asymmetric performance pattern. Generally, option owners will exercise their right only when it is to their benefit. As a result, an option owner faces limited downside risk (the premium or amount paid for the option) and theoretically unlimited upside reward. The option seller faces theoretically unlimited downside risk (an option is usually exercised at a disadvantageous time for the option seller) and limited upside reward (if the holder does not exercise the option). This is one of the most difficult risks to capture from both an earnings and valuation perspective within the context of a bank's treasury risk management activities.

Exhibit 6.2 Sources of interest rate risk

Source: Author's own.

Funding liquidity risk. In addition to managing traditional call risk, maturity gap risk and transaction settlement risks (purchase/sale/fail), the treasury's liquidity desk must analyze the degree to which it is overly reliant on wholesale or otherwise volatile fund providers. Scenarios should be evaluated that stress test reliance on liquidity providers subject to triggers such as rating downgrade, legal actions, compliance impacts, operational shut-downs, and other scenarios. In addition, the firm must put into place a contingency funding plan that can be invoked in the event of a run on deposits, or other liquidity crisis. This requires identifying and measuring back-up funding need, establishing appropriate back-up lines, and periodically testing readiness.

Investment and derivatives portfolio risks. Treasury is normally responsible for managing the firm's structural investment portfolio, including the available for sale and held to maturity portfolios. It is around this book of business, and the wholesale funding book, that the treasury should build reasonable models to measure value-at-risk exposure. These are not necessarily as rigorous as required within the trading portfolio, given that these positions are not marked-to-market through earnings. Approximations of value-at-risk are normally sufficient to understand risk exposures that accrue to these portfolios today and over time. In best practice, a principle components analysis is used to create a range of interest-rate scenarios that are used to value portfolio positions. The output from these scenarios can then be used to create a distribution of portfolio returns. Sound practice includes simple measures such as account-level effective duration and convexity metrics and then relating exposure to rate scenarios and measuring the potential change in value relative to capital (see Exhibit 6.3 for a hypothetical portfolio risk report).

Counterparty credit risk. Very little reporting is typically generated around treasury relationships with dealer counterparties. However, important risks and concentrations should be evaluated, and limits established, to ensure potential exposure, expected exposure and credit risk mitigation agreements are well controlled. The treasury division should establish proper documentation, controls and reporting around master agreements, confirmations, broker/dealer correspondence and other activity.

	Market value	Base case effective duration	Base case effective convexity	Base case price						
				-300	-200	-100	0	100	200	300
NON-AGENCY ABS	$200,000,000.00	0.88	-0.20	101.75	101.39	101.10	100.89	100.36	99.71	98.96
				0.85%	0.49%	0.20%	0.00%	-0.53%	-1.17%	-1.92%
AGENCY MBS POOL	$2,500,000,000.00	1.65	-2.19	104.74	103.99	103.51	103.28	100.91	97.49	93.53
				1.42%	0.69%	0.22%	0.00%	-2.30%	-5.60%	-9.43%
AGENCY CMO	$550,000,000.00	2.02	-1.82	104.12	103.34	102.77	102.09	99.53	96.16	92.37
				1.98%	1.23%	0.66%	0.00%	-2.51%	-5.81%	-9.53%
AGENCY NOTE	$150,000,000.00	0.40	-0.18	102.57	102.24	101.94	101.72	101.18	100.05	98.55
				0.83%	0.51%	0.22%	0.00%	-0.53%	-1.64%	-3.12%
TREASURY NOTE	$272,000,000.00	1.02	0.07	104.53	103.45	102.56	101.91	101.00	100.13	100.13
				2.57%	1.51%	0.63%	0.00%	-0.90%	-1.75%	-2.60%
NON-AGENCY CMO	$3,500,000,000.00	1.89	-1.68	102.85	102.28	101.77	101.17	98.84	95.92	92.68
				1.65%	1.09%	0.59%	0.00%	-2.30%	-5.19%	-8.39%

TOTAL PORTFOLIO	$7,172,000,000.00
TOTAL ASSETS	$20,491,428,571.43

Leverage capital	$1,254,075,428.57
Exposure at +200bp	-5.07%
Current leverage ratio	6.12%
Net leverage at +200bp	4.88%

Exhibit 6.3 Hypothetical portfolio risk report

Source: Author's own.

Capital risk. Fundamentally, this is the management of the instruments contained within the capital base. It is becoming more common for the treasury division to integrate economic capital sensitivity measures into its balance sheet scenario testing, including measures of credit risk and credit transitions over the earnings forecast horizon, which requires firms to derive models to allocate balances to the allowance for loan and lease losses, non-accruals, and losses. Many treasury divisions do not manage these risks directly, but instead take input projections for these elements from the portfolio credit risk management and controller divisions. Treasury also may dedicate staff to better deployment of capital through hybrid and other capital instruments, as well as managing any share buy-back program.

Enterprise risk management (ERM): ERM has recently become a topic of considerable interest among financial organizations, bank rating agencies and bank supervisors. However, the phrase "enterprise risk management" is often overused and misunderstood. ERM is not a product that can be purchased, a policy that can be mandated or a regulation that can be prescribed. The Committee of Sponsoring Organizations of the Treadway Commission (COSO)[4] offers the following definition:

> *ERM is a process, effected by an entity's board of directors, management and other personnel, app*lied in strategy setting and across the enterprise, designed to identify potential events that may affect the entity, and manage risk to be within its risk appetite in order to provide reasonable assurance regarding the achievement of entity objectives. [Emphasis added]

An evolutionary process, ERM requires the adoption of risk management as a core value within an organization. While it is not the domain of treasury to implement ERM, a treasury division that establishes sound risk management practices should be encompassed within and complementary to an effective ERM framework.

---

[4] *Enterprise Risk Management—Integrated Framework*, September 2004.

The Dominance of Earnings

For most financial organizations, the dominant driver of earnings is net interest income (NII) and a critical management activity is creating stability of the earnings stream across a wide variety of economic scenarios. To achieve this, it is common for a bank's board of directors to orient treasury around the governance of consolidated earnings performance, particularly net interest income and the net interest margin (NIM). The board's policies typically require the treasury division to simulate earnings over specified time horizons and to stress test and sensitivity test earnings forecasts, subject to potential and expected market and economic environments. While opinions vary as to the applicability of stochastic versus deterministic simulations, the use of scenario analysis is critical and should be understood and monitored by senior management of the firm.

In most large financial organizations, the scenarios seek to limit risk to earnings in such a manner that forecast earnings, based on consensus estimates of market factors and balance sheet volumes, would produce sustainable earnings over time. In addition, banks typically seek to limit exposure to extreme movement in market factors such that may place the firm's earnings or value in undue peril. In practice, this normally incorporates a neutral position relative to movement in market risk factors, with a dominant focus on measuring and managing earnings at risk (EAR).

Earnings at Risk (EAR)

As mentioned previously, net interest income (NII) is often the dominant portion of overall bank earnings, usually representing more than 60 percent of total revenues. The NII is sometimes referred to as the "spread" or rate-sensitive component of a bank's revenue stream, as the quality and sustainability of this revenue depends on the spread between the yield on assets and cost of liabilities.

The net interest spread is influenced by the volume, mix and quality of rate-sensitive assets and liabilities, today and over time. Within today's balance sheet, there are products that will reprice over 12 months; this repricing will be based on rates that exist at an event date in the future.

For example, consider a firm that holds within its current position balance sheet a commercial loan that originated several years ago. This loan was fixed-rate at 6 percent for three years; after this fixed period, the loan reprices at 200 basis points off the US dollar Libor curve, currently at a rate of 5.15 percent. Today's balance is US$1m and the repricing date is 188 days in the future. Once the loan reprices, it will do so every 60 days for a period of 12 months, at which point it will mature. The firm then funds this position with a term deposit fixed at 3.5 percent. The following Exhibit 6.4 expresses the income earned on this position over the next three repricing dates, 7 August, 6 October and 5 December.

From an earnings perspective, the firm has six more months of earnings at 6 percent, at which point the loan reprices to 7.15 percent. Over this horizon, the earnings per share sums to US$0.77. This is an incomplete picture of risk, however, as it assumes that the two-month US dollar Libor rate in August will be 5.15 percent, the rate that prevails today on January 31, 2007. If rates change between January 31, 2007 and August 7, 2007, the reported earnings over this horizon will be incorrect. Let us consider the impact of rates declining by 200 basis points over this horizon.

This reduction in rates produces a new EPS of US$0.55, a decline of approximately 29 percent from the US$0.77 level. This dramatic drop in earnings is a red flag and would certainly motivate the organization to seek strategies to mitigate or offset this risk exposure, assuming that the probability attached to the scenario (i.e., a decline in rates of 200 bp) was considered sufficiently high to warrant taking remedial action.

Regardless of likelihood, this type of measure is easy to understand. The firm can place a risk limit and corporate policy around this measure, and report to the board, senior management and the A/L committee on a routine basis (at minimum quarterly, but often monthly). Strategies to offset exposure, such as new pricing campaigns, purchasing or entering into a financial hedge or other such action would be evaluated and presented to the appropriate governance committee on a routine basis.

It is this spread relationship, and the timing and magnitude of repricing events between assets and liabilities, which drives a financial firm's NII. Managing the sensitivity of net interest spread is one of the core functions of the treasury group and many of its other activities are geared toward

	31/01/07	07/08/07	06/10/07	05/12/07	03/02/08
Commercial loan, hybrid 3:2M Libor:	$1,000,000	$1,000,000	$1,000,000	$1,000,000	$1,000,000
Interest income	$5,000	$31,333	$11,917	$11,917	$11,917
Time deposit	$1,000,000	$1,000,000	$1,000,000	$1,000,000	$1,000,000
Interest expense	$2,917	$18,278	$5,833	$5,833	$5,833
Net interest income	$2,083	$13,056	$6,083	$6,083	$6,083
Average earning assets	$1,000,000	$1,000,000	$1,000,000	$1,000,000	$1,000,000
NIM (annualized)	2.50%	2.50%	3.65%	3.65%	3.65%
EPS	$0.12	$0.12	$0.18	$0.18	$0.18

Exhibit 6.4 Base case analysis

Source: Author's own.

	31/01/07	07/08/07	06/10/07	05/12/07	03/02/08
Commercial loan, hybrid 3:2M Libor:	$1,000,000	$1,000,000	$1,000,000	$1,000,000	$1,000,000
Interest income	$5,000	$31,333	$10,250	$9,417	$8,583
Time deposit	$1,000,000	$1,000,000	$1,000,000	$1,000,000	$1,000,000
Interest expense	$2,917	$18,278	$5,833	$5,833	$5,833
Net interest income	$2,083	$13,056	$4,417	$3,583	$2,750
Average earning assets	$1,000,000	$1,000,000	$1,000,000	$1,000,000	$1,000,000
NIM (annualized)	2.50%	2.50%	2.65%	2.15%	1.65%
EPS	$0.12	$0.12	$0.13	$0.10	$0.08

Exhibit 6.5 Down 200 bp over horizon

Source: Author's own.

measuring, monitoring, controlling and protecting the spread. These objectives are achieved through direct influence as well as through the establishment of a market-oriented fund transfer pricing (FTP) regime, profitability, relationship pricing, and loan/facility pricing spreadsheets/models.

The Importance of Value

While measures of earnings at risk are the dominant and proper orientation of effective balance sheet management for the accrual book, EAR scenarios and stress testing are insufficient. Suppose bank management offered only one-year certificates of deposit (CDs) at 4 percent and in turn used the deposits to fund five-year fixed rate, callable loans at 8 percent. The bank has created a nice 4 percent margin, right? However, what happens if interest rates increased three percentage points so that in one year, when the CDs mature, it costs 7 percent to bring in new money?

The 4 percent margin will soon reduce to 1 percent when the deposits renew at the higher rate. This margin compression is earnings at risk. However, there is even worse news for the bank. The loans that were made for five years could now be made for a higher rate, perhaps as high as 11 percent; the original 8 percent plus the 3 percent increase in rates. The loan customers would be thankful that they had locked in their loan rate at 8 percent. But what has happened to the value of the loans? If the market rate for similar loans is 11 percent, the bank is holding relatively low-coupon instruments. In effect, they are giving up an additional 3 percent for four years (four years as one year has passed). Should the bank decide to sell the lower-coupon loans in the current interest rate environment, they would have to sell at a deep discount. This is what is known as economic value-at-risk, or the risk that the market value of assets and liabilities will change due to changes in interest rates.

If the transaction is viewed in a more "technical" sense, you can quantify the exposure and characterize the distinguishing features between EAR and economic value of equity (EVE). For example, assume that we have two banks: A and B. The transactions they each make on day 1 are as follows

Obviously, Bank A is in a better income position, earning a full 100 basis point spread over Bank B. A naïve analysis would look at the one-year earnings and conclude that Bank A is managing its business more effectively. Focusing solely on short-term earnings, which many banks are inclined to do, we make this assumption. But then consider what happens when interest rates increase dramatically, by say 300 basis points. What happens to the value of each bank's position? Which bank is in a better position?

Bank B continues to earn a 3 percent spread while the spread earned by Bank A is now 1 percent. Said differently, Bank A has "lost" 300 basis points for four years. The present value of this lost 3 percent annuity (i.e., US$3 over four years) is 9.31 (exactly equal to the discount on the loan). This "opportunity cost" of capital is not illusory.

Should Bank A attempt to readjust its position, it would only be able to sell its loan for US$90.69 and reinvest at the new market rate of 11 percent. Even if no repositioning occurs (i.e., take your loss today), the "unrealized loss" is nonetheless real. If Bank A maintains its holdings, it will have lower long-term earnings than Bank B (the long-term earnings potential of the company has been impaired). This said, EVE is not without its flaws.

Bank	Transactions
A	• 5-year loan at 8%; short call • Funded by 1-year money at 4%
B	• 1-year loan at 7% • Funded by 1-year money at 4%

Exhibit 6.6 *Comparative interest rate risk exposure*

Source: Author's own.

Bank	Transactions
A	• PV of a 4-year loan at 8% when market rates are 11% is 90.69 • The face value of the deposit at the end of year one remains 100 since it is repriced at the market rate
B	• PV of a 4-year loan at 11% when the market rates are 11% is 100, or par • As above, the value of the deposit is 100

Exhibit 6.7 *Comparative value at risk*

Source: Author's own.

Economic Value of Equity

In practice, EVE has been interpreted to mean the net present value of discounted cash flows (DCF) across a bank's balance sheet. So, for example, if you hold a mortgage loan, the method would require the bank to create a base-case scenario that reflects the principle and interest (P&I) cash flow schedules that are expected to occur over the remaining life of the instrument. For a measure of risk, this cash flow schedule will change as interest rates change. For a traditional fixed-rate mortgage, the schedule of P&I will decline as rates rise and increase as rates fall. As the value of the mortgage is a function of these cash flows, as interest rates increase and cash flows decline, the PV will decline due to discounting a lower volume of cash flows in the early years, and more cash flows in the later years. This seems reasonable. To see what is wrong with this method, however, consider a bank that owns a one-year floating-rate loan and has sold a five-year cap on the loan, a product very similar to the adjustable rate products that have proliferated on today's balance sheets. The bank's position is:

Capped Floater Loan = Non-Capped Floating Rate Loan. 5-Yr Cap Option

Assume then that the cap option is 200 bp out of the money at origination and that the loan originated at 3M Libor flat when the 3M Libor was 3.80 percent. The cap is, thus, 5.80 percent. Once the 3M Libor exceeds 5.80 percent at a reset date, the loan becomes a fixed-rate product and no longer adjusts upward. We are going to assume that volatility is flat at 15 percent for the purpose of this illustration. If you compute EVE as a discounted cash flow, which is the current approach used by many banks, the option has no effect on cash flows until the 3M Libor exceeds 5.80 percent. In the base case, you would see no effect. If a +200 bp shock were to occur you would likewise see no effect. The following Exhibit 6.8 highlights the coupon and EVE/NPV (Net Present Value) impact.

A market practitioner will immediately observe that the option value is misrepresented in this approach. As expected, the yield on the position floats until the interest rate passes the cap strike rate of 5.80 percent. However, if you are only discounting cash flows (i.e., principal and income streams), the cap "value" is unobserved in any rate environment

	Dn 100	Base case	Up 100	Up 200	Up 300
Base rate	3.80%	3.80%	3.80%	3.80%	3.80%
Rate shock	−1.00%	0.00%	1.00%	2.00%	3.00%
Net rate	2.80%	3.80%	4.80%	5.80%	6.80%
Cap level	5.80%	5.80%	5.80%	5.80%	5.80%
Net rate	2.80%	3.80%	4.80%	5.80%	5.80%
EVE/NPV	$ 100.00	$ 100.00	$ 100.00	$ 100.00	$ 95.79

Exhibit 6.8 *Impact of rate movement on loan coupon*

Source: Author's own.

	Dn 100	Base case	Up 100	Up 200	Up 300
Floating rate note	$ 100.00	$ 100.00	$ 100.00	$ 100.00	$ 100.00
Option value	$ (0.41)	$ (1.38)	$ (3.33)	$ (6.34)	$ (9.83)
OAV	$ 99.59	$ 98.62	$ 96.67	$ 93.66	$ 90.17
EVE/NPV	$ 100.00	$ 100.00	$ 100.00	$ 100.00	$ 95.79
Difference	$ (0.41)	$ (1.38)	$ (3.33)	$ (6.34)	$ (9.83)

Exhibit 6.9 *Impact of rate movement on value*

Source: Author's own.

below the cap strike. The more appropriate method would be to measure the value of the embedded option along with the instrument. In doing so, the values in Exhibit 6.9 are obtained.

These differences are far from trivial. Risk managers and bank supervisors should be hesitant to specify a methodology as simple as the NPV/EVE method, which is, arguably, the method advocated if interpreted according to existing regulatory guidance, as well as the majority of US industry practice. This situation has festered over the years due to two main factors:

- The acceptance of the EVE/NPV metric as a less than ideal but sufficient measure of risk; and

- The dominance of income simulation and income forecasting as the principle metric for measuring structural accrual-book risk.

These are powerful arguments against better methodologies; however, they hinge on the issue of "sufficiency." That is, is it accurate to say that the EVE/NPV measure is a "sufficient" measure of risk? Is EVE sufficient when coupled with an income simulation measure? Good arguments can be made that for many accrual-book positions EVE is an insufficient measure, even when coupled with income simulation measures. Given the growing complexity of embedded options, particularly in the mortgage space in the United States, and recognizing technology advances that permit more rigorous measurement of position risk, there is a case that can be made to enhance structural position risk measurement.

Consider, for example, the effective duration of the position under an EVE measure and calculated relative to the +/ñ 100bp shock from Exhibit 6.9 (shown earlier). Clearly, the effective duration (ED) is 0 under the EVE method. That is, there appears to be no price risk. In reality, the effective duration for this instrument is around 1.48 percent. While seemingly a small number, assume for a moment that this is the only position held by the financial organization. Further, assume the bank is funded with 90 percent quarterly reset funds (for simplicity, assume this is equivalent to an ED of 0.25) and 10 percent equity. In this case, Duration of Equity (D_E) is solved in the following manner:

$$TA \times D_A = \left[\frac{TL}{TA} \times D_L + 1 - \left(\frac{TL}{TA} \right) \times D_E \right]$$

where

TA = total assets
TL = total liabilities
D_A = duration of assets
D_L = duration of liabilities
D_E = duration of equity.

Solving for D_E when D_A and D_L are 0 and 0.25, respectively, leads to a D_E of 2.25 percent; however, when the asset duration is reflected at the more accurate 1.48 percent, D_E becomes 12.56 percent. In this case, the change in equity given a change in rates is D_E = 12.56 percent*Δy*Price.

If you assume this D_E can be scaled by a change in yield, then a 200 bp change in rates, without considering effective convexity, gives 25.12 percent. Under the most recent Basel proposals for supervision of interest rate risk, this exposure level would qualify as an "outlier" bank. What at first may have appeared to be a rather benign position turns out to be high risk. Looked at another way, perhaps more cynically, there appears to be plenty of room to "game" the rules if permitted to use simple measures rather than being asked to apply more rigorous and modern valuation algorithms to structural balance sheet positions. In practice, it could be argued that a portion of the gaming already takes place in more opaque portfolios, such as the deposit book of business where rules are unclear, practices wildly divergent and measurement methods inconclusive.

Clearly, the quality and integrity of balance sheet measurement methodologies are pivotal for a reasonable portrayal of risk. To achieve this, and as seen in the previous example, reasonable pricing of embedded derivative(s) should be required as a part of the measure being considered. Under the DCF/EVE measure, options are not fairly represented.

Pulling the Balance Sheet Puzzle Together

Static and Dynamic Models

Static models are based on positions at a given point in time. Typically, this is a firm's current position (CP) report. Gap, economic value of equity and duration-based models are typically considered static models. These models rely on current position balances and the cash flows expected to be produced from those balances over the life of the transaction.

Dynamic models, on the other hand, attempt to capture how a bank's management and its customers are expected to react to a changing interest rate environment. These models are more useful for active management of position risk over time. That is, within the model, balance sheet footings (i.e., volumes within asset/liability classes) are allowed to change according to behavioral rules that are built by the analyst. It is important that the A/L group has control over this process, and that it is not unduly influenced by the sales and/or budgeting/financial control side of the firm. The A/L group needs to be able to independently evaluate planned behavior in the context of historical performance and with an eye toward future market conditions. For example, if the national prime lending rate is rising, management may raise loan rates by a certain percentage and, consequently, future loan volumes may be assumed to decline, although existing business would be allowed to reprice at the higher rate. In such a circumstance, it is often the case that neither the sales side or the budgeting side will want or be motivated to recognize or account for this behavior until the impact is virtually certain.

Given the flexibility and more realistic conditions that dynamic models can explore, most firms find that dynamic income simulation models are more informative than static models. While short-term focused, the dynamic income simulation helps the proactive organization forecast the results of active decision making and develop strategies under various potential rate scenarios. While this sounds great, be aware that such forecasting is laden with assumptions that must be made about the direction of interest rates, how customers will react, how business strategy would change under each environment and how other key variables would be impacted. Thus, income simulation modeling is only as good as the quality of the assumptions and staff running the system. Some banks with very simple tools outperform banks using the most sophisticated models offered by vendors. Often, nothing replaces good professional judgment, market intuition and experience.

Major Assumptions Used Within a Balance Sheet Model

In general, most dynamic simulation models will estimate cash flows for most standard instruments including fixed/floating rate securities, loans, deposit products, and funding sources. Most models can incorporate various types of amortization schedules, rate quote conventions, spread assumptions, term assumptions, call and sinking fund provisions, and payment frequencies—assuming the data are accurate and available. In this regard, all models are simply "toolkits" to build accurate cash-flow forecasts.

There are other important considerations in developing a balance sheet model, however, which include:

- *Architecture.* Does the model allow for easy distributed and/or grid compute to leverage technology? Is the model easily scalable? Is the technology based on component architecture such as a service-oriented architecture?
- *Modularity.* Does the model port well into other systems to take advantage of possible points of integration? Are reporting dimensions dynamic and does the model allow for on-the-fly changes?
- *Reporting.* Is it relatively easy to get assumptions into the model and customizable information out? Are tools available for multidimensional analysis?
- *Usability.* Does the model make the performing of calculations relatively easy?
- *Schedulability.* Can processes be batch-controlled and automated?
- *Benchmarking.* Can the model be easily benchmarked and tested against known quantities?

Regarding calculations, the usefulness of simulation techniques—earnings and value—depends on the validity of the underlying data and assumptions and the accuracy of the basic structure on which the model is run. The results obtained will not be meaningful if these assumptions do not fairly reflect the bank's internal and external environments. Some of the major assumptions and/or inputs that are basic to all simulation models include the following.

Starting Balance Sheet

It is imperative that the bank ensures that the beginning balance sheet used for projecting earnings is accurate and captures all material positions and their characteristics. The old axiom "garbage in, garbage out" applies here. Internal audit can usually validate the integrity of the data. Critically important is how balance sheet accounts, and/or instruments, are aggregated into the model chart of accounts (COA). The classic example of poor aggregation is to separate all mortgages into two worlds; for example, all fixed-rate products over 7 percent and all under 7 percent. Such wide aggregation groups, if the positions are significant, are probably conducive to poor modeling results.

Selection of Rate Scenarios and Driver Rates

The driver rates should be comprehensive and properly assigned to the account pools or instrument profiles. Moreover, the interest rate scenarios that are run should contain both realistic rate paths (i.e., where and when the bank expects rates to move, such as the forward rate path) as well as stressed rate paths (i.e., +/− 200 bp shocks). Regardless, the input of rate paths should be consistent with expectations and the scenario under consideration. In some cases, the bank may be looking at reports that claim to be rate increases when in fact the analyst forgot to change one or more paths, or has made nontransparent overrides to modeled rates or spreads. Therefore, having checks and balances around these inputs is important. With some models, the process for entering market data and rates can be convoluted and overly complex. A rule of thumb in any modeling environment is to try to keep things as seamless and simple as possible, but not too simple. Unnecessarily complex input processes can result in lower integrity and may expose the modeling effort to higher levels of potential error.

New Business Assumptions

It is critical to know whether and how the model incorporates new business, or if it is a "constant scale" (i.e., constant) balance sheet model (i.e., this means that any run-off is replaced but only to the point that it brings the position back in balance with the starting position account level). Notably, new business assumptions can mask/hide inherent interest rate risk. For example, if the model assumes that loans grow by 30 percent funding by a similar increase in core monies, when in fact they each only grow by 5 percent, the assumed growth may mask earnings deterioration in a rising rate environment, as the higher rate production never actually occurs. It is for this reason that some practitioners recommend running both static and dynamic simulations to gauge the range of exposure. No matter your perspective, it is important to understand the level of new business assumed to roll onto the book (i.e., "new business assumptions"), how it is priced when it hits the book, how it is funded and its assumed life.

Repricing Attributes

If analysis is performed at the pool level, rather than at the instrument level, the analyst will need to make assumptions about how the pool reprices. Even in the case where instrument-level attributes are captured, assumptions will need to be made for existing and new business where there are either gaps in the data or a need to create behavioral characteristics. If 100 percent reprice every three months, it might be reasonable to assume that 33 percent will reprice each month. Such assumptions may lead to inaccurate results and, thus, should be documented. Another example may be a 30-year adjustable-rate mortgage. It has a 30-year maturity but reprices each year. Repricing assumptions also are important for products with caps and floors. In the ARM example, many ARMs have periodic and lifetime rate caps/floors. Thus, if rates increase 300 basis points within one year, the ARM could only adjust up, for example, by 200 basis points (i.e., the periodic cap). Another important point is how the new business is assumed to come onto the book. If you assume that the spread to your driver rate for indirect loans is 150 basis points when, in fact, it is only 75 basis points, the new business will look more profitable than it is. Being able to model this "spread" risk may be an important consideration.

Run-Off Schedules

When will a loan cease to be outstanding? Answering this question is especially important for products with embedded options. One cannot assume a static amortization schedule for loans with prepayment options. Similar run-off issues exist for CDs if modeled on a pool level. For example, if you have a pool of six-month CDs, it may be reasonable to assume that one sixth of the pool runs off each month.

Core Deposit Behavior

How the bank models its core deposits will influence the accuracy of the model. It is for this reason that the core deposit assumptions should be thoroughly understood, documented, and validated. The modeling of core deposits is an art, not a science, and opinions as to the best methods to use are wide and diverse. Given varying approaches, risk managers and A/L analysts should ensure that the assumptions are documented, rational, consistent with observed behavior (i.e., supported by analysis), and are not "manipulated" (e.g., altered to produce a desired outcome). In one bank, the treasurer was very quick to alter repricing beta assumptions in order to "manage" the model results to the output he desired. This manipulation of the model output was always "defensible" but not well communicated, documented or supported by empirical analysis. These apparently minor changes had major effects and in this case there was never any discussion of such change in the governance forums that existed. In practice, such "gaming" of model results should be avoided or, at minimum, any changes to critical assumptions should be required to be defended—with empirical research/analysis—at high-level risk governance forums.

Prepayment Assumptions

Loans that are subject to prepayment must be simulated to consider the prepayment option embedded in the contracts. The most common method is to use generic prepayment speeds obtained from an external source, such as Bloomberg. In certain instances, the bank will take these generic speeds and adjust them to account for idiosyncratic factors that characterize the bank's local market. Underlying such adjustments should be documented analysis, even if it is fairly basic. The more preferred method for modeling prepayment risk is to use econometric models to project prepayment speeds. These models are often fairly complex and many ALM tools source the prepayment speeds from third-party specialist firms. A good example of such a firm is Andrew Davidson & Co., Inc. The advantage of using these models is that the speeds produced can be at the transaction level and include individual loan characteristics, including things such as age, location, origination channel, spread at origination, curve at origination, and other items.

Conclusion

Financial theory and practice have converged at a rapid rate within the last decade. While attribution for this enhanced alignment is wide and various, it is clear that the increased acceptance of advanced financial concepts, dramatic improvements in computing power and improved data management have been primary motivators for this change.

This evolution in financial practice shows no signs of slowing. The world is getting smaller and advanced risk management capabilities more pervasive; markets are more liquid than ever, spreads narrower and pricing more competitive; transactions and information are arriving at ever-faster speed, with ever more complexity, and decisions need to be made on the fly. For firms to gain strategic advantage, it is no longer sufficient to merely measure, report, and avoid risk. Today, the field of participants in the financial services business is too diverse to allow for such a relaxed approach toward risk management. Successful firms are those that proactively manage risk, not just avoid it.

The importance of more comprehensive risk measurement and management is echoed by former US Federal Reserve Bank Chairman, Alan Greenspan. In his October 5, 2004 speech to the American Bankers Association, Chairman Greenspan noted:

> It would be a mistake to conclude (from these comments) that the only way to succeed in banking is through ever-greater size and diversity. Indeed, better risk management may be the only truly necessary element of success in banking.

Although commonly assumed to be so, size is not the critical element of success. Rather, the ability to rapidly, accurately, and dynamically manage your portfolio of risks is the dominant success factor.

Being nimble and reactive toward risk and risk management has never been as approachable to all financial firms as it is today, thanks to better data models, pervasive access to data and information and much faster computers and computer technology. These increased capabilities are allowing firms to price risk across products, relationships and geographies with an eye toward the "market price" of risk rather than the traditional banking model of pricing risk to peer.

The next step in the evolution of financial intermediation is one that will require active "portfolio" management rather than traditional reactive "transaction" management. It requires the implementation of processes and procedures that ensure that the bank is being compensated for the risks it assumes. Active portfolio management should allow the bank to determine where value is being created and where it is being destroyed. It involves the ability to routinely (perhaps on a daily basis) attribute the correct amount of capital at any level desired, often at the level of the transaction. It provides an ability to more actively buy, hedge, sell or hold risks, choosing which risks to keep and which risks to mitigate or eliminate. Perhaps, most importantly, it allows for the opportunity to align incentives and business behaviors with risks being underwritten.

CHAPTER 7

The Risks Within the Hedge Fund Industry

Diccon Smeeton

ABN AMRO

Introduction

A quick scan of the financial press reveals many influential pundits still consider the hedge fund industry to be a cabal of rapacious, Gordon Gecko types, or "locusts" hell-bent on financial Armageddon!

Incontrovertibly, the hedge fund industry has witnessed explosive growth since the early 1990s. It no longer bears any resemblance whatsoever to the cottage industry of a decade ago, however, and is a respected alternative asset class essential to an institutionalized investment portfolio, with risks better understood and managed by all participants. Growth has been fuelled largely by significant fund development in Europe and in Asia, albeit from low bases, although the longest established, most institutionalized and largest funds remain North American. The total amount of capital invested in these alternative investments now significantly exceeds US$1tn, and the capital inflow shows no signs of abating. As the industry has grown, and ancillary services around it have mushroomed, the range of strategies and investment styles has also expanded and with them the associated risks. Significantly, the pressures on banks to engage with hedge funds has also increased and, consequently, bank exposure to the sector has increased, although we believe this remains overstated and more diffuse.

Nevertheless, the risks of doing business with this unregulated, leveraged client group remain significant but perhaps are overstated—and are certainly often misunderstood. The nature of the business undertaken by hedge funds means that they often invest in significant concentration, or in illiquid securities. The lack of transparency can cause problems when managing risk and is perhaps the biggest hurdle in any assessment of the risk of any particular hedge fund.

Leverage does contribute to the risks of the industry but managers now demonstrate greater caution in utilizing leverage than they did pre-1998 and rarely utilize the levels offered by banks and brokers, contrary to spectators who appear to believe in the widespread misconception that leverage is directly proportional to investment success. The lack of controls around leverage, the "herd mentality" of many hedge fund managers and the resultant herd-like behavior of their funds may cause problems for the financial markets as a whole. Additionally, as hedge funds potentially combine high levels of leverage with their increased involvement in increasingly complex OTC products, the industry could be susceptible to a systemic reduction in liquidity. Potentially aggravating this are capacity constraints that are evident in thinly traded markets or securities. This could potentially be exacerbated by the anecdotal pressures that are beginning to become apparent among certain service providers, particularly administrators. The industry has changed phenomenally, however, since the collapse of LTCM in 1998 and huge advances have been made in risk management, technology, and market practice that considerably reduce the possibility of such a mammoth recurrence.

Due Diligence

As the industry has grown, many strategies of hedge funds have become less opaque and more complex to the risk professionals whose job it is to monitor their activities, and the tools available to manage the risks have improved. The "traditional" reliance on unsophisticated, nuclear-option additional termination events in master documentation, in which a fund manager is faced with catastrophe, and front-office pressure on the risk "cost centers" to maintain a profitable account can be very forceful, has been replaced with an array of risk management options that includes frank, regular, and open relationships with hedge fund managers, risk measurement models sensitized to liquidity and concentration restraints, collateral management systems that can actually call for initial margin as well as the daily mark, plus greater education of and increasing risk tolerance by senior credit risk management in banks for hedge fund risks. Risk professionals in many of the leading banks and financial institutions now have the appropriate tools necessary to assess the risks incurred and have gained greater access to hedge fund management companies.

In general, hedge fund managers have a symbiotic relationship with banks, a crucial factor not always appreciated fully by the deep-pocketed bureaucratic behemoths, nor readily acknowledged by the canny "hedgies" that have skillfully played brokers off against each other for years. The liquidity and the credit limits provided by banks are vital to funds in order to enable them to achieve their investment objectives and ensure their survival during liquidity crunches by keeping funding in place. By appreciating the significance of banks to their investment objectives, hedge fund managers have begun to improve the level of disclosure that they provide to their counterparties. The more enlightened have also begun to appreciate the benefits of treating the risk departments of banks as "partners," and the "best practices" hedge fund managers now go to great lengths to ensure that counterparty credit officers have a solid understanding of all aspects of their business activities. A good relationship with a key credit officer, who has been kept well informed of business activities, has proved beneficial to many fund managers in times of difficulty.

There are two major owners of risk in hedge funds (other than the risks borne by the principals and employees): investors and counterparties. The risks incurred through investment are manifold and are largely overcome through significant levels of both initial and ongoing due diligence to ensure solid understanding that higher returns necessitate a higher risk-taking appetite and an appreciation of investment portfolio diversification. The largest risk to investors tends to be either poor performance or fraud. Hedge fund managers, particularly in "start-up" phase, are keen to attract and retain investor assets. As a result, they tend to be forthcoming with requests for information when approached by potential investors. Risks, therefore, other than performance or fraud, are relatively easily understood and mitigated. Trading relationships tend to be more complicated, as fund managers are sometimes reluctant to provide "proprietary" information to other market participants, despite almost universal adherence to Chinese Walls policies in place at all banks. The primary foundation of good risk management when dealing with hedge funds in any capacity is extensive initial and ongoing due diligence. This would normally involve site visits to the offices of the management company in order to satisfy oneself that the operations are sufficiently robust to handle the proposed activities of the hedge funds under management. The due diligence process would normally involve meetings with the CEO/CIO of the fund in order to fully understand the strategy and the means that will be employed to achieve the fund's investment objectives. In addition, a thorough due diligence process would require a meeting with the fund manager's COO and chief risk officer in order to fully understand the operational infrastructure, as well as the risk-control measures in place to protect the fund and its activities.

Regulation

The lack of regulation of the majority of hedge funds is often cited as a key contributor to the risks run by the sector, yet as the market-timing scandals among mutual fund managers, Enron and WorldCom, even the collapse of Barings, demonstrate that regulation offers minimal protection against a determined fraudster. Many hedge fund managers, however, are regulated by the local financial regulator (e.g., the FSA in the UK and the CFTC or the SEC in the United States). It is a fact that the absence of regulation does not noticeably contribute to the risks run, but it does mean that hedge funds tend to operate below any kind of regulatory radar. In addition, the presence of a regulator (which, despite best efforts, is almost always under-resourced) could give both investors and service providers a false sense of comfort or imply a degree of sanction that reduces the fundamental "caveat emptor" caution relating to any investment decision and fundamental due diligence that investors and counterparties are now continually upgrading and refining.

The fact that hedge funds tend to be incorporated in offshore financial jurisdictions means that the burden of regulation is unlikely to extend to the funds themselves, thus preserving the tax benefits of investors and maintaining an active industry of brass-plate manufacturers in some corner of the West Indies. The involvement of a local regulator, however, governing the activities of a fund manager should, and does, provide some comfort to both investors and counterparties. These regulators tend to provide a measure of protection against fraudulent activities, particularly the FSA in the UK, which conducts a thorough investigation of principals before providing registration. Once a fund is established and trading, it is doubtful that a regulator will uncover fraud or illegal activity before investors incur a loss.

Investment companies registered with the US Securities and Exchange Commission (SEC) are subject to a high level of scrutiny with regard to their activities concerning (amongst other things) the short-selling of securities and the use of leverage. Consequently, many hedge fund managers have historically opted to operate as .unregistered investment companies. As of February 2006, the SEC implemented a rule change that required almost all US hedge fund managers, as well as those hedge fund managers located in jurisdictions other than the other things) the short-selling of securities and the use of leverage. Consequently, many hedge fund managers have historically opted to operate as "unregistered investment companies." As of February 2006, the SEC implemented a rule change that required almost all US hedge fund managers, as well as those hedge fund managers located in jurisdictions other than the United States, but with US investors, to register with the SEC as investment advisors, under the Investment Advisors Act. This requirement applies to firms managing in excess of US$25m and which are open to new investors. This rule is currently under review, having been subject to successful challenges in US courts. In June 2006, the US Court of Appeals for the District of Columbia overturned the rule and ordered the SEC to review it. Nevertheless, it is a matter of time before hedge fund regulation mark II is revealed. An interesting aside: many fund managers opted to return money to investors or to close their funds and thus avoided the need to register with regulators. Making themselves so exclusive has served to increase their appeal and investors appear to pay eye-popping management fees for the privilege of having these titans manage their money.

Most UK-based hedge fund managers are registered with the Financial Services Authority (FSA) and, as a result, regulatory developments have not had a significant impact on their activities. Given the require-ment of UK-based fund managers to register with the SEC if they have US investors, some European managers have forcibly redeemed their US investors. In June 2005, the FSA published discussion papers on hedge funds, focusing on systemic risk and consumer protection. In 2005, the FSA also created an internal team to monitor the activities of the 25 hedge funds doing business in the UK that are perceived to represent the highest levels of risk to the financial industry. It is widely agreed that the FSA's use of guidelines, adherence to recommended best practices and encouragement of dialogue as opposed to a prescriptive set of rules is a model worth expanding.

Recent pronouncements by the European Central Bank (that the threat of the potential risks to the financial markets as a result of hedge fund activities are comparable to an epidemic of bird flu—not surprising given the rhetoric adopted by some local politicians to describe hedge funds) and by the Bank of England (which, in what can perhaps be described as a more measured and less knee-jerk reaction, has engaged with market participants in an attempt to highlight specific risks posed by hedge fund activity) illustrates that the issue of hedge fund regulation remains a live topic and that the various issues are not always adequately highlighted and any discussion is still clouded with a lack of solid under-standing around the industry. It is likely that hedge funds will continue to be further embraced by regulation as the industry grows (particularly if hedge funds are increasingly offered to retail investors). As the industry has become more sophisticated and risk management techniques have increased so substantially, however, the risks to investors could be over-stated. Regulation would be unlikely to prevent the occurrence of a sig-nificant market event and the victims of such an event would probably include hedge funds as well as banks and other financial institutions.

What Would Be the Impact on the Industry of a Failure of a Hedge Fund?

Surprise, surprise—the sun would still rise tomorrow, the resilience of the industry would again be demonstrated and certain hedge funds could even make outsize profits. It is a truism that the "Wall Street community" proved themselves to be the lender of last resort to the hedge fund sector, after agreeing to the Federal Reserve-orchestrated bail-out of LTCM. It is likely that the industry participants would once again resolve a similar crisis.

Perversely, it may be a blessed, "normalizing," relief should a counterparty suffer a loss from dealing with a hedge fund. Almost unique among any sector to which it extends financial services, banks are terrified of incurring a hedge fund loss yet expect it as a normal cost of doing business in the retail, commercial, and corporate sectors. This continuing fixation with "zero loss" has its roots in the hoary sound bite among senior risk management that all hedge funds are "correlated," meaning any single loss is magnified into a financial tsunami. We observe, however, how the hedge fund industry and its service providers have continued to thrive since the 1998 LTCM debacle, the bursting of the tech and dotcom bubbles, and the Ford/GM downgrade in 2005.

Hedge funds fail for any number of reasons and attrition is a regular occurrence. By far the most common failure, however, is associated with poor performance. In the event that a fund performs badly, it is difficult for the fund managers to attract sufficient investor assets. In turn, this makes it difficult for the manager to retain or attract staff due to the lack of fee income (either in the form of performance, but also in the form of management fees). The lack of fee income also makes it difficult for the fund manager to invest in state-of-the-art risk management systems. When this happens, hedge funds tend to die quietly and disappear which shows maturity among participants, rather than the unrecognizable stereotype of a desperate gambler taking a last chance outsize risk.

Since the Federal Reserve-sponsored rescue of Long Term Capital Management in 1998, banks have become a great deal more sophisticated in their risk management process. In addition to the general level of due diligence conducted prior to permitting trading limits, banks demand collateral to support the counterparty risk, as well as tighter levels of documentation to govern the trading relationship between the fund and its trading counterparties. The development of cross-margining and cross-netting systems enables banks to benefit from a balanced book of business from a hedge fund, in exchange for favorable margin treatment for the hedge fund. These measures have served to protect individual banks from risk of loss in the event of a counterparty default. In addition, the widespread use of risk management techniques has also reduced the risk of systemic loss across the wider banking industry.

A recent phenomenon has been liquidations of hedge funds as a result of the weight of capital flowing into the industry or the crowding of certain strategies. As the market has become more crowded, hedge fund managers have found that their ability to generate superior return has become threatened by the sheer number of counterparties chasing the same deals. This has had two effects: first, managers may be forced to invest in higher-risk transactions in order to meet investors' return expectations; and second, funds are failing, having been unable to justify their stubbornly consistent management and performance fees in the face of lackluster investment returns.

Ongoing Risk Management

Hedge funds represent a significant, and increasing, client base for many banks. The activities of hedge funds now touch on many different business activities undertaken by investment banks and provide liquidity in many markets. As their importance to banks increases, the risks that banks face when doing business with funds also grow. Internal pressure to remain competitive, as well as to minimize capital utilization, and thus bolster profitability has caused the risk departments of banks to look for inventive risk solutions to protect the banks from the risk of loss.

A thorough and ongoing due diligence process is the best means of protection against risk of loss, as it bolsters collateral management and trade capture systems. The ability to conduct stress testing on the bank's portfolio of trades, both with individual hedge funds and with the sector as a whole, is an area banks continue to enhance. Banks with a prime brokerage operation are in a stronger position when it comes to risk management than those without. This is due to the levels of transparency that a prime broker is able to exercise, which enables the prime broker to control and manage their own risks in a more holistic way.

There is no substitute for "knowing the customer." It is important that risk departments are able to establish their own relationship with the principals or risk managers at the hedge fund management companies, instead of relying on the relationship that is in place between the fund and the business areas of the bank. Risk departments should insist on receiving financial disclosure from funds on, at least, a monthly basis. This disclosure should, at a minimum, include information relating to the NAV of the fund, NAV per share as well as performance information. Quality is, of course, better than quantity. Most fund managers are content to provide the same information to counterparty banks as they are prepared to provide to their investors. This should not be viewed in isolation and should be compared to other funds following the same strategies, in order to establish some kind of peer comparison and perhaps be scrutinized in some detail after counterparty and portfolio stress-testing exercises have been conducted.

As the flow of institutional capital into hedge funds increases alongside the rising incidence of fraud cases that have caused losses for investors, there has been heightened focus on operational due diligence. Operational risk is particularly relevant with hedge funds, due to the wide disparity between the resourcing of each management company, which can vary between small private offices to deeply resourced, institutional money management companies. The increase of availability of outsourcing providers has gone a long way to improving the operational risks run by hedge funds, as there are now a variety of robust middle-office functions available on an outsourced basis.

Perhaps the area most vulnerable to operational risk, and therefore one that should be subject to particular scrutiny by market participants, is that of portfolio valuations. This is an area that can be susceptible to manager manipulation. There is a risk that unscrupulous managers will use asset valuations artificially to boost fund performance, or to smooth over mark-to-market losses of the fund portfolio. A legitimate source of valuation risk arises if an investment strategy is to invest in thinly traded or illiquid securities. If this is the case, the fund has little choice but to accept the risk that valuations might be hard to come by, or might reflect very wide bid/offer spreads. Some unscrupulous managers, however, might exploit illiquidity in order to falsify performance records. This can be avoided by ensuring that there is a robust, independent valuation process in place (i.e., that the back office or third-party valuation agent calculates month-end valuations, independent of front-office involvement.

This helps to prevent the risk that investment managers might be able to "mark" their own book). Investors and credit counterparties should demand transparency over the valuation process, as well as evidence that the prices are achieved consistently. The most practical solution to this issue is to ensure that the fund manager has appointed a third-party fund administrator to provide valuations. Best practice would suggest that the administrator calculates the NAVs using data derived exclusively from independent sources and with no reference to the fund manager. We must be realistic, however, that third-party administrators are straining under unprecedented demand, high staff turnover and "exotic" trades that inevitably compromise the integrity of the valuation process. In many cases, any prices are hard to obtain for esoteric investments.

How Is the Banking Industry Coming to Terms with This Growing Investment Class?

Hedge funds represent a significant proportion of investment banks' revenues. This is due to their demand for a wide range of products, ranging from cash instruments to structured finance transactions. Increasingly, banks are having to be creative in their product offerings in order to meet the demands of this sophisticated client base and industrialize the process of managing their hedge fund risks. As another example of the symbiotic relationship, banks increasingly see hedge funds as an investor base ready, at a price, to assume some of their own risk.

A major impact of the development of the global hedge fund sector has been that banks have had to evolve in order to retain trading personnel. This has meant that banks have had to revise the remuneration offered to proprietary traders in order to match the pay packages offered by hedge funds.

The risk management (encompassing both credit and market risk) departments of banks have been obliged to become more sophisticated and responsive in the ways that risk is managed and measured. Increasingly, banks use sophisticated stress-testing techniques in order to measure and monitor portfolio concentrations and correlation risks. The use of VaR and cross-product margining further reduces the banks' exposures to portfolio risks, as well as providing a true measure of counterparty exposure. The days of idiotic panic-stricken fire drills where staff sacrificed weekends to prepare impressively comprehensive (but incomprehensible) spreadsheets are surely numbered.

Stress testing is becoming a more widely used tool by both hedge funds and banks. The significance of severe market events is measured using a variety of scenarios. These scenarios tend to be based on both hypothetical scenarios and real events. While it can be argued that hedge fund managers are paid to manage money in a variety of risk scenarios, stress testing is an increasingly useful means of measuring the likely impact of specific risk events on funds. The results of stress tests are used as a risk management tool on both sides, and their importance must increase.

Operational risk is a significant source of risk for hedge fund managers, who are increasingly demanding higher levels of operational competence from counterparties as well as service providers (such as administrators, prime brokers, custodians, and valuation agents). Hedge funds are susceptible to operational risk at every level and as they invest in more illiquid or complicated products. Therefore, the abilities of prime brokers and administrators to obtain accurate market pricing is becoming more important. In addition, hedge funds themselves are looking to diversify their risk by entering into multiple prime broker agreements, as well as entering into trading limits with a diversified selection of banking counterparties.

What Might Happen Going Forward?

It is inevitable that "alternative investments" will continue to grow in importance. Increasingly, "real money" or long-only fund managers are utilizing investment techniques (insofar as regulations permit) that have traditionally been seen as being reserved for hedge fund managers only. In addition, many of the traditional asset managers are establishing hedge funds for a number of reasons: to retain investment management talent, to retain investors seeking superior investment returns, to generate hedge fund fee income, and to diversify their investors' risk profiles, as well as to allow these investors to benefit from investment returns in falling markets.

It is also likely, however, that we will see an increase in the number of closure rates as fund assets increase. This is for a number of reasons, but most significantly because there is likely to be too much cash chasing too few opportunities. This underperformance will result in dissatisfied investors, and lead to redemptions, a natural "Darwinian" occurrence. Additionally, hedge funds are investing in assets that represent high risk of loss. An example is that these funds invest in distressed securities and, as interest rates rise and defaults increase, those funds that have bought the highest-risk, lowest-grade securities start to experience significant losses. The risks of loss are particularly high, given that most major hedge funds invest in fixed-income securities, even if this is not their main investment strategy. Should a significant credit event cause a loss of confidence in the corporate bond market, funds are likely to find that many of their investments become increasingly illiquid.

Another significant risk facing the industry is complacency from banks themselves, evidenced by the continued penny pinching on trade capture, collateral management and risk management systems. As hedge funds become more important to banks, it is likely that risk departments will face increasing pressure to relax standards and lower the barriers to entry with regard to credit quality and collateral measures. A wholesale reduction in standards will make banks more susceptible to systemic risk, irrespective of the quality of a bank's individual hedge fund portfolio.

It is most likely that hedge fund growth will slow due to pressure from banks themselves. The banking sector appears to be facing two distinct trends: first, an increased drive for profitability; and second, continued consolidation. Banks are increasingly looking to improve their return on equity and, as their shareholders demand reduced volatility of earnings, consequently they limit their exposure to any particular sector. This rule also applies to exposure to trading counterparties. Some estimates claim that global assets under management in the entire hedge fund sector will total US$6tn within the next decade. Growth of this magnitude will put pressure on bank credit lines, particularly if further industry consolidation results in fewer market participants. Given the various risk mitigators required by banks when trading with hedge funds, the volumes of business can be high but the "actual" risk (measured to a specific confidence level) comparatively low. Nonetheless, the risk appetite is likely to be finite. As pressure on credit limits grows, it would seem inevitable that banks will provide credit to those funds that either represent a comparatively low level of risk or that generate significant revenue for banks. As a result, it is likely that the growth of the hedge fund industry will be constrained by the banks' ability to provide credit.

The risks of dealing with hedge funds remain the same as they always have. Both banks and investors, however, are benefiting from both improved standards of disclosure and the latest advances in risk management techniques.

CHAPTER 8

Derivatives Risk—OTC and ETD

Errol Danziger

Danziger Structured Finance

Introduction

"Risk" is a synonym for uncertainty or unfamiliarity. Something that is unfamiliar or unknown is more risky than something that is familiar.

All investments are based on a forecast of some kind, that is, on some assumption about the future. Every investment has uncertainty built into it and every investor is exposed to risks of various kinds. Investment return is therefore uncertain by definition and is thus the inevitable by-product of taking risk.

There are three categories of investment risk or financial risk: market risk, credit risk, and operational risk. Market risk is the risk of incurring losses due to changes in market factors—prices, volatilities, and correlations. It includes asset liquidity risk and the credit risk associated with investments. Market risk can, in turn, be subdivided into interest rate risk, equity risk, currency risk, commodity risk, and liquidity risk.

The omnipresent existence of financial risk means that risk management is essential to investment management. The overriding purpose of risk management is the preservation of wealth. In the long term, an investment manager focuses on expected return on investment. A risk manager, on the other hand, maintains that one cannot manage expected return, but one can manage risk. There is a trade-off between risk and expected return and one cannot be considered without reference to the other. This means that all risks that are associated with an investment have to be balanced with the investment opportunity and there should ideally be a balance between the intentional assumption of risk and the hedging of risk. The perception that there is a relationship between investment and risk is widely accepted in the banking sector. Modern banks do not manage investment portfolios: they manage risk—their long-term investment strategies are to define the risks to which they wish to be exposed and to manage that exposure appropriately.

The Role of Derivatives in Risk Management

A derivative contract is a bilateral agreement that provides for payment to be made by one contracting party to the other, the amount of such payment to be quantified at a future date based on the value of an asset, index, or rate at that future date. The asset, index, or rate, which determines the amount to be paid, is referred to as the derivative's underlying. The underlying of a derivative is a specified interest rate, security price, commodity price, foreign exchange rate, index of prices or rates, or some other variable. A derivative is thus a financial instrument the value of which depends on the future performance of an asset of variable value, usually a cash market security or commodity, financial or commodity index, or notional amount. The notional amount of a derivative is a number of currency units, shares, bushels, pounds, or other units specified in the contract. A derivative requires no initial net investment or an investment that is smaller than would be required for a cash market investment and it permits net settlement or performance that is equivalent to net settlement. The settlement of a derivative contract with a notional amount is determined by the interaction of the notional amount with the underlying: the interaction may be by multiplication, or may be formulaic.

The main economic advantage of derivatives is that they facilitate the transfer of financial risks. Derivatives facilitate efficient and cost-effective risk management. The need for such risk management arises because participants in investment markets have different perceptions of risk. They may wish to reduce or eliminate risk, they may accept a certain level of risk but wish to stabilize risk at that level, or they may wish to increase the level of risk that is assumed. They do this by transferring risk to other market participants or by assuming risks of other participants that are transferred to them.

Derivatives are thus used for trading, hedging, and arbitrage. Trading with dividends involves entering into risk positions, with the object of earning profits when forecasts are met. Most derivative trading involves traders and hedgers, who secure the equilibrium and liquidity on the exchange-traded futures and options markets. A trader wishes to assume the very risk that the hedger wants to eliminate. Hedging is the process of securing an existing or planned portfolio against market fluctuations. Hedgers use derivatives to reduce funding costs, diversify sources of funding or avoid market volatility. Arbitrage constitutes the making of trades in order to exploit market imbalances for the purpose of making risk-free profits. Arbitrageurs ensure that the prices of forward transactions deviate minimally, if at all, and for a short time only from their theoretical values.

The success of derivatives has been attributable to the market risks embodied in the high volatility and associated risks relating to currency, equity, and bond markets. Managing those risks is critical for investment success. An investor may wish to avoid the risk of incurring losses on his portfolio. A speculator may wish to deliberately undertake increased risk in order to earn profits from forecasting market development correctly. They enable investors to transfer unwanted risks to other market participants.

Although derivatives allow investors to manage the financial risks associated with their investment transactions, there are also risks inherent in the use of derivative products, many of those risks being market-related.

The Classification of Derivatives

Derivative contracts are classified based either on the manner in which they are entered into, or based on the type of rights and obligations that they bring into existence.

Based on the manner in which derivative contracts are entered into, there are two broad classes of derivatives: ETD (or exchange-traded derivatives); and OTC (or over-the-counter derivatives).

Exchange-traded derivatives, such as commodity futures and listed equity options, are standardized contracts that are actively traded on public exchanges. A clearing house acts as the central counterparty for each transaction. In order to protect itself from default by any market participant, the clearing house requires each market participant to pledge collateral called "margin" for each open position, that is, for each contract for which performance is pending. Profits and losses on each contract are calculated and netted at the end of each trading day and, at the opening of the market on the following trading day, the exercise price of the contract is adjusted to match the previous day's closing spot price of the underlying.

Margin covers the maximum expected loss that might be incurred by the market participant on the following exchange trading day. Unlike payment against delivery for cash market transactions, which must take place within two or three days of the completion of the transaction contract, settlement of exchange-traded derivatives takes place on specific dates, called the settlement date. Thus exchange-traded futures and options contracts provide for settlement on just four specific dates during the year.

Exchange-traded derivatives have standardized contract specifications, and are revalued marked-to-market—or margined daily by the clearing house. By entering into a counter transaction, an investor can neutralize (close out) his contractual rights and obligations prior to the maturity date of the contract. Any profits or losses incurred on a contract that has not been closed out are credited or debited daily. Organized derivatives exchanges thus provide investors with the facilities to contract based on market perception and in accordance with appetite for risk, but without having to buy or sell the underlying commodities, securities, or equities. Exchange-traded derivatives comprise a mature market that has been active for decades and the traded instruments that are traded on the exchanges are regulated by the exchanges on which they are traded as well as by governmental securities authorities. Because exchange-traded derivatives are actively traded, the market performs a constant pricing function.

OTC derivatives are derivative contracts that are individually negotiated and customized for the specific needs of a particular investor. They meet a specific investment or trading requirement more easily than a standardized derivative. OTC derivatives often have an element of both risk hedging and speculation, so that the same derivative contract may be a hedge for one end-user and a speculation for another. OTC derivatives are repriced periodically, usually monthly or six-monthly, by a process called "marking-to-market." Customized OTC derivatives may have a limited or no trading market and, therefore, no market price. Market participants determine prices themselves, using complex and often proprietary pricing models.

Every derivative contract has either a forward-based format or an option-based format. Forward-based derivatives include forward contracts, futures contracts and swap agreements. A forward-based derivative has a symmetrical risk profile, in which the seller's loss equals the buyer's gain, and vice versa.

Forward contract. A forward contract is an OTC derivative that is customized for the needs of the contracting parties. It provides that one party will buy and the other party will sell a designated quantity of the underlying at a pre-agreed price on a specified future date. Contractual performance takes place at maturity of the contract, on which date either cash settlement, that is, the cash value of the contract, or the underlying is conveyed through physical delivery by the seller to the buyer. A forward contract functions in the same way as an insurance policy, limiting both profits and losses. This is called reduction of variance, where "variance" is defined as the extent to which possible outcomes depart from the expected return, so that an event with only one outcome has zero variance. Because a forward contract limits losses as well as profits, on account of the requirement to make a fixed payment to the counterparty notwithstanding favorable or unfavorable price variations in the underlying, possible outcomes will depart less from the expected return when a forward is used to limit risk exposure.

Because a forward contract calls for bilateral future performance, however, it involves significant credit risk, in the form of risk of loss for both parties resulting from the contracting counterparty failing to perform. As the value of the forward contract is only conveyed at maturity, price changes can lead to large gains or losses on the contract by either party. The gain to one counterparty in a forward-based transaction is always equal to the loss incurred by the other party. This is called symmetry of risk and it is the most important feature that distinguishes forward-based transactions from option-based transactions.

Futures contract. A futures contract is a forward-based derivative that is standardized and exchange-traded. Standardization of futures contracts results in the quantity and quality of the underlying, the time and place of delivery of the underlying and the method of payment in respect of each contract of the same series of futures contracts being identical, with only the price being negotiated. Standardization of a futures contract implies that it is fungible and can therefore be transferred from investor to investor.

Standardization and fungibility results in futures markets being highly liquid. This market liquidity, together with small contract size, facilitates the ability of a large number of investors and speculators to be able to trade in futures. Futures contracts are settled by physical delivery or close out, so that where the price of a futures contract rises, the contract buyer can realize a profit by selling the contract: closing out by entering into a counter-transaction releases both contracting parties from their contractual obligations.

Swap agreement. A swap agreement is a notional principal contract that obligates the two contracting parties to exchange payment streams that are based on a notional amount, on periodic payment or settlement dates. The notional amount, which is the underlying of the swap, is not usually exchanged and the two payment streams are usually netted, with only the difference being paid by the party who is the net debtor to the creditor party.

Economically, a swap is the equivalent of a series of forward contracts. Each swap payment date or swap settlement date effectively represents the maturity date of one forward contract and the commencement of a new contract that will mature on the next settlement date. Swaps are individually negotiated and are not exchange-traded.

Option contract. An option is a contract or financial instrument under which the grantor or writer of the option gives the option grantee or holder the right, but not the obligation, by exercising the option, to buy—in the case of a call option—or to sell—in the case of a put option—a specified asset at a predetermined price, called the strike price of the option, at either a fixed future date, or on one or more of a specified number of future dates, or on a date chosen by the option holder not later than the last day for exercise of the option.

The option holder pays a fee, called the option premium, to the grantor for the rights conferred by the option contract. Where the holder of the option has not exercised it by the last day fixed for exercising the option, the option expires unexercised and the option premium remains the property of the option grantor. Because the option holder can choose to either exercise the option or let it expire unexercised, the holder benefits from favorable price movements in the underlying, but loses only the premium paid for the contract in the event of unfavorable price movements. The option grantor, on the other hand, has committed to a firm obligation with respect to the underlying: he has no discretion with regard to the exercise of the option, and must stand ready to sell to or buy from the option holder, in the event that the holder chooses to exercise the option. Consequently, option-based derivatives involve asymmetrical risk, because the option buyer risks only the option premium, while the seller's potential loss is unlimited.

Option-based derivatives are used mainly for hedging and for speculation. Speculators use options because of the leverage that options grant relative to the value of the underlying, "leverage" meaning that a percentage change in the underlying will result in a greater percentage change in the value of the option. Speculating in options can, therefore, be more profitable and more risky than investing directly in the underlying. Speculators seek to increase risk, and thus return, and profit from market price fluctuations in the option contract itself. An option can also be used for reducing or maintaining risk through hedging. Hedgers seek to reduce the risk of current or anticipated investments through the use of an offsetting option position.

Risks Associated with Derivatives

The risks of using derivatives—market risk, credit risk, legal risk, operational risk, liquidity risk, and systemic risk—are not unique and are also encountered in traditional lending or investment. But it should be noted that the use of OTC derivatives is often particularly risky, because these contracts are customized for the needs of a particular counterparty with the result that risks associated with the use of the contracts may be assembled in new and unexpected ways.

Market risk is the risk of loss from adverse price movements in the market for the underlying asset. Investors typically manage market risk on a portfolio basis, combining offsetting positions to determine net risk exposure, and hedging any net excess risk by entering into futures or options contracts. To determine the net risk of a portfolio, an investor deconstructs the contracts that make up the portfolio according to their underlying market risk factors—delta, elasticity, convexity, volatility, time decay, basis and discount rate risk—so that those risks can be netted or managed in some other way.

Delta is the name given to the rate of change in the value of a derivative contract for a given change in the value of the underlying asset. For example, the value of an option with a delta of 0.5 changes to the extent of 50 pence for every £1 that the value of the underlying changes. A derivative contract or investment portfolio is said to be "delta hedged" or "delta neutral" if a derivative has been entered into to offset the value of the underlying in proportion to the delta of the contract or the portfolio. Delta is always a value between 0 and 1, which means that, ignoring other distortive factors, the value of a derivative cannot change to a greater extent in absolute terms than the value of the underlying. A swap usually has a delta of 1, so that a price movement in the underlying produces an equivalent price movement in the swap. The delta of an option moves less linearly from 0 to 1, as the option moves from having a negative value to having a significantly positive value; in other words, the closer that an option is to having a positive value, the faster delta changes. Convexity risk is the rate of change in delta relative to changes in the price of the underlying.

In percentage terms, the price fluctuations of futures and options, relative to invested capital or to pledge collateral, are much greater than those of the underlying instrument. This is called the leverage effect. Leverage may also be defined as the ability of an investor to control a large notional amount of an underlying through a relatively small capital outlay. Both forward-based and option-based derivatives are leveraged, because at a comparatively small capital cost in the form of margin or premium, the investor is exposed to a significantly larger amount of the value of the underlying. This means that investing or pledging a small capital amount can control larger amounts. The trading of derivatives can thus offer great profit potential, but can also offer an extensive exposure to risk. In the context of options, leverage or elasticity is a measurement of the percentage change in the price of an option given a 1 percent change in the price of the underlying. Elasticity of options is usually positive, so that for example, a 1 percent change in the price of the underlying option is usually accompanied by a percentage change greater than 1 percent in the option premium. This relationship is called the "leverage factor" of options.

The existence of liquidity implies that the derivative contracts can be entered into at any time, in any volume, without overly affecting market prices. The trading of standardized contracts in public derivative markets ensures market liquidity because it results in a concentration of order flows. Flexibility is thereby ensured, so that investors and speculators can contract based on market assessment and appetite for risk.

Volatility risk is the degree to which the value of an option is affected by changes in volatility levels, in other words, price movements of the underlying asset. Volatility is an important factor in option pricing, because the more volatile the price of an underlying, the underlying rate or the return generated by the underlying, the greater the value of the option in respect of that underlying. Common measures of volatility are historical volatility and implied volatility. Historical volatility measures past market movements, but may not be an accurate indicator of future volatility and, consequently, is seldom regarded as an accurate index for use in option pricing. Implied volatility is derived from all the known characteristics of an option that must have been used in establishing and maintaining the option's market price. Because volatility is the only pricing input other than short-term interest rates that is not directly observable, its source requires subjective determinations and estimation. Volatility is a critical measure in the hedging of an option portfolio, because implied volatility often changes without any change occurring in the price of the underlying asset.

Time decay is the loss in value of an option due to the passage of time, assuming constant price and implied volatility of the underlying. An option that has the same price as the value of the underlying asset, or a price which is below that of the underlying asset, loses value over time, because, as the option approaches maturity, the probability that it will acquire positive value decreases.

Basis risk or correlation risk is the risk of market inefficiency, that is, the risk that the price of a derivative will not be perfectly correlated with the price of the underlying asset in its cash market. Basis risk translates into the risk that hedges composed of offsetting contracts in the cash and derivatives markets may become unbalanced, thus resulting in hedge imperfection.

Discount rate risk is the risk that the value of a derivative will be affected by changes in the market interest rate used to discount future cash flows to present value. For options, a higher discount rate usually means a higher value for call options and a lower value for put options, due to the lower present value of the exercise price.

The Management of Market Risk

There are many different ways in which derivative holders, whether dealers or end-users, manage market risk. Dealers mark contracts to market at least daily, or calculate the market risk of a derivatives portfolio daily, while taking into account all major market risk components, and comparing the result to pre-established market risk limits.

The price of a forward-based derivative is based on the price of the underlying asset, adjusted for the time differential between the contract date and the settlement date. The reason for such adjustment is that the buyer earns interest on the deferred purchase price during the period for which the contract is open and avoids incurring costs of carry during that period, while the seller may derive a convenience yield benefit by holding the underlying in inventory during the contract period. Forward-based derivatives are subject mainly to the market risk factor of delta and are not usually susceptible to elasticity, time decay, volatility, or convexity risk, so that changes in the price of the underlying produce proportional changes in the value of the derivative.

Although forward-based derivatives are subject to basis risk and discount rate risk, these risks are seldom hedged. The hedging of a forward-based derivative involves the aggregation as a group of derivatives of similar asset classes, so that forwards offset other forwards and any residual risk is delta-hedged. Forward-based derivatives have relatively straightforward market risk profiles, so that the hedging and monitoring of risk is easier than is the case for option-based derivatives. A forward-based derivative can thus be hedged with a proportional amount of the underlying and the hedge will remain stable.

The exposure of option-based derivatives to market risk factors results in greater complexity. Because option-based derivatives are subject to convexity risk, the relationship between the option price and underlying asset price is not constant. Options are also subject to volatility risk and time decay risk, even if the price of the underlying remains constant. The basis of an option, however, is usually left unhedged. Consequently, a delta-hedged options portfolio is not static and is monitored and readjusted over time, in a process called "dynamic hedging." Dynamic hedging involves its own risks; thus, the cost of hedging may be greater than expected, or prices may move significantly before positions can be adjusted, resulting in losses. A decision must be taken how often to rehedge as a result of price changes in the underlying or expected price volatility. The more frequently the hedge is balanced, the greater the protection against loss, but frequent adjustments involve expense. This means that successful dynamic hedging depends on accurate forecasts of both market volatility and interest rates. Option-based derivatives of similar classes are thus aggregated and managed as a group, by the offsetting of options with options and dynamic hedging of any residual risk arising from mismatches in the options portfolio.

Basis risk or correlation risk is caused by inefficiencies between the derivatives market and the underlying market. This risk is beyond the control of the investment manager and cannot therefore be hedged. Interest rate risk can be hedged by acquiring short-term securities, such as UK government gilts.

Market risk may also be measured as value-at-risk or capital at risk, using probability analysis based on a common confidence interval and time horizon, with "capital at risk" defined as the maximum loss expected to be exceeded with a set probability over a fixed period.

An Assessment

The widespread use of exchange-traded derivatives had a modest start in the mid-20th century, when most transactions were in respect of commodities. Since then, the number and subject matter of standardized derivative contracts, both commodity-based and financial, has increased significantly and the use of such contracts, both by producers and commodity users, as well as by speculators, has grown dramatically. In tandem with this development, the use of OTC derivatives has also grown hugely, as more opportunities for harnessing the benefits of derivatives have been identified.

The growth in derivative use, however, has not been uneventful. Major losses have been incurred by derivative market participants and these losses have been widely publicized. In the 1980s, the London borough of Hammersmith and Fulham, which had contracted interest rate swaps for speculative reasons, defaulted on these contracts after having incurred large losses due to an adverse movement in interest rates; the House of Lords subsequently held that the borough was not liable on the contracts as it had lacked the statutory authority to enter into them. In the early 1990s, US company Gibson Greetings lost substantial amounts on interest rate swaps that it had contracted in an attempt to control its interest expenses. At about the same time, Procter & Gamble incurred large losses on complex total-return swaps that it had entered into in an attempt to alter the profile of its interest receipts and expenses, and Orange County of California filed for bankruptcy after it incurred huge losses, having entered into reverse repos and inverse floaters, which were less usual derivative contracts but were highly leveraged, and generated enormous losses due to adverse market interest rate movements. In 1995, short straddles entered into by Nick Leeson in relation to financial futures traded on Asian markets resulted in the failure of his employer, Barings Bank. In 1998, hedge fund Long Term Capital Management incurred large losses as a result of having entered into total-return swaps based on the value of Russian government securities, which defaulted; LTCM was rescued by the US treasury authorities and a number of large banks, which sought to avoid any domino effect on other financial sector firms. The bankruptcy of Enron in 2001 was partly due to its failed market-making attempts with regard to commodity derivatives.

These events have given rise to a degree of nervousness mixed with skepticism, regarding both the usefulness of derivatives and the extent of the corporate and systemic risks that their use has created, both for end-users and for the financial system in general. Suspicion about derivatives is typified by a 2003 claim by Warren Buffett that derivatives are time bombs and financial weapons of mass destruction.

The other side of the picture is that prophesies of derivative-triggered doom have neither been realized, nor is there any real sign that they ever will be. The numbers of derivatives contracted and the value of underlying and notional amounts is constantly increasing. New investment-related uses for derivatives are frequently being explored and offered to market participants. Trading companies are becoming more accustomed to compiling a risk balance sheet and to harnessing derivatives in order to lay off non-core risks to others more willing and able to bear those risks.

Moreover, there is a growing awareness on the part of corporate managements of the potential of derivatives to increase desirable risk and to attenuate risk that managements seek to avoid. This has been exemplified by the widespread use by large banks of interest rate swaps to manage interest rate risk and of credit default swaps to avoid sectoral and customer-centered credit limits.

The challenge for the future will be to educate managements in other sectors about the benefits of derivatives and to increase the usefulness of derivatives through lateral creativity with regard to the ways in which derivatives can usefully be put to work. All of these factors point to a burgeoning future role for derivatives, as more and more interest is focused on the commercial usefulness of the contracts.

Editors Update

Recognize that this was drafted in 2007 just prior to the crisis and indeed derivatives (in particular, OTC derivatives) performed amazingly well during the crisis. However, regulators were concerned about a perceived lack of transparency in the market. I am far from sure where they obtained these concerns from since in a professional's market such market making activities are clearly of general benefit. Rather than implementing a systems of post trade notification, which would have been both cheap and would not have distorted the market, regulators have instead tried to shoehorn the OTC market into an STD structure.

This is a mistake which they will regret. It was unnecessary. The previous structure enabled professional firms to utilize credit mitigation techniques to minimize the risk. That has now been replaced with placing collateral in the form of margin at exchanges. This undermines the financial pricing of derivatives and had rendered some parts of the market moribund. As we move into an increasingly risk volatile world the importance of derivatives for both currency and interest rates has never been clearer. When the next crisis comes, which is likely to be a too small to survive crisis, these new regulations will be seen to hinder the solutions we would wish to employ.

I provide one final parting shot. There is no transaction that you need to send to central counterparty if you think through what you are trying to achieve. There are better and more cost-effective alternatives available if only you allow yourself to consider them. As regulations change the solutions change with them and innovation is required. That this is in part innovation back to the past is perhaps even more surprising. The risk managers need to drive and be part of this movement and not just be another part of the ban k allowing regulation to dictate decisions which will be seen with hindsight to have been inappropriate.

Bibliography

Eurex Frankfurt, A.G. 2002. *Fixed Income Trading Strategies*. Frankfurt, Germany: Eurex Communications.

Eurex Frankfurt, A.G. 2005. *Trading Strategies*. Frankfurt, Germany: Eurex Communications.

Financial Accounting Standards Board (FASB). 2004. *Accounting for Derivative Instruments and Hedging Activities*. Norwalk, CT.

Ineichen, A.M. 2003. *Absolute Returns: The Risk and Opportunities of Hedge Fund Investing*. Hoboken, NJ: Wiley.

Krawiec, K.D. 1997. "More than Just New Financial Bingo: A Risk-based Approach to Understanding Derivatives" *Iowa Journal of Corporation Law* 23, p. 1.

Merton, R.L. November 2005. "You Have More Capital than You Think." *Harvard Business Review* 85.

CHAPTER 9

The Simple Art of Monte Carlo

Aaron Brown

Morgan Stanley

Introduction

Monte Carlo is a beautifully simple and counterintuitive idea: when a problem is too hard to solve rationally, do something random. It has application beyond applied mathematics. In the introduction to *The Simple Art of Murder*,[1] Raymond Chandler explained the secret to keeping the plot moving in hard-boiled fiction, "[T]he demand was for constant action; if you stopped to think you were lost. When in doubt, have a man come through a door with a gun in his hand." Thirty-three years later, the television show *The A Team* faced a similar problem. The show's innovation was to have constant action sequences; there was no tolerance for thinking, investigating, or waiting. The screenwriters were forced to make such frequent use of the phrase "It's so crazy, it just might work" to explain essentially random actions by the main characters, it became a tagline of the show. Of course, by that time the action stakes had been raised. A man with a gun was not enough—the A Team's plan was usually something like build an armored assault vehicle out of a can of tuna fish and a used-up cigarette lighter, then drive down Main Street and hope the bad guys shoot and reveal their hideout.

---

[1] Chandler, Raymond, *Simple Art of Murder*. Vintage, (reissue edition September 12, 1988) ISBN-13: 978-0394757650.

Older readers will remember hand-soldered electronics with vacuum tubes. When these worked badly, people learned that a sharp slap on the side often corrected the problem. We used to tap meters and feather dials to get more accurate results. With modern solid-state components, randomness usually hurts rather than helps performance, but we still randomly jiggle papers to get them to line up and gently shake powders to get them smooth. Improvisational theatre teaches actors to respond to everything with, "yes, but . . . ," and add some random element. "Yes" and "no" both stop the action. You need added randomness to keep the skit going and, of course, random mutations are the reason this chapter has been included in this book.

Pi and Canfield

A classic early application of Monte Carlo analysis is described in Hammersley and Handscomb's *Monte Carlo Methods*.[2] In 1864, an army officer named Fox was wounded in the American Civil War. He amused himself while recovering by tossing a needle onto a lined sheet of paper to determine the proportion of times the needle intersected a line. Georges-Louis Leclerc, Comte de Buffon, tried to calculate this proportion in 1777, so the experiment is known as "Buffon's Needle." Pierre-Simon Laplace derived the correct mathematical expression in 1812. The probability is equal to two times the length of the needle divided by pi times the distance between the lines. Fox reversed the logic and used the experimental result to estimate pi (two times the length of the needle divided by the proportion of hits times the distance between the lines should equal pi in the long run). This is the key idea of Monte Carlo analysis, to use a random experiment to get an approximate answer to a mathematical problem.

Eighty years later, Stanislaw Ulam was convalescing from an illness and wondering about the probability of winning a game of Canfield Solitaire. After failing to get an analytic solution, he thought about playing a large number of games to get the answer. There were three reasons that Ulam's

---

[2] Hammersley, D.C., and J.M. Handscomb. 1965. *Monte Carlo Methods*. Methuen & Co Ltd. ASIN: B000I177TA.

musings led to Monte Carlo analysis while Fox's needle tossing remains a historical footnote. First, Ulam had computers, which make the Monte Carlo idea much more powerful. Even primitive computers could toss a lot more needles than a wounded Army captain. Secondly, Ulam knew a lot of important physics problems that could be attacked profitably with Monte Carlo methods. People already knew pi to more accuracy than any experiment could produce. Thirdly, Ulam knew John von Neumann and Nicholas Metropolis, who helped with the mathematical development (and Metropolis had a gambler grandfather who coined the term "Monte Carlo," after the famed gambling resort, which did much to popularize the technique).

Unfortunately, there are three problems with the Canfield example, which blur important distinctions and have led to considerable confusion. Fox did pure Monte Carlo. He had a deterministic mathematics problem (what is the ratio of the circumference of a circle to its diameter?) and he introduced randomness in order to get an answer. There was no randomness in the initial problem.

Ulam's problem can be viewed as deterministic. The probability of winning a game of Canfield Solitaire is a deterministic constant, just like pi. But it can also be viewed as a question about a random variable; what is the expected value of X where X = 0 if you lose a game of Canfield and X = 1 if you win? Estimating the expected value of a random variable by taking the mean of observed values is not Monte Carlo, it is inferential statistics. This may seem like hair-splitting in this example, but the distinction is crucial in other problems.

Another confusion is that Fox did only Monte Carlo, while Ulam did Monte Carlo followed by simulation. Fox only recorded the observations of his experiments, the calculation to get pi happened only after the results were in. Ulam randomly shuffled a deck of cards and then went through a complex simulation to figure out if the arrangement was a winning or losing one. He did calculations on each random draw, not only at the end of the experiment. Even worse, you can regard his entire experiment as a simulation; he simulates someone playing a game of Canfield, including the shuffling. As there is no introduced randomness, he does not need the idea of Monte Carlo. He could describe his experiment entirely as a simulation of what he wanted to measure

Monte Carlo and Simulation

While Monte Carlo simulation is a powerful combination of tools, it is essential to understand the two distinct ideas and do each one correctly. Moreover, many Monte Carlo problems need no simulation, and many simulation problems need no Monte Carlo. Fusing the two ideas into one weakens both of them.

To see the distinction, consider the Monte Carlo part (shuffling the deck) and the simulation (playing out a game of Canfield) separately. Why use Monte Carlo? Because it would take too much computer time to try all 52 (8×10^{67}) arrangements of a deck of cards. If there were fewer cards in the deck, or if there were symmetries that could reduce the number of combinations that had to be considered, we would get a better answer by stepping through all relevant combinations, one at a time. If we had a fast enough computer, we would not need Monte Carlo.

Why simulate? Because it is the fastest way to determine whether a combination of cards results in winning or losing a game of Canfield. If a clever person figured out a faster way, we would use it. It would not matter how fast our computer was, or whether we wanted an exact or approximate answer. If the game were simpler, for example, if we could tell whether a deck arrangement was winning or losing by locating the ace of spades in the deck, we would not bother simulating a game.

So for small decks and simple games, we need neither Monte Carlo nor simulation. For large decks, we need Monte Carlo. For complicated games, we need simulation. When we have complicated games played with large decks, we use Monte Carlo simulation.

Captain Fox did not need simulation. Once he saw whether the needle crossed the line or not, no further analysis was necessary. But he did need Monte Carlo. Whether the needle crosses the line depends on two factors: the distance from the center of the needle to the nearest line and the angle of the needle with respect to the lines. He could try to measure these systematically. He could place the needle at different distances from the line and rotate it to estimate the range of angles that would cause it to intersect a line. His error would depend on the fineness of his grid and the accuracy of his measurements. If he were only concerned with one dimension, either the position of the center of the needle or the angle of the needle, the systematic measurement would probably give smaller error for the same effort. Two dimensions make Monte Carlo more attractive; the simpler measurement saves so much effort that it more than compensates for the lower efficiency of random versus systematic sampling. With more dimensions, say he was also interested in making the needle length random and using paper with irregularly spaced lines, Monte Carlo would be no harder, but systematic sampling would increase dramatically in difficulty.

Moving from pi and solitaire to more general applied mathematics, we can say the same thing. We need Monte Carlo when a problem has many dimensions. It takes too much computer time to try every combination of many variables, even if each variable can only take on a few values. Monte Carlo gives only an approximate answer, but if done properly, the quality of that approximation is independent of the number of dimensions.

We need simulation when we cannot solve a differential equation analytically or (what amounts to the same thing to an applied mathematician) when the analytic solution requires numerical evaluation that takes longer than simulation. The differential equation tells us how to get from one state to the next, just like the rules of Canfield Solitaire. Solving it allows us to look at the boundary conditions (the arrangement of the shuffled deck in Canfield) and determine directly whether it is winning or losing. If we can't solve the differential equation, we can still simulate, going from the boundary conditions one step at a time until we discover the result we want. A differential equation is like a recipe, a series of instructions that get you from boundary condition to solution; an analytic solution is like a blueprint. Both tell you how to make something, but the recipe requires going through all the steps in order while a blueprint illustrates the finished product directly.

This brings up the third problem with the Canfield example. The rules of Canfield are not a differential equation (or a difference equation, in this case, because the moves are discrete). The player has choices. One state does not determine the next; it only determines a range of next states from which the player makes a choice. A straightforward exact solution requires playing every game every possible way, which is why the Canfield Solitaire problem remains unsolved. People have pretty good estimates of the winning probability, but they rely on a combination of analysis, guesswork, and simulation. You might think the player choice only adds another dimension to the problem so, as Monte Carlo is independent of the number of dimensions, it shouldn't make the problem harder. The problem is you cannot treat a choice as a random event (i.e., a common mistake in finance).

Derivative Pricing

Derivative pricing has the same three features that make Canfield Solitaire a bad example from which to learn Monte Carlo.

- The problems contain their own randomness (the unknown future price movements of the underlying), which is easily confused with the artificial randomness injected into the problem for Monte Carlo.
- Complex derivatives are often valued by simulation, with or without Monte Carlo, which can blur the distinction between the two tools.
- Many derivatives, such as American options, involve some choice by one or both parties to the contract. This creates another potential confusion, between randomness and choice.

Unfortunately for finance, derivative pricing is the way many quants are introduced to Monte Carlo, so they learn the latter incorrectly. This leads to problems when they later tackle problems other than pricing.

The most basic derivative pricing technique is the binomial tree, which involves neither Monte Carlo nor simulation (although it is often confused with those two things). Suppose a stock sells for US$100 today and tomorrow I know it will be either US$101 or US$99. The risk-free rate of interest is 0.02 percent per day. A one-day European call option on 100 shares with a strike price of US$100 will be worth either US$100 tomorrow (if the stock price is US$101) or zero (if the stock price is US$99). I can get the same result by buying 50 shares of stock and borrowing US$4,949 for one day. Tomorrow I will need US$4,950 to repay the loan. If the stock price is US$99, my 50 shares will just cover the repayment. If the stock price is US$101, I have US$100 profit. As the cost of buying 50 shares (US$5,000) minus the US$4,949 borrowed is US$51, that must be the price of the call option, or arbitrage is possible.

Notice that there is no randomness in this argument. It does not matter what the probability of the stock going up or down is, just what the two possible values are. There is also no simulation, just a calculation. The argument depends on some financial assumptions and simple arithmetic.

There is a convenient shortcut, however, that people often use to solve problems like this. If you invest US$10,000, the price of 100 shares, at the risk-free rate of 0.02 percent for one day, you have US$10,002. If the stock has a 51 percent chance of going up to US$101 and a 49 percent chance of going down to US$99, the expected value of 100 shares of stock is also US$10,002. If we compute the expected value of the option under this "risk-neutral probability," we get the correct US$51 price (51 percent of US$100 and 49 percent of zero). The risk-neutral probability is not the actual probability, but it gives the correct derivative price.

The value of this shortcut can be seen if we imagine the stock continuing to move up or down US$1 in value every day for N days. I can price an N day option using the method outlined earlier, but I need to simulate $(N+1) \times (N+2)/2$ nodes in a binomial tree. If I remember the risk-neutral probability trick, I can just compute the expected value of the derivative until a binomial distribution with p = 0.51 and discount it back to the present at the risk-free rate of interest.

Beyond Binomial Pricing

Simulation enters the picture when it is not enough to consider only the terminal nodes of the tree, when the path the security price takes makes a difference to the derivative valuation. This can happen because the derivative itself is path-dependent, that is to say the payoff depends not only on the terminal price of the underlying, but on previous prices. Asian options, for example, depend on the average price of the underlying over the interval and barrier options pay off or not depending on the maximum or minimum price reached. Another reason is the path might affect the option holder's action, as in an American option that can be exercised any time up to expiry. Finally, we are often evaluating a dynamic position, say a hedged option position, so the outcome of the strategy depends on the path even if the derivative itself does not. Another common term for this is "non-recombining tree." That means if the underlying ticks up in price and back down, it creates a different state of the world than if the underlying ticks down in price and back up; although the underlying price is the same, the world states do not recombine.

We try tricks to avoid considering every path. We include additional state variables, use Brownian bridges or collapse portions of the tree. But sometimes, simulation is the fastest way to price a derivative. A binomial tree with N time steps has N+1 final nodes and (N+1) (N+2)/2 total nodes, but 2^{N-1} possible paths through the tree. That makes exhaustive simulation practical only for small N. For some problems we can get away with a coarse time step and small N, but often we get more accuracy with a larger N, but only simulating a fraction of the possible paths.

Monte Carlo is a way to reduce the number of paths. You simulate the derivative price on some paths selected at random and hope that the average of the sampled paths is close to the average of all paths. In this case, the Monte Carlo randomness and the selection of random paths is the same randomness as the underlying security. We can think of the underlying security as picking a path at random through the tree, in which case we can think of our pricing algorithm as pure simulation, mimicking the behavior of the underlying, rather than Monte Carlo simulation.

It is usually better, however, to select another form of randomness to reduce the number of paths considered. This is particularly true when we are not doing pricing but another application such as risk management, hedge design or trading strategy analysis. Analysts who know only Monte Carlo simulation may not think about this.

Consider, for example, estimating the one-day 99 percent VaR of a short down-and-in call option (i.e., we want X, such that the contract will lose US$X or more 1 percent of the time; a down-and-in call option is one that pays off only if the underlying price falls below the knock-in level, then rises above the strike price; as we are short the option, our VaR is set in situations when the option increases in price). Monte Carlo simulation is wasteful, because we only care about a few paths (the ones that fall to the knock-in point, then go up a lot). Moreover, we have to simulate all the way to option expiry, which could be months or years away, in order to estimate the distribution of the option's value after one day.

A more important problem with Monte Carlo simulation is we need to use the actual probability distribution of the underlying (which we typically do not know very well) to determine whether or not it knocks in, and the risk-neutral probability (which we can typically measure with precision) to compute its value at the end of one day. Any simulation with a single set of probabilities will give inaccurate answers (and it does not work to switch from actual to risk-neutral after the knock-in barrier is hit).

A better approach is to consider the nodes one day in the future that have high values for the vanilla version of the call (the same option without the knock-in feature). All we need to know is the actual probabilities of getting to these nodes after knock-in and we only need to compute enough nodes (counting down from the highest) to add up to a 1 percent probability of knock-in. Depending on the complexity of our actual probability model, this is something we might be able to compute, but if not, we could estimate it from an efficient Monte Carlo integration. This is not Monte Carlo simulation, because we are not simulating the price movements of the underlying and we are not pricing the option from the path the underlying takes. We are taking a random selection of paths in order to estimate the probability that a path from the origin to the selected one-day node hits the knock-in point. There are other ways to attack this problem, some of which involve Monte Carlo, some of which do not. My point is the Monte Carlo simulation is not a good approach, but that is no reason to reject Monte Carlo entirely.

Beyond Binomial

The other major reason trees get big in derivative analysis is when we have more than two forward branches out of each node. An N step tree with K choices at each node can have up to K^{N-1} terminal nodes. Recombining reduces this number, but it still can be more nodes than can be easily processed even if K and N are moderate-sized.

For example, suppose I have an underlying that can tick up or down by 0.1 percent each step (i.e., it can be multiplied by 1.001 or divided by 1.001) but that the tick size (the volatility) can increase or decrease by 10 percent each step (so 0.1 percent can go to 1.1 × 0.1 percent = 0.11

percent or 0.1 percent/1.1 =0.0909 percent). After 100 times steps, that gives 1.3 billion different terminal values for the underlying. That is too many to examine individually. This causes problems even if we are pricing a vanilla derivative whose payout is determined only by the underlying price at expiry.

Simulating paths of the underlying just increases our computation effort without benefit, as only the terminal value of the path matters. We can use Monte Carlo for this problem, however. We can select terminal values at random and compute their probabilities. This will allow us to integrate the vanilla derivative payoff to get an expected value. Note that our randomness is not the randomness of the underlying security. We pick terminal values without regard to their probabilities (in fact, we do not know their probabilities until after we pick one).

There is a crucial financial distinction among multinomial tree models. If we have K paths out of every node, we need the prices of K securities at each node in order to generate arbitrage prices for all securities (and those K securities must not be linearly dependent among the paths). In simple binomial option pricing, we use the price of the underlying security (which we know at each node because that is what goes up and down) and the risk-free security (which we know because it depends only on time step, not node within time step) to price all the options on the underlying. The assumption is sometimes called "complete markets," as in complete markets for each possible state we can construct a security that pays US$1 in that state and nothing in all the other states.

One of the main reasons for going to multinomial trees is different derivatives on the same underlying have inconsistent prices in a binomial tree. With K paths out of each node, we can calibrate the tree to K—2 derivatives (plus the underlying price and the risk-free asset). If we do this we can obtain an arbitrage price for each remaining derivative (i.e., if the actual market price differs from our computed price, we can construct a riskless portfolio with a return better than the risk-free rate). Of course, that is only in theory; if we have to calibrate to 40 different instruments, only an optimist believes that the 41st instrument will fall perfectly into line. These models are sometimes called "local volatility" because, in principle, the entire future tree is known today.

Multinomial trees are also used for the opposite reason; that markets are not complete. In order to model the essential unhedgeable risk of positions, we need more paths leaving a node than we have securities to use as hedges. These are called "stochastic volatility" models. They do not give arbitrage prices for derivatives; instead they give a probability distribution of future values from which a price can be estimated.

In the first case, we can use Monte Carlo to determine the risk-neutral terminal distribution on the underlying that prices all our calibration instruments correctly, then use that risk-neutral distribution to price any other path-independent derivative. A superior approach recognizes there is an error in the measurement of market prices and calibrates to minimize the squared error with more calibration instruments than paths out of each node. In the second case, we use Monte Carlo to determine the actual probability distribution directly.

Going Farther with Monte Carlo

The objective of this chapter has been to give a clear idea of what Monte Carlo is and how it can be used effectively, or inefficiently. Whenever you use it, ask yourself what is the full experiment you would do if you had infinite computer time, and make sure you have a good random sample of that very large or infinite experiment. Make sure you introduce the precise randomness you need, rather than taking whatever randomness happens to be lying around. Ask yourself why the problem is high-dimensional, and if Monte Carlo is the best way to get around that. Do not automatically use Monte Carlo because you are simulating and do not neglect to consider Monte Carlo because you are not simulating. And most importantly, learn to say, "It's so crazy, it just might work," with a straight face.

There are many other things to learn about Monte Carlo. Some important ones are variance reduction, dimensionality reduction, proxy distributions, quasi-random numbers, control variates, antithetic variates and stratified sampling. These are all simple and easily implemented ideas that will reduce your Monte Carlo error and processing time. To paraphrase an old saying about the game of poker, "I can explain Monte Carlo in five minutes, to understand it takes a lifetime."

CHAPTER 10

Correlation Causes Questions: Environmental Consistency Confidence in Wholesale Financial Institutions

Michael Mainelli

Z/Yen Group Limited

Introduction

Wholesale financial institutions have tried a number of approaches for managing and modeling operational risk, with limited success. Z/Yen Group Limited, for example, has developed an approach called environmental consistency confidence (ECC) meaning, basically, if you can predict incidents and losses with some degree of confidence, then your modeling is useful. It is often said, "correlation doesn't demonstrate causation." That is true, but "correlation should cause questions." The core of environmental consistency confidence is using modern statistical models to manage financial institutions through the examination of correlations between activity and outcomes. This chapter sets out how environmental consistency confidence works, how it differs slightly from other approaches, its basis in system dynamics, its fundamental concept of predictive key risk indicators for losses and incidents (PKRI⇔LI) and two early trials showing promising results.

Wholesale financial institutions have tried applying system dynamics and modeling techniques from at least the 1970s with minimal returns.

Investment banks have modeled trading floors in order to see how to optimize trade flows; large payments processors have tried modeling their multipath networks in order to optimize processing time and security. Further, Basel II initiatives led numerous wholesale institutions to document their operations in order to show their control of operational risk. Nevertheless, a few decades on, it is clear that the application of formal system dynamics modeling tools is rare in finance, at least in the minds of systems modeling experts, when compared with some other industries.

Wholesale financial institutions may have smaller transaction volumes than retail institutions, but even a modest investment bank can process 250,000 equity trades a week (Z/Yen global investment banking benchmarks). The very largest investment banks might handle 40 million equity trades a year (Z/Yen global investment banking benchmarks) and large amounts of foreign exchange, money markets, and other instruments. With large numbers of transactions, numerous paths, and variable activity levels this should be a fruitful environment for the application of system dynamics, yet most wholesale operations managers do not believe that system dynamic techniques bear fruit. A number of factors contribute to this lack of apparent benefit. First, wholesale trading finance is a fast-changing environment with little time for analytical reflection and a need for quick payback on investment in operations. Secondly, there has been only a modest amount of emphasis on the back-office processing operations. Instead, most of the emphasis has been on supporting the front-office trading floor. Thirdly, wholesale institutions tend to respond positively to regulatory initiatives setting out operations standards, but otherwise do what everyone else is doing. Thus, despite a few trials of system dynamics approaches, as almost no one has a big success story in an environment where rapid, perhaps overly rapid, decisions are taken, almost no one will undertake a systems modeling project.

Operational Risk

According to §644 of the "International Convergence of Capital Measurement and Capital Standards"[1] from the Bank for International

---

[1] June 2004.

Settlements, known as Basel II,[2] operational risk is defined as the "risk of loss resulting from inadequate or failed internal processes, people and systems, or from external events." Since operational risk became a regulatory discussion topic in the early 1990s, a number of approaches have been tried to both measure it and manage it, and all have been found wanting. Arguably, the evolution of current thinking about operational risk has already had three stages:

- *OpVAR (operational value-at-risk).* This was an early approach that attempted to treat operational risk in the same manner as market and credit risk. The basic idea was to build a large, stochastic model of the various operational risks and use Monte Carlo simulations to calculate a "value-at-risk" that would allow a financial institution to set aside an appropriate amount of capital. This approach requires probability distributions of operational risk, in the same way that banks analyze market movements or credit defaults. A few industry initiatives attempted to collect large datasets of operational risk losses, for example, defalcation by employees, but found that the data were heterogeneous and difficult to extract because of its sensitivity—who wants to admit publicly that they have been defrauded? In our opinion, OpVAR still has a place as a useful analytical check, but not as a primary means of measuring and managing operational risk.
- *Process modeling.* Many financial institutions documented their operations in order to analyze their operational risks. Many of the tools used to document the operations were also the same tools used to input models to system dynamics simulation software. While this also led many institutions to experiment with system dynamics techniques, they then encountered problems of validating the models and chaos theory effects, that is, extreme sensitivity to initial conditions. Further, this approach failed to provide a useful measure for banks to calculate an appropriate amount of capital to set aside to cover operational risk.

---

[2] See http://bis.org/publ/bcbs107.htm

- *Risk dashboards or "radar."* Some financial institutions explored the application of compliance tools that required operational managers to prove that they had followed procedures that minimized operational risk. While this heuristic approach is culturally suited to banks (it has the bureaucratic "tick-bashing" and form-filling with which they are so familiar), it also fails to provide an overall measure of operational risk. Further, there was little consideration of the human systems within which this approach was being applied so, for instance, people just repeatedly answered questions with the desired answer, for example, "is your computer room secure?"—"yes," thus negating any benefit. Finally, this approach results in a lot of RAG (red-amber-green) type reports that cannot be readily summarized numerically and are incapable of contrasting different risks other than by their frequency or place in the taxonomy. So, with little account taken of the severity, five open computer room door incidents may be rated more important than a single total power outage.

Elements of these three approaches are still used, and useful, but on their own they do not provide measurement and management of operational risk. There are some other approaches worth noting. Though these have not been as popular, they may have more long-lasting benefits:

Culture change. As operational risk is primarily risk generated by people internally (people fail to follow processes, deliberately sabotage or make poor decisions), a culture that promotes reduced operational risk should provide significant benefits.[3] This approach, however, does not provide a measure of operational risk for capital purposes.

Cost-per-transaction variance. This approach attempts to contrast operational risk across products by fully allocating costs to each transaction,

---

[3] Howitt, J., M. Mainelli, and C. Taylor. May 2004. "Marionettes, or Masters of the Universe? The Human Factor in Operational Risk." *Operational Risk* (a special edition of *The RMA Journal*), pp. 52–57, The Risk Management Association.

thus generating a more typical distribution curve for risk.[4] This approach does find system dynamic modeling useful, to help allocate pooled costs based on activity levels (activity-based costing), and does appear to work in practice and across the industry. However, this approach has not been widely adopted, possibly because the full-blown version requires extensive, and expensive, systems modeling, and possibly because the regulators have been slow to see that it does help them provide comparable metrics; though those metrics are not traditional.

Another approach worth evaluating, which leads to a slightly different view of how system dynamics is applied to the organization, is the use of key risk indicators.

What Is a Key Risk Indicator (KRI)?

Key Risk Indicators: risk indicators are statistics and/or metrics, often financial, which can provide insight into a bank's risk position. These indicators should be reviewed on a periodic basis (often monthly or quarterly) to alert banks to changes that may be indicative of risk concerns. Such indicators may include, for example, the number of failed trades, staff turnover rates, and the frequency and/or severity of errors and omissions.[5]

KRIs are measurable metrics (sic) or indicators that track different aspects of operational risk.[6]

A working definition is "regular measurement based on data which indicates the operational risk profile of a particular activity or activities." KRIs can be environmental, operational or financial. For instance, environmental indicators (that might turn out to be KRIs) could be such

---

[4] Mainelli, M. May 2004. "Toward a Prime Metric: Operational Risk Measurement and Activity-Based Costing." *Operational Risk* (a special edition of *The RMA Journal*), pp. 34–40, The Risk Management Association.

[5] Basel Committee on Banking Supervision, *Sound Practices for the Management and Supervision of Operational Risk*, December 2001.

[6] The Risk Management Association, *The KRI Banking Study*, 2005, page 5.

things as trading volumes and volatilities on major commodities or foreign exchange markets. Operational indicators (that might also be KRIs) could be general activity levels in the business, number of deals, mix of deals, number of amendments, staff turnover, overtime or IT downtime. Financial indicators (that might also be KRIs) could be things such as deal volatility, dealing profit, activity-based costing variances or value of amendments.

The key link is to apply a more scientific approach to managing risk. Firms must test the usefulness of operational risk data collection by using losses or incidents to discover what the indicators should have been. In other words, what drives operational risk? We describe this approach as predictive key risk indicators to/from loss/incidents prediction (PKRI⇔LI).

The important point to note is that people can suggest many possible risk indicators (RIs), but they are not KRIs unless they are shown to have predictive capability for estimating losses and incidents. A KRI must contribute to the predictability of losses and incidents in order to be validated as a KRI. If an RI does not predict losses or incidents, it remains an interesting hypothesis, someone's unvalidated opinion. Experience does help to identify the true drivers of operational risk and should help focus attention and control actions, but the PKRI⇔LI approach supports and validates (or invalidates) expert judgment of true drivers of operational risk losses. The intention of this approach is not to replace expert judgment, but to support that judgment in a more systematic way in an ever-changing environment.

Why Are KRIs Important?

KRIs are important for at least four reasons:

- KRIs measure probable operational risk arising over a time period, as opposed to tracking operational risk, and thus make an appropriate management tool for operational risk;
- KRIs help to form an input for economic capital calculations by helping to produce estimates of future operational risk losses and thus helping to set a base level of capital for operational risk;

If all goes well:

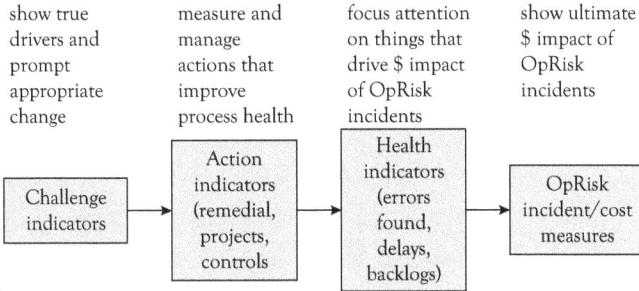

show true drivers and prompt appropriate change	measure and manage actions that improve process health	focus attention on things that drive $ impact of OpRisk incidents	show ultimate $ impact of OpRisk incidents

Challenge indicators	→	Action indicators (remedial, projects, controls)	→	Health indicators (errors found, delays, backlogs)	→	OpRisk incident/cost measures

But if not:

we do not respond, or respond inappropriately	we select actions that do not improve results	we manage things that do not matter much, at the expense of things that do	we are misled about true impact and need for action

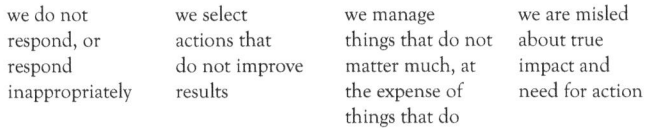

Exhibit 10.1 How should KRI's work?

Source: Z/Yen Group Limited.

- KRIs are increasingly examined by rating agencies, for example, Moody's or Standard & Poor's, and financial analysts; and
- KRIs are increasingly important to regulators.

Without capturing incidents and loss data, there is nothing to predict. Sound incident-data capture is a prerequisite for anything but the most basic capital allocation under Basel II. It is worth quoting at length from Basel II[7] as this shows what regulators expect both for operational risk and for key risk indicators.

In addition to using loss data, whether actual or scenario-based, a bank's firm-wide risk-assessment methodology must capture key business environment and internal control factors that can change its operational risk profiles. These factors will make a bank's risk assessments more forward-looking, more directly reflect the quality of the bank's control and operating environments, help align capital assessments with risk management objectives, and recognize both improvements and deterioration in operational risk profiles in a more immediate fashion. To qualify

---

[7] See http://bis.org/publ/bcbs107.htm for full text

for regulatory capital purposes, the use of these factors in a bank's risk measurement framework must meet the following standards:

- The choice of each factor needs to be justified as a meaningful driver of risk, based on experience and involving the expert judgment of the affected business areas. Whenever possible, the factors should be translatable into quantitative measures that lend themselves to verification.
- The sensitivity of a bank's risk estimates to changes in the factors and the relative weighting of the various factors need to be well reasoned. In addition to capturing changes in risk due to improvements in risk controls, the framework must also capture potential increases in risk due to greater complexity of activities or increased business volume.
- The framework and each instance of its application, including the supporting rationale for any adjustments to empirical estimates, must be documented and subject to independent review within the bank and by supervisors.
- Over time, the process and the outcomes need to be validated through comparison to actual internal loss experience, relevant external data, and appropriate adjustments made.

There are a number of KRI initiatives in the financial services industry to share best practice on KRIs and loss/incident reporting or collection. A leading initiative is the Risk Management

Association's *KRI Banking Study*, KRIeX,[8] in which some 50 banks defined 1,809 KRIs, though the relevance of these has not been tested using PKRI⇔LI prediction (to be fair, there has been some talk of doing something at an unspecified point in the future). Some examples of the Risk Management Association's KRIs are the percentage of transactions requiring manual input, percentage of unsettled transactions after due dates and theft per 1,000 ATMs. A breakdown of the KRIs by category and number is set out in the following Exhibit 10.2.

---

[8] See www.kriex.org

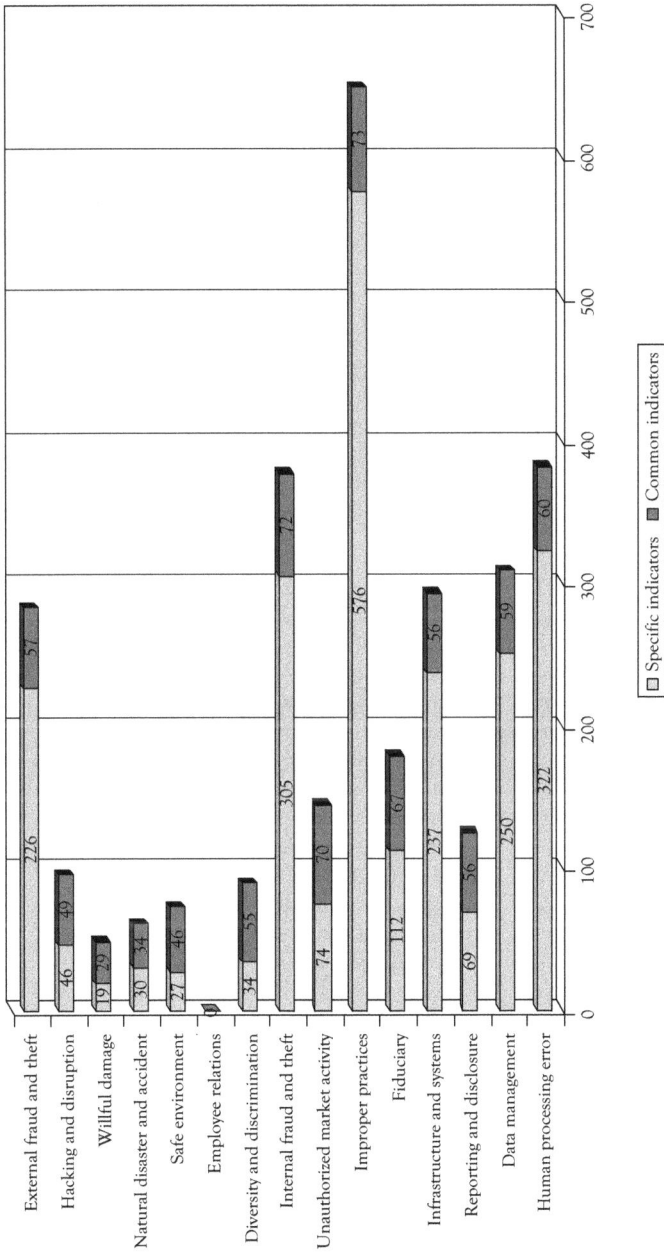

Exhibit 10.2 KRIeX RIs by category

Source: Risk Management Association (author's chart).

It is implausible to ask any organization to track 1,809 key risk indicators. To be fair, only 74 indicators are common and apply to virtually all risk points. Further, only (sic) 533 are "high-risk points." While some activities are "done to be seen" by regulators, KRIeX remains a valuable resource. This is an exhaustive approach at an early stage that does help by providing a starting set of RIs, but the KRIs for different institutions must evolve from individual institutional experience, rather than being imposed over-heavily from a template. Exhibit 10.3 sets out the characteristics of a KRI as seen by the Risk Management Association.

In a sense, the choice is between what is currently done informally (no significant business lacks RIs) and what could be done better through more formality, statistics and science to make them KRIs. For each KRI, there needs to be definition and specification. The Risk Management Association's template specification structure (see Exhibit 10.4) gives a flavor of what this means.

Effectiveness	Comparability	Ease of Use
Indicators should....	Indicators should....	Indicators should....
1. Apply to at least one risk point, one specific risk category and one business function.	1. Be quantified as an amount, a percentage or a ratio.	1. Be available reliably on a timely basis.
2. Be measurable at specific points in time.	2. Be reasonably precise and define quantity.	2. Be cost-effective to collect.
3. Reflect objective measurement rather than subjective judgement.	3. Have values that are comparable over time.	3. Be readily understood and communicated.
4. Track at least one aspect of the loss profile or event history, such as frequency, average severity, cumulative loss or near-miss rates.	4. Be comparable internally across businesses.	
5. Provide useful management information.	5. Be reported with primary values and be meaningful without interpretation to some more subjective measure.	
	6. Be auditable.	
	7. Be identified as comparable across organisations (if in fact they are).	

Exhibit 10.3 KRI characteristics

Source: Risk Management Association.

Definition	Specification	Guidance
• KRI number	• Specification version	• Usage
• KRI name	• Term definitions	• Collection
• Description	• Value kind	• frequency
• Rationale/Comments	• Dimensions	• Reporting frequency
• Nature	• Limitations on scope	• Frequency of change
• Type	• Buckets	• Collection level
• Typography	• Bucket variants	• Variants
• Ratings	• Definition thresholds	• Directional
	• Measurement rules	• information
	• Underlying KRIs	• Extraneous
	• Calculation method	• influences
	• Benchmark rules	• Control indicator
	• Aggregation method	• Source
	• Scaling denominator	
	• Scaling rules	

Exhibit 10.4 KRI template

Source: Risk Management Association.

PKRI LI Issues

One could readily conclude that a fairly static KRI cannot be "key." For example, a KRI such as the number of lawsuits received by a particular function might change very little for long periods. In this case, one might wish to examine "lawsuits in period," "estimated settlement values" or other more sensitive measures than just a very slow-changing "outstanding lawsuits." However, what matters is whether or not the KRI contributes to the capability of predicting operational losses/incidents, not its variability.

There is overlap between KRIs and key performance indicators (KPIs). It would be easy to say that KRIs are forward-looking and KPIs are backward-looking, but far too simplistic. There are clearly overlaps. For instance, high trading volumes and high volatility on one day might be good performance indicators predicting a high likelihood of good future financial performance turnout for that day, but also indicative of emerging operational risks from that day.

KRIs that increase in some ranges and decrease in others can cause confusion as KRIs are not necessarily linear. For example, staff overtime might be an example of a KRI with a bell-shaped curve. No overtime may indicate some level of risk as people aren't paying attention or do tasks too infrequently; modest levels of overtime may indicate less risk as staff are now doing a lot of familiar tasks; and high rates of overtime may indicate increased risk again through stress. KRIs help to set ranges of acceptable activity levels. There can be step changes in operational risk associated with a KRI. For instance, a handful of outstanding orders at the close of day may be normal, but risk might increase markedly when there are over a dozen outstanding orders. KRIs should vary as risk changes, but they do not have to vary linearly.

What about all the stuff that is taken for granted? For example, electricity and water supplies may seem to be an important consideration when looking at KRIs for developing world locations, yet do not really feature in criteria in the developed world. In the major financial centers, many things are assumed, for instance, an absence of natural threats such as hurricanes or flooding, yet London used to have a significant flood risk, and may again as the Thames Barrier comes to the end of its projected usefulness. Geological issues such as earthquake-prone faults or health issues such as malaria do not seem to feature. Nor does terrorism risk seem strong in people's perceptions of what really matters. There are also numerous personal issues that do not feature—work permits, opening bank accounts, arranging for utilities, schools, personal safety—any of which could scupper a trading floor.

Somewhat naturally, people tend to care about those things of which they are most conscious. Any of a number of issues could have us looking back several years from now and grimly nodding about how trading ceased to function when "people wanted to avoid concentrating terrorism risk" or "infectious diseases just became too dangerous to have people so highly concentrated." The PKRI⇔LI approach is an approach for regular management, not extreme events.

It is a combination of factors that makes a set of KRIs successful, not just a single factor. Jared Diamond derives an Anna Karenina Principle from the opening line of Tolstoy's novel: "Happy families are all alike; every unhappy family is unhappy in its own way."[9] Diamond believes the principle describes situations where a number of activities must be

---

[9] Jared Diamond, *Guns, Germs, and Steel*, Random House, 1997.

done correctly in order to achieve success, while failure can come from a single, poorly performed activity. This is certainly the case for KRIs—the evolving set of KRIs is important, not a single one at a point in time, nor too many all the time.

Environmental Consistency Modeling Using Support Vector Machines

Two examples of environmental consistency confidence projects using PKRI⇔LI are explained a bit later (a European investment bank and a global commodities firm), but it is worth looking at the support vector machine approach that underlay the modeling. Both projects used classification and prediction tools based on support vector machine mathematics to undertake predictive analysis of the data. Support vector machines (SVMs) are algorithms that develop classification and regression rules from data. SVMs result from classification algorithms first proposed by Vladimir Vapnik in the 1960s, arising from his work in *Statistical Learning Theory*.[10] SVMs are based on some wonderfully direct mathematical ideas about data classification and provide a clear direction for machine learning implementations. While some of the ideas behind SVMs date back to the 1960s, computer implementations of SVMs did not arise until the 1990s with the introduction of a computer-based approach at COLT-92.[11]

SVMs are now used as core components in many applications where computers classify instances of data (e.g., to which defined set does this group of variables belong?), perform regression estimation and identify anomalies (novelty detection). SVMs have been successfully applied in time-series analysis, reconstructing chaotic systems and principal component analysis. SVM applications are diverse, including credit scoring

---

[10] Vapnik, V.N. 1995. *The Nature of Statistical Learning Theory*. New York, NY: Springer-Verlag; Vapnik, V.N. 1998. *Statistical Learning Theory*. John Wiley & Sons.

[11] Boser, B., I. Guyon, and V. Vapnik. 1992. "A Training Algorithm for Optimal Margin Classifiers." In Fifth Annual Workshop on Computational Learning Theory (COLT-92), pp. 144–52, Pittsburgh, ACM.

(good or bad credit), disease classification, handwriting recognition, image classification, bioinformatics, and database marketing, to name a few.

SVMs are said to be independent of the dimensionality of feature space as the main idea behind their classification technique is to separate the classes in many data dimensions with surfaces (hyperplanes) that maximize the margins between them, applying the structural risk minimization principle. The data points needed to describe the classification algorithmically are primarily those closest to the hyperplane boundaries, the "support vectors." Thus, only a small number of points are required in many complex feature spaces. SVMs can work well with small datasets, though the structure of the training and test data is an important determinant of the effectiveness of the SVM in any specific application.

SVMs compete forcefully with neural networks as well as other machine-learning and data-mining algorithms as tools for solving pattern-recognition problems. Where SVMs do not perform well, it is arguable that the algorithmic rules behind the support vector algorithm do not so much reflect incapabilities of the learning machine (as in the case of an overfitted artificial neural network) but rather regularities of the data. In short, current opinion holds that if the data in the domain are predictive, SVMs are highly likely to be capable of producing a predictive algorithm. Importantly, SVMs are robust tools (understandable implementations, simple algorithmic validation, better classification rates, overfitting avoidance, fewer false positives, and faster performance) in practical applications. "The SVM does not fall into the class of "just another algorithm" as it is based on firm statistical and mathematical foundations concerning generalization and optimization theory."[12] However, comparative tests with other techniques indicate that while they are highly likely to be capable of predicting, in applications SVMs may not be

---

[12] Burbidge, R., and B. Buxton. "An Introduction to Support Vector Machines for Data Mining." Keynote YOR 12 (Young Operational Research 11th Conference, University of Nottingham, 28 March 2001), Computer Science Department, University College London, Gower Street, WC1E 6BT, UK.

the best approach for any specific dataset. "In short, our results confirm the potential of SVMs to yield good results, especially for classification, but their overall superiority cannot be attested."[13]

Environmental Consistency Confidence

The conjunction of SVMs with traditional system dynamics may seem unorthodox, but it gives organizations the capability of regularly applying scientific management. Our hypothesis is that certain KRIs predict future losses and incidents, so let us test that using modern statistical tools. If our environmental factors are consistent with the outcomes, then we can be confident we are tracking the right things. From the fact that we are tracking the right factors, we should then develop projects to eliminate or mitigate the causes. If we fail to predict, we are not tracking the right things and need to explore further, and fairly rapidly as it indicates that things may be "out of control."

If we look at the wider system of wholesale financial institutions, we see similar high-level systems that can be predicted, not just operational risk. The following exhibit sets out a simple model of finance as one where risks are selected through positioning and marketing and then priced by attempting to ascertain the difference in value to customers and the cost of capital.

At each point in this abstract model of finance, we can use a KRI system, for example:

- Marketing: can we predict sales?
- Pricing: can we predict profitability?
- Underwriting/trading: can we predict incidents and losses?

A KRI system, as with any system, has basic components:

---

[13] Meyer, D., F. Leisch, and K. Hornik. November 2002. "Benchmarking Support Vector Machines." *Adaptive Information Systems and Modelling in Economics and Management Science Report Series*, No. 78, Vienna University of Economics and Business Administration.

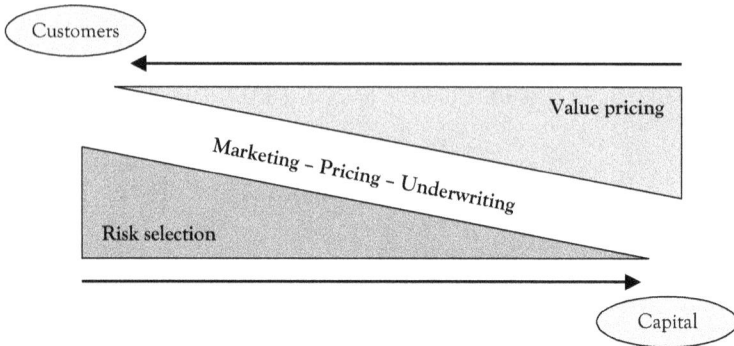

Exhibit 10.5 Financial services risk/reward cycle

Source: Author's own.

- *Governance.* Working from the overall objectives of the business, set out a definition of the operational risk framework, the calculation of economic capital and a basic set of essential KRIs.
- *Input.* Gaining stakeholder commitment, assembling resources, and appointing a team that then work to establish the potential KRIs.
- *Process.* Supporting the operational risk managers through data collection, statistical validation, statistical testing, correlations, multivariate prediction, cross-project discussion, training, template materials, and methodologies.
- *Output.* Evaluating KRIs, focused on a "customer" point of view (how does this help me manage my business better?), so that people learn from both successes and failures.
- *Monitoring.* Providing management information up to governors, over to customers, down to project managers and across project managers so that they are coordinated. Monitoring also uses feedback from KRI outcomes to feed forward into new KRI ideas and re-plan the shape of the KRI portfolio. An integral part of monitoring is evaluating KRIs at a technical level—do they predict? PKRI⇔LI prediction is one direction, and LI⇔PKRI is another.

The KRI system is a classic feedback and feed-forward cybernetic system. KRIs help managers to manage by reducing the amount of measures they need in both feed-forward and feedback. So the crucial distinction is between RIs and KRIs using PKRI⇔LI, as KRIs help to combat information overload:

What information consumes is rather obvious: it consumes the attention of its recipients. Hence a wealth of information creates a poverty of attention, and a need to allocate that attention efficiently among the overabundance of information sources that might consume it.[14]

By giving managers a clear focus on the operational risk drivers, they can commission further work to reduce them. The KRI system can be represented diagrammatically as shown in Exhibit 10.6.

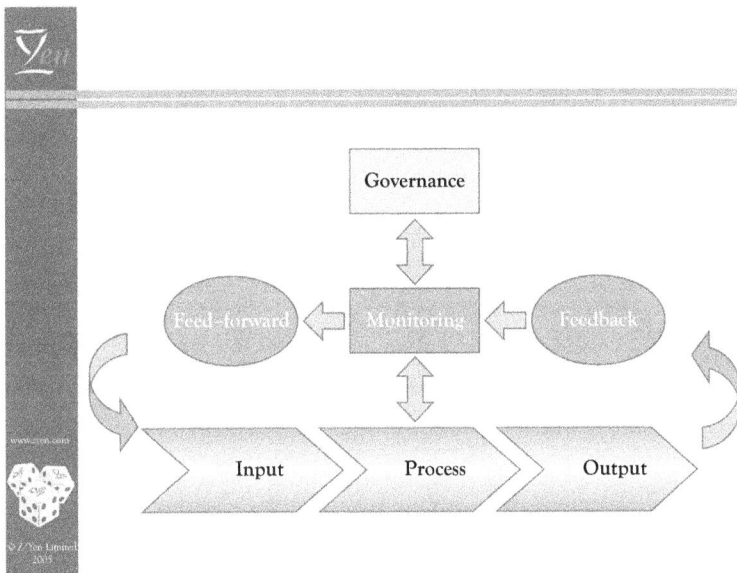

Exhibit 10.6 KRIs as a system

Source: Z/Yen Group Limited.

---

[14] Simon, H.A. 1971. "Designing Organizations for an Information-Rich World." In *Computers, Communication, and the Public Interest*, ed. G. Martin. Baltimore: The Johns Hopkins Press.

Thus, in many ways, the PKRI⇔LI approach is a classic system dynamics approach, but the use of the SVM to link inputs (KRIs) with outputs (incidents and losses) focuses on establishing predictive relationships rather than presuming that the dynamic modeling paradigm is intrinsically important to either how those relationships are validated or how they are interpreted.

The PKRI⇔LI approach is a dynamic process, not a project to develop a static set of KRIs. This means that a team, possibly aligned with other "scientific" management approaches such as 6Σ, needs to be constantly cycling through an iterative refinement process over a time period. This leads to the development of cyclical methodologies. For example, Z/Yen's Z/EALOUS methodology is one such, and diagrammatically illustrated overleaf.

What Is Current Practice? Two Early Examples

Scientific management of wholesale financial operations is increasing. Investment banks have increased their operational benchmarking markedly since the late 1990s. Managers in many investment banks (e.g.,

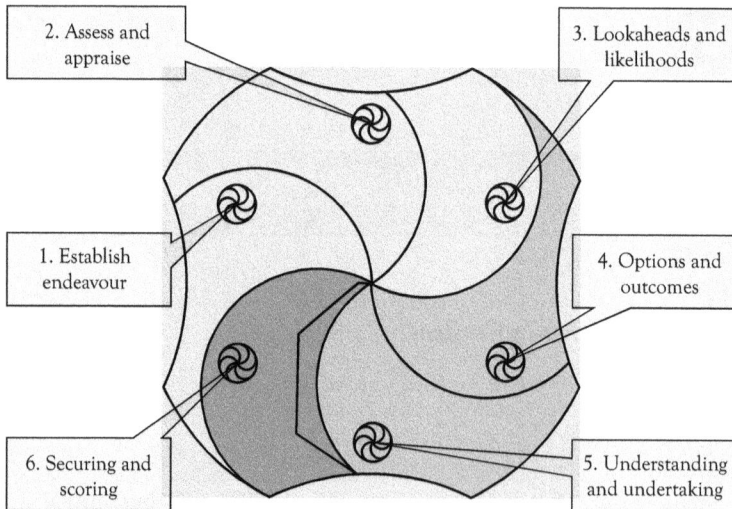

Exhibit 10.7 Environmental consistency confidence in wholesale financial institutions

Source: Z/Yen Group Limited.

Bank of America, JPMorgan Chase, Citigroup and Merrill Lynch, among others, have publicly announced their pursuit of 6Σ at conferences and on websites) follow the DMAIC or DMADV 6Σ approaches (originally from GE) when they have losses/incidents that they want to eliminate by eliminating root causes.

6Σ is clearly related to a dynamic system view of the organization, a cycle of tested feed-forward and feedback. This has led to greater interest in using predictive analytics in operational systems management. Several leading investment banks, using 6Σ programs and statistical prediction techniques (predicting trades likely to need manual intervention), have managed to reduce trade failure rates for vanilla products from 8 percent to well below 4 percent within three years. As the costs per trade for trades requiring manual intervention can be up to 250 times more expensive than trades with straight-through processing transactions, this is a very important cost-reduction mechanism, as well as resulting in a consequent large reduction in operational risk.

Predictive analytics also feature where investment banks are moving toward automated filtering and detection of anomalies (dynamic anomaly and pattern response, DAPR).[15] Cruz notes that a number of banks are using DAPR approaches not just in compliance, but also as operational risk filters that collect "every cancellation or alteration made to a transaction or any differences between the attributes of a transaction in one system compared with another system. . . . Also, abnormal inputs (e.g., a lower volatility in a derivative) can be flagged and investigated. The filter will calculate the operational risk loss event and several other impacts on the organisation." He continues, "the development of filters that capture operational problems and calculate the operational loss is one of the most expensive parts of the entire data collection process, but the outcome can be decisive in making an operational risk project successful."[16]

---

[15] Mainelli, M. October 2004. "Finance Looking Fine, Looking DAPR: The Importance of Dynamic Anomaly and Pattern Response." In *Balance Sheet*, The Michael Mainelli Column, Vol. 12, No. 5, pages 56–59, Emerald Group Publishing Limited.

[16] Cruz, M.G. 2002. *Modelling, Measuring and Hedging Operational Risk.* John Wiley & Sons.

Stage	Objectives
Define	Define the project goals and customer (internal and external) deliverables
Measure	Measure the process to determine current performance
Analyze	Analyze and determine the root cause(s) of the defects
Improve	Improve the process by eliminating defects
Control	Control future process performance

Exhibit 10.8 DMAIC—*Existing product/process/service*

Source: www.isixsigma.com

Stage	Objectives
Define	Define the project goals and customer (internal and external) deliverables
Measure	Measure and determine customer needs and specifications
Analyze	Analyze the process options to meet the customer needs
Design	Design (detailed) the process to meet the customer needs
Verify	Verify the design performance and ability to meet the customer needs

Exhibit 10.9 DMADV—*New product/process/service*

Source: www.isixsigma.com

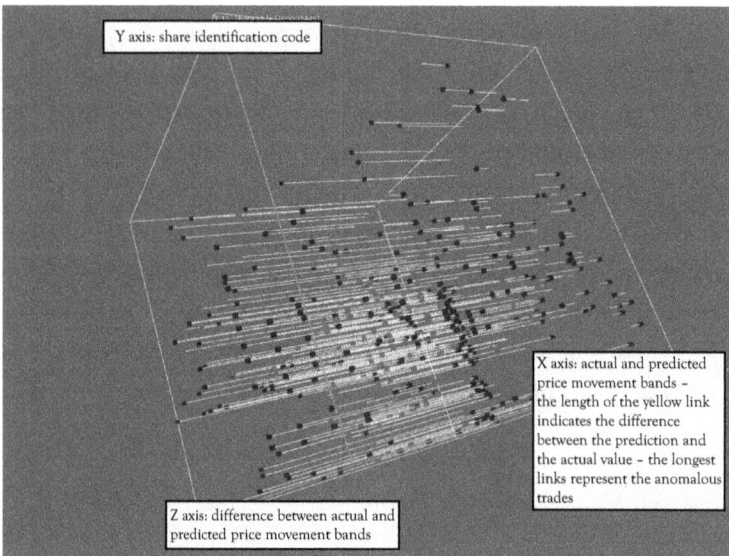

Exhibit 10.10 DAPR *support vector machine example: contrasting a subset of actual versus predicted trade price bands*

Source: Z/Yen Group Limited.

location ID	HR-Headcount #	HR-Joiners in month	HR-Leavers in month	IT-System Disruption Incidents	IT-System Downtime	FO-Trade Volume #	FO-Trade Amendments #	OPS-Nostro Breaks #	OPS-Stock Breaks #	OPS-Intersystem Breaks #	OPS-Failed Trades #	OPS-Unmatched Trades #	RIS-Market Risk Limit Breaches #	AU-High Risk O/S Overdue Audit Issues #	AU-High Risk O/S Audit Issues #
1	136	6	11	2	35:07	19218	317.1	3	9	6	463	52.77778	0	0	4.5
2	121	6	11	2	3:13	8999	0	17	4	2	26	0	3	0	4.5
3	23	6	11	0	0	661	8.7	3	0	0	0	7.444444	0	0	4.5
4	30	6	11	0	0	4307	80.5	7	1	1	17	0	1	0	4.5
...															
n															

Exhibit 10.11 Sample investment bank KRI data

Source: Z/Yen Group Limited.

PKRI⇔LI aligns with this interest in using predictive analytics to improve operational management. While interest in the PKRI⇔LI approach may be rising, particularly among investment banks, there has been a paucity of data available for these purposes. As operational risk units are growing and developing data collection and measurement systems, PKRI⇔LI projects are growing in number.

European Investment Bank

One European investment bank used three years' data to predict losses/incidents from data such as deal problems, IT downtime, and staff turn-over over a six-month period. It achieved reasonable predictive success, an R^2 approaching 0.9 at times, though more frequently 0.6 (i.e., 60 percent of losses can be predicted). A high-level snippet gives a flavor of the data.

Note that some of the items in this snippet, for example, HR joiners/leavers or IT disruption at the system level, can in practice be very hard to obtain. It was also noteworthy that, as a data-driven approach, PKRI⇔LI projects are only as good as the data put into them—"garbage in, garbage out." In some areas, the data may not be at all predictive. More rigor needs to be used as the data become more important. Data quality can vary over time in hard-to-spot ways and interact with wider systems, particularly the people in the systems. For instance, in this trial of PKRI⇔LI, the IT department was upset at IT downtime being considered a "key risk indicator" and unilaterally changed the KRI to "unplanned" IT downtime, skewing the predicted losses. This change was spotted when using the DAPR system to run the reverse LI⇔PKRI prediction as a quality control. Another example of Goodhart's Law, "when a measure becomes a target, it ceases to be a good measure" (as restated by Professor Marilyn Strathern).

Global Commodities Firm

A large global commodities firm active not only in a number of commodity markets but also foreign exchange and fixed income piloted the PKRI⇔LI approach in one large trading unit. While the predictive success was not especially great in the pilot, an R^2 approaching 0.5, the approach was seen to have merit and they decided to roll the PKRI⇔LI methodology out globally across several business units. It was telling that the PKRI⇔LI approach helped them to realize the importance of good data collection and use, and to identify areas where their data specification, collection, validation and integration could be markedly improved. It is also important to note that the SVM approach did not add much value in the early stages; many of the predictive relationships were straightforward, for example, large numbers of deal amendments can lead to later problems.

The PKRI⇔LI approach has become part of a more scientific approach (hypothesis formulation and testing) to the management of operational risk.

Modern (organization) theory has moved toward the open-system approach. The distinctive qualities of modern organization theory are its conceptual-analytical base, its reliance on empirical research data, and, above all, its synthesizing, integrating nature. These qualities are framed in a philosophy which accepts the premise that the only meaningful way to study organization is as a system.[17]

Conclusion

At its root, environmental consistency confidence means building a statistical correlation model to predict outcomes and using the predictive capacity both to build confidence that things are under control, and to improve. The correlations should raise good questions. KRIs are a continuous, evolving system, not static, hence the focus on the cyclical PKRI⇔LI approach. Today's KRI should be tomorrow's has-been as managers succeed in making it less of an indicator of losses or incidents by improving the business. Likewise, managers have to consider emerging KRIs and validate them. Wholesale financial institutions can impress regulators with PKRI⇔LI, perhaps reducing regulatory overhead, but far more important is to use KRIs to improve their businesses and reduce operational risk.

---

[17] Kast and Rosenzweig in *Systems Behaviour*, Open Systems Group, Harper and Row, 1972, 3rd edn (1981), p. 47.

Bibliography

Beer, S. 1966 (1994 ed). *Decision and Control: The Meaning of Operational Research and Management Cybernetics*. Hoboken, NJ: John Wiley & Sons.

Mainelli, M. June 2005. "Competitive Compliance: Manage and Automate, or Die." In *Journal of Risk Finance*, The Michael Mainelli Column, Vol. 6, No. 3, pages 280–84, Emerald Group Publishing Limited.

Mainelli, M., I. Harris, and A. Helmore-Simpson. June 2003. "The Auditor's Cross Subsidy' (Statistical Modelling of Audit Prices)." *Strategic Planning Society E-Newsletter*, Article 1. Also published as "Anti-dumping Measures & Inflation Accounting: Calculating the Non-Audit Subsidy." www.mondaq. com (June 19, 2003).

Michie, D., D.J. Speigelhalter, and C.C. Taylor. 1994. *Machine Learning, Neural and Statistical Classification*. Hemel, UK: Ellis Horwood, out of print. See http://amsta.leeds.ac.uk/~charles/statlog/

Thanks

I would like to thank Matthew Leitch, Justin Wilson, Ian Harris, Jürgen Strohhecker, Jürgen Sehnert and Christopher Hall for helping to develop some of the thinking behind this article, though not to claim they agree with all of it.

PART III
Credit Risk

CHAPTER 11

Regulation and Credit Risk

Rod Hardcastle

LloydsTSB[1]

Introduction

This chapter will discuss the development and implementation of Basel II[2] in order to examine issues in the regulation of credit risk. The chapter looks at the reasons for bank regulation, explores the growth in both the volume and complexity of regulation in recent years, and proposes three principles that could be adopted to improve the implementation of future regulatory initiatives. The minor changes rendered by Basel III for these purposes can be ignored but should be considered by a firm to the extent to which they are relevant.

Reasons for Bank Regulation

Banks are regulated because they occupy a special position in the economy. The role of banks as financial intermediaries means that if they fail the impact is greater than that of the failure of other types of businesses, due to the knock-on effect of depositors losing their savings and the potential impact on other banks and businesses that may have large trading or settlement positions with the failed bank.

---

[1] The following represents the views of the author and is not necessarily the view of LloydsTSB Group.

[2] *Basel II: International Convergence of Capital Measurement and Capital Standards: A Revised Framework—Comprehensive Version*, Basel Committee of the Bank for International Settlements, June 2006.

Regulators (and central banks) are particularly interested in the integrity of commercial banks, given that if a commercial bank gets into difficulty, it is the regulators who may end up in the position of "lender of last resort," that is, they may have to pick up the bill if banks fail.

For these reasons, the operation of a bank is subject to a range of regulations designed primarily to protect depositors and to protect the integrity of the financial system as a whole.

A recent, more detailed definition of the goal of banking regulation[3] (from a regulator's perspective) states that it should:

- ensure financial stability of the (banking) system as a whole through a focus on the safety and soundness of individual institutions;
- protect consumers through the oversight of individual institutions and the provision of safety nets;
- include clear arrangements for crisis management;
- provide a level playing field, to ensure that competition and innovation can flourish;
- respond to market developments in a timely manner;
- not disadvantage EU institutions in their global operations;
- be carried out in a transparent manner with appropriate accountability arrangements; and
- be cost-effective and efficient.

From a banker's perspective, Alessandro Profumo,[4] in a presentation to the European Banking Committee on July 5, 2005, said that regulation should provide:[5]

- a framework which ensures a level playing field among financial firms throughout the single market, whilst meeting the criteria of efficiency and effectiveness.

---

[3] *Supervisory arrangements: The next 5 years.* European Banking Committee, EBC/020/05, October 28, 2005, page 5.

[4] CEO, Unicredit.

[5] *Ibid*—EBC/020/05, page 5.

- Where *efficient* means it should minimize supervisory costs, either direct or indirect, and *effective* means it should guarantee the objective of financial stability, by lowering the probability of ineffective monitoring and inconsistent decisions . . .
- equal treatment for all firms across the EU irrespective of the country of origin . . .
- neutrality toward strategic and organizational choices of financial firms.
- Regulatory and supervisory requirements should not create incentives which might distort the behavior of private actors. (bullets added for emphasis)

Setting aside the slightly EU-centric elements of both descriptions mentioned earlier, what is striking is the similarity between the two positions, especially in the areas of equality of treatment, cost-effectiveness, efficiency, and not influencing behavior inappropriately. This should not surprise anyone—it is not in the best interests of banks to operate in an inappropriately risky manner, nor do banks want to see regulatory frameworks that give an advantage to any subset of a competitive market.

The Current State of Regulation

If banks' and regulators' aims are so closely aligned, how have we managed to get into a situation where "too much regulation" is considered by many to be the biggest risk facing banks today?[6]

That is the view from the Centre for the Study of Financial Innovation's (CSFI) annual "banana skins" survey. The exhibit overleaf shows graphically the increasing concern over the burden of regulation.

It should be noted that the importance of "too much regulation" differed between the three sub-audiences in the CSFI survey: bankers ranked it no. 1; industry commentators ranked it no. 2; and regulators, perhaps predictably, ranked it rather lower, at no. 9.

---

[6] *Banking Banana Skins 2006—The CSFI's annual survey of the risks facing banks.* The Centre for the Study of Financial Innovation, 2006, page 11.

There is, nonetheless, something fundamentally wrong with the state of regulation when the view from bank executives is that it is the biggest risk facing banks—for two years in a row.

The reason the CSFI's respondents feel this way is that since 2000, both the volume and the complexity of regulation has increased dramatically. This has come about for three main reasons:

The decision by the Basel Committee of the Bank for International Settlements (BCBS) to revise the Basel Capital Accord to make it more risk-sensitive;

The convergence of several pieces of EU legislation, including MiFID,[7] and the Consumer Credit Directive[8] to name just two; and

The response from the regulatory community to several high-profile corporate failures in the late 1990s and early 2000s, including Enron, WorldCom, Global Crossing and Parmalat.

Increasing Volume

To give an idea of the change in volume of regulations, let us look at the BCBS. In the six years leading up to the publication of Basel I,[9] the BCBS published 13 papers,[10] including one consultation on Basel I.

In the corresponding period leading up to the publication of Basel II, the BCBS published 147 papers,[11] including three major consultations on Basel II.

---

[7] Official title: DIRECTIVE 2004/39/EC OF THE EUROPEAN PARLIAMENT AND OF THE COUNCIL of April 21, 2004 on markets in financial instruments amending Council Directives 85/611/EEC and 93/6/EEC and Directive 2000/12/EC of the European Parliament and of the Council and repealing Council Directive 93/22/EEC.

[8] Modified proposal for a DIRECTIVE OF THE EUROPEAN PARLIAMENT AND OF THE COUNCIL on credit agreements for consumers amending Council Directive 93/13/EC.

[9] *International convergence of capital measurement and capital standards*, Basel Committee of the Bank for International Settlements, July 1988.

[10] http://bis.org/bcbs/index.htm and subsidiary links.

[11] Ibid.

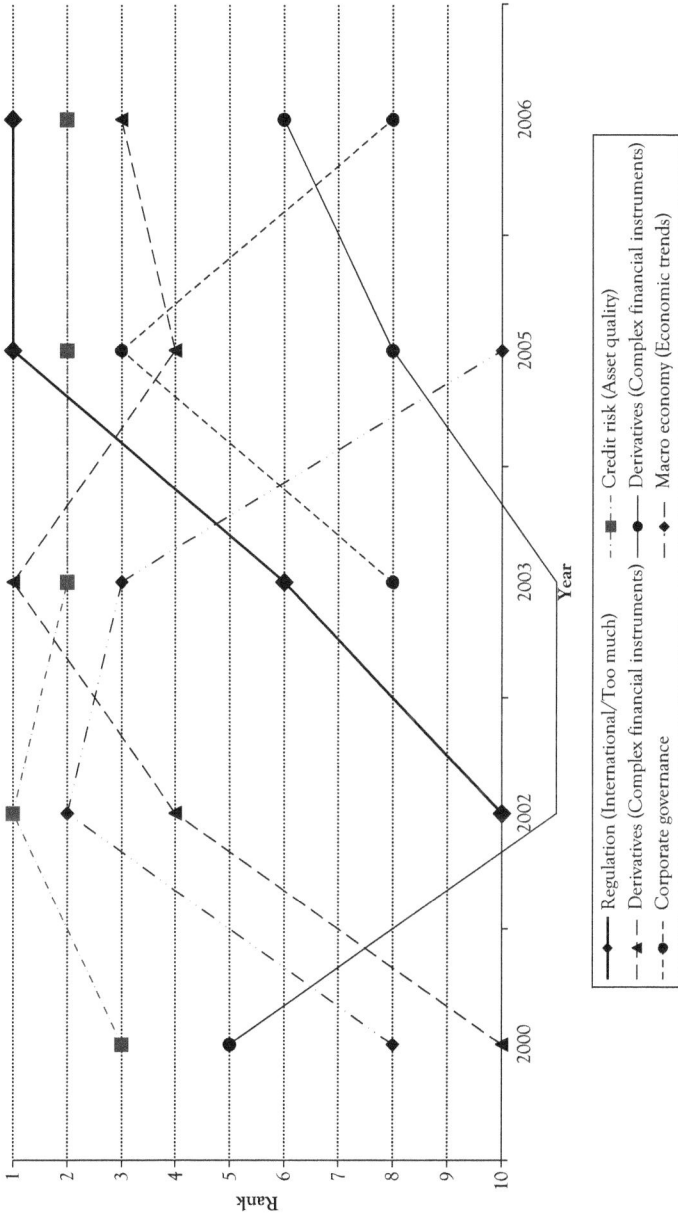

Exhibit 11.1 Banking banana skins

Source: CSFI Banking Banana Skins, 2006.

It is not just the number of publications that has increased: Basel I (1998 updated version) totals 26 pages; Basel II (*Final Framework*, June 2006 version) runs to 347 pages. Taking these numbers as indicative, this represents a 150-fold increase in the volume of regulatory paper issued by BCBS from Basel I to Basel II.

Given the increase in globalization of banks since the mid-1980s, bankers also face the issue of keeping up with multiple regulatory bodies and the various pronouncements they make.

In the UK, this is manifested in the path that Basel II has taken: from the BCBS (347 pages), through the European Union's Capital Requirements Directive (255 pages) to the FSA's General and Banks & Investment Firms Prudential Sourcebooks[12] (GENPRU and BIPRU) (868 pages).

Increasing Complexity

To give an idea of the change in complexity of requirements using the Basel I versus Basel II example, Basel I is based around a capital calculation that can be summarized as:

$$Capital\ Required = \Sigma\ Risk\text{-}Weighted\ Assets \times 8\ percent$$

where: risk-weighted assets = exposure[13] × exposure class risk weight; and exposure class risk weight is looked up on the following exhibit.

By contrast, the capital calculation for corporate borrowers at the heart of the internal ratings-based (IRB) approaches under Basel II can be represented as follows:

$$Capital\ Required = \Sigma\ Risk\text{-}Weighted\ Assets \times 8\ percent\ Risk\text{-}Weighted\ Assets$$
$$= EAD \times K \times 12.5$$

---

[12] *Consultation paper 06/3***—Strengthening Capital Standards 2*, Financial Services Authority, February 2006.

[13] For the sake of simplicity, the treatment of off-balance sheet exposures through credit conversion factors has been omitted from the exposure definition.

Exposure class	Risk weight
Claims on OECD central governments and central banks denominated in national currency and funded in that currency	0%
Claims on domestic public sector entities, excluding central government, and loans guaranteed by or collateralised by securities issued by such entities	0%, 10%, 20% or 50% at discretion
Claims on banks incorporated in the OECD and claims guaranteed by OECD incorporated banks	20%
Loans fully secured by mortgage on residential property that is or will be occupied by the borrower or that is rented	50%
Claims on the private sector Claims on banks incorporated outside the OECD with a residual maturity of over one year All other assets	100%

Exhibit 11.2 Existing Basel 1 risk weights*

Source: BCBS *International Convergence of Capital Measurement and Capital Standards*, 1998, pp. 17–18.

---

* *International convergence of capital measurement and capital standards*, Basel Committee of the Bank for International Settlements, July 1988, updated to April 1998, pages 17–18 (summarized).

where:[14,15]

$$K = LGD \times N \frac{1}{\sqrt{1-R}} \times G(PD) + \sqrt{\frac{R}{1-R}} \times G(0.999)$$

$$-PD \times LGD \times \frac{\left(1+(M-2.5)\times b\right)}{(1-1.5\times b)} \times 12.5 \times 1.06$$

and

$$R = 0.12 \times \frac{\left(1-e^{-50\times PD}\right)}{\left(1-e^{-50}\right)} + 0.24 \times 1 - \frac{\left(1-e^{-50\times PD}\right)}{\left(1-e^{-50}\right)}$$

$b = (0.11852 - 0.05478 \times \ln(PD))^2$

$N(\cdot)$ stands for the standard normal cumulative distribution function

$G(\cdot)$ stands for the inverse standard normal cumulative distribution function.

This is the IRB formula for corporate customers under Basel II; there are four other categories of credit-risk customers (see the following Exhibit 11.3), each with its own different formula.

In addition, for IRB banks, there are specific calculations required (or optional treatments available) for leasing, purchased receivables, equity exposures, specialized lending, counterparty credit risk (trading book) and securitization (see Exhibit 11.4).

Pushing Banks Toward a Precipice?

One of the major consequences of Basel II is that if a bank wishes to adopt the more advanced options available for credit risk assessment under Basel II, they are required to be able to model a number of quantitative measures of risk, specifically:

- Probability of default (PD);
- Loss-given default (LGD);

---

[14] Ibid. paragraph 272, except as noted below.
[15] The "x1.06" at the end of the formula for K is from DIRECTIVE 2006/48/EC OF THE EUROPEAN PARLIAMENT AND OF THE COUNCIL of June 14, 2006 relating to the taking up and pursuit of the business of credit institutions (recast), Annex VII, Part 1, paragraph 3.

Corporate	Corporate SME	Retail mortgage	Qualifying revolving retail	Retail other
As above	As above, different R factor	As above, no b factor, 0.15 R factor in all cases	As above, no b factor, 0.04 R factor in all cases. (portfolio must pass earnings volatility test before using this treatment)	As above, no b factor, different R factor
Basel 2: paragraph 272	paragraph 273	paragraph 328	paragraph 329	paragraph 330

Exhibit 11.3 Risk weights for customer classes

Source: BCBS: *Based II International Conference of Capital Measurement and Capital Standards: A Revised Framework,* June 2006 (paragraphs as indicated).

Leasing	Purchased receivables	Equity exposures	Specialised lending	Counterparty credit risk (Trading book)	Securitisation
Must be treated as loan, with collateral. EAD equal to discounted lease payments. Residual value added, weighted by remaining term	Must calculate dilution risk, unless specifically permitted to disregard	May be exempted to use 100% / 150% risk weight if criteria met. Otherwise a simple approach with 300% / 400% risk weight applies, or a model must be created, with a 200% / 300% risk weight floor	Must use specific risk weights (the "slotting criteria") unless specifically permitted to use general IRB formula above	May calculate exposure value using internal models ("expected positive exposure") instead of existing MTM plus add-on approach	Must use external ratings where available, or infer an equivalent internal rating if possible. If not, supervisory formula approach is available, but it is highly complex and data-dependent.
Basel 2: paragraph 523. Residual value weighting added in the EU Capital Requirements Directive (CRD) Annex VII, Part 1, paragraph 27.	paragraph 369	paragraphs 340–358	paragraphs 275–279	paragraphs 777(xi), 777(xii)	paragraphs 538–643

Exhibit 11.4 Treatments for different products

Source: Ibid. (paragraphs as indicated).

- Exposure at default (EAD); and
- Maturity (M).

Given the "use test"[16] requirements under Basel II, there is then a requirement for banks to incorporate these models into the decision-making processes of the bank, with the consequence being that the output of the models assumes a significant weight in the management of the firm.

Relying blindly on risk models to make decisions for a bank cannot be correct—the potential costs of type I and type II model errors[17] are too significant to allow banks to leave credit decisions to models alone, particularly in the commercial and corporate banking markets.

Chorafas (2000) states "...analytical models are no substitute for sound judgement...."[18] This is logically correct. Models can only react, in the prescribed way they have been built, to the inputs that they have been designed to assess.

By contrast, an experienced lender, who is well informed about the market, can make assessments that a model cannot, by virtue of the unconstrained nature of his or her thought processes.

For this reason, it is important that both banks and regulators recognize, respect and attribute proper weight to the value of expertise and experience in making credit decisions.

Regulators do recognize the risks of over-reliance on models. John Tiner, Chief Executive of the Financial Services Authority in the UK recently said:

> ...I am concerned about the realities of ever more complex financial instruments, accounting rules and prudential capital rules ... There is no let-up in the stream of increasingly complex

---

[16] See paragraph 444 of the Basel II final framework document.

[17] JimÈnez, G., and J. Saurina. 2006. "Credit Cycles, Credit Risk, and Prudential Regulation," *International Journal of Central Banking*, p. 66. (In the context of credit risk, a type I error, also referred to as "false negative," is the possibility that a good credit is rejected and a type II error (a "false positive") is the possibility that a bad credit is accepted.)

[18] Chorafas, D. 2000. *Managing Credit Risk Volume 1: Analysing, Rating and Pricing the Probability of Default.* London: Euromoney Books.

instruments emerging from firms. We should be in no doubt that this is generally a good thing—innovation feeds customer choice and competition. *But as the ranks of quants and rocket scientists in financial firms continue to grow, we must not lose sight of the limitations of complex and sophisticated financial modeling techniques.*[19] (italics added for emphasis)

There is another risk in the drive toward risk modeling, which comes from the increasing tendency of regulators to look for consistency in risk models across banks.

The more regulators encourage consistency, the more they are in danger of building up a high level of systemic risk. This arises from the potential for "herd mentality" whereby models that are too similar may react in the same way to an unforeseen circumstance.

Regulators should certainly understand the differences between banks' models and approaches, but they should be encouraging differences in bank strategy and approach, not eradicating them.

Much Ado About Nothing?

By the time Basel II reaches its final implementation date of January 1, 2008[20] (for advanced IRB in the European Union) it will be four years past its initial implementation deadline[21] and will have taken a decade to develop and implement. In spite of this, in the run-up to the initial implementation date in Europe (January 1, 2007), a number of key areas remained unclear, including:

---

[19] John, T. 2005. Chief Executive of the Financial Services Authority in the UK, from a speech at the FT Banker Awards in September.

[20] As this chapter went to print, 2009 was the proposed implementation date for Basel II in the US, although the implementation approach remained markedly different in the US to anywhere else in the world.

[21] *The new Basel Capital Accord: An explanatory note.* Basel Committee of the Bank for International Settlements, January 2001, page 1.

- The way "downturn"[22] LGD and EAD figures are to be calculated, justified and implemented;
- The way that Pillar 2 will work in practice;
- "Home/host"[23] regulator issues; and
- The impact and resolution of procyclical effects.
- These are all issues that create real concern within the banking industry, particularly in terms of how they impact on the concerns listed at the start of this chapter.

A further major concern in respect of Basel II relates to the costs of initial implementation and ongoing compliance. PricewaterhouseCoopers undertook a study on behalf of the European Union in 2004 where they estimated that it would cost Euro 20bn – Euro 30bn to implement the CRD across Europe.[24]

The implementation cost estimated by PwC is a staggering sum of money. One then considers:

- the impact of capital floors (in place for the first three years of Basel II at least);
- product level restrictions (such as the LGD floor for retail mortgages);
- the numerous and additive requirements for banks to demonstrate "conservatism" in their PDs;
- The requirement to use "downturn" LGDs and EADs; and
- the as-yet-unknown impact of Pillar 2 add-ons.

---

[22] For a description of downturn LGD, see paragraph 468 of the Basel Final Framework document.

[23] "Home/host" refers to a situation where a bank that is incorporated in one country and which has operations in another country may find itself having to satisfy the regulators in both countries in order to be able to utilize the more advanced approaches under Basel II. Banks have maintained that it should be the home regulator that makes this decision, and a host regulator should not require more or different information in order to endorse the home regulator's decision.

[24] MARKT/2003/02/F *Study on the financial and macroeconomic consequences of the draft proposed new capital requirements for banks and investment firms in the EU*, PricewaterhouseCoopers Final Report, April 8, 2004.

The accumulated impact of the aforementioned points calls into question the ability of banks to realize capital reductions as a result of Basel II. Banks have numerous stakeholders to satisfy, some of whom have their own view on the adequacy of capital resources (e.g., rating agencies). However, given the aforementioned, there is a question as to when quantifiable benefits from Basel II will find their way to the bottom line for banks.

Basel II Is Not Alone

The previous examples have focused on Basel II. It is important, however, to recognize that there are several other regulatory change programs that are currently underway or which have been completed in the last few years, including:

Sarbanes-Oxley;[25]

The adoption of IFRS standards;[26]

Anti-money-laundering regulations contained within, for example, the US Patriot Act;[27] and

The Markets in Financial Instruments Directive (MiFID).

Each of the aforementioned represents a significant expenditure of time and resource on a regulatory, and therefore mandatory, program of work. Each is complex, and in some cases they have not been well coordinated between the relevant regulatory authorities.

It is the combination of increasing volume and complexity represented by the regulatory programs listed earlier (plus Basel II) that causes concerns among bankers.

This is well summed up by Hank Paulson, the US Treasury Secretary, who stated in one of his first speeches after taking office that ". . . the regulatory 'pendulum' had swung too far in response to the Enron and

---

[25] Official short title: The Sarbanes-Oxley Act of 2002, H.R.3763.

[26] International Financial Reporting Standards. Comprising 41 separate standards, the implementation of IFRS (replacing Generally Accepted Accounting Practices, or GAAP) is a major task for all firms, not just banks.

[27] Official short title: Uniting and Strengthening America by Providing Appropriate Tools Required to Intercept and Obstruct Terrorism (USA PATRIOT ACT) Act of 2001, H.R.3162.ENR.

WorldCom corporate scandals . . ."[28] and "the challenge before us now is how to achieve the right regulatory balance to enable us to be competitive in today's world."[29]

Mr Paulson's wording about "the right regulatory balance" neatly encapsulates the basis of the rest of this chapter—how the development and implementation of regulations might be improved.

Improving the Process

There would seem to be three high-level principles that regulators and banks should follow to ensure that future regulatory initiatives are implemented as smoothly as possible.

Principle 1: Regulations Should Be Based on Principles Not Rules

Regulations should be driven by mitigation of clearly defined risks that impact the regulators' key areas of responsibility: protecting depositors and the integrity of the financial system.

Too many of the discussions that have gone on in recent years in respect of the consultations and negotiations around Basel II have been to do with reviews of detail in lengthy documents rather than about substantive issues of how to reduce or manage the risks about which regulators are legitimately concerned.

Both regulators and banks must recognize that there are significant implications involved with moving toward principles-based regulation. To give just two examples, one from each "side":

- Regulators will need to spend more time reviewing banks' operations, policies and processes to ensure that principles are being adhered to—this means that the cost of regulation will increase, as regulators will need both more people and people with a different skill set;

---

[28] *Financial Times*, Wednesday, August 2, 2006, page 1.
[29] Ibid.

- Banks will have to accept that it will be possible to face enforcement action for breach of a principle, rather than a rule.

For these reasons, among others, principles will not be the appropriate solution to all regulatory requirements. In particular, where the possible enforcement action includes the prospect of individual censure (fines or imprisonment) for senior management, clarity of boundaries will be required.

Principles-based regulation would require a change in mindset on the part of both parties and would necessitate more of a relationship approach between regulators and banks. This is reflected in the second principle.

Principle 2: Regulators and Bankers Need to Understand That We Are in This Together

It is normal for banks and regulators to have differing opinions on a range of issues—if they did not it would be a cause for concern. However, it is important that regulators trust that banks will not deliberately operate in an unsafe manner, and it is equally important the banks trust that regulators will not impose inappropriately restrictive rules on them.

It is in the best interest of banks to behave in a responsible manner, given the potential for significant reputational damage if they do not.

It is in the best interests of regulators to set and interpret regulations in a practical, pragmatic manner. This will help to avoid unintended consequences such as stifling innovation or restricting competition.

An example of a difference of opinion between regulators and banks to illustrate this point is a recent discussion on whether there is a difference between a bank's support for a branch of the bank overseas, and support for an overseas subsidiary.

- Regulators maintain that branch status puts a different legal requirement on the bank to support a branch, as opposed to a subsidiary (and from a strictly legal perspective, the regulators are right).

- Banks say that the reputational impact of allowing any related entity to fail is so catastrophic that the niceties of legal structure are irrelevant to the bank when assessing whether to support an overseas part of the bank or not. From a practical perspective, the banks' point is compelling.

The difference of opinion will remain. What is needed is for banks and regulators to find a way to agree on rules, and interpretations of rules, that do not drive banks, for example, to constitute their overseas operations in a particular legal form merely because they believe that their choice will result in a more or less stringent treatment.

Principle 3: Regulators and Banks Need to Communicate More Clearly

Regulators in general (and the FSA in particular) have been making real changes in the way they operate the process of communicating with industry in respect of changes arising out of Basel II.

It should be noted, however, that from the start the debate on Basel II has taken place at a technical level. This came about in part because it was technical people (e.g., portfolio managers and economic capital experts), rather than senior management with a more strategic focus, who led the debate on Basel II. This is true of both the banks and regulators.

In line with the first two principles, the communication process could be further improved by focusing the discussions on the risks that regulators are concerned about, coming up with principles (where that is appropriate) and sharing with banks, before regulation is drafted, what the risk is and why new regulation is required.

Banks understand the risks that regulators are concerned about. Closer, earlier dialogue may well enable new regulations to be avoided by agreeing to change practices.

What Is Next for Risk Regulation?

Looking even further forward, when looking at what is next for the regulation of credit risk, let's start with a question: which is the odd one out?

Financial markets are:	global
Financial institutions are:	global
Basel II was designed to be:	global
Regulators are:	local

Over the last decade, the financial services landscape has evolved, becoming more globally integrated. In order for regulators to keep up with the banks, markets, and regulatory regime that Basel II represents, it seems logical that regulators must start to act and think globally. There is a real chance that they will fail in their duties to depositors and financial stability if they do not.

It is indisputable that acting globally raises issues for regulators. The most important of the issues is probably legislative—many regulators are required by law to act in the best interests of local depositors and for the protection of the local financial system.

This is a point that is at the heart of the "home/host" issue, and which affects another major issue with regulation: consistency. Both regulators and bankers, in their respective assessment of the goal of regulation, noted the need for a level playing field. This is currently being hampered by a lack of global consistency in the implementation of Basel II.

The 1.06 multiplier for IRB risk weights in the EU CRD is an example of this. The BCBS calculated a "scaling factor" of 1.06 following the decision to calibrate Basel II to unexpected losses only, and based on data from QIS3. Crucially, the BCBS has never explicitly changed the Basel formula to incorporate the multiplier. The EU did explicitly change its risk weight formula (see formula on p. 116), opening the way for EU banks to be required to hold more capital than non-EU banks, whose regulators adopt the formula as published by Basel.

In order to act globally, regulators may need to seek changes in their legislative responsibilities. This may not be popular in some jurisdictions, especially those where protectionist instincts are strongest; however, the increasingly global nature of the banks they are regulating makes it necessary for regulators to take a more global view in order that they fullfill their local obligations. If a regulator is unaware of an impending problem in another jurisdiction, the problem could end up catching them unawares at home.

Even without immediate change in legislation, regulators can make the most of the freedoms they do have, working within their existing legislative responsibilities, to develop, foster and increase cooperation with their peers in other regulatory organizations.

The EU, and in particular the Committee of European Banking Supervisors (CEBS), have been working on improving consistency and transparency of regulation within the EU. This is demonstrated by the inclusion of Article 129[30] (requiring home, or "consolidating," supervisors to manage the approval process for IRB and AMA approaches) in the Capital Requirements Directive and the publication of CEBS' Consultation Paper 09.[31]

Notwithstanding the aforementioned, one senior regulator's attitude has been related as: "we will listen to what (another regulator) has to say, but it is our decision and we reserve the right to require more or different documentation as evidence of compliance." This is indicative of the issues in trying to get regulators to work together.

Basel III

Assuming that there will be a Basel III, what should it look like?

The three-pillar structure is a good framework for a regulatory regime and should be retained. To make a real advance on Basel II, the revised framework should be constructed as follows.

Pillar 1: Minimum Capital Determined by Banks' Internal Risk Models

Many banks already model varying risk types at a fairly granular level. Where economic capital models, or their equivalent, are in use there is

---

[30] Directive 2006/48/EC of the European Parliament and of the council of June 14, 2006 relating to the taking up and pursuit of the business if credit institutions (recast) Article 129, page 48.
[31] CEBS Consultation Paper 09: *Guidelines for Cooperation between consolidating supervisors and host supervisors.*

often a high degree of senior management support and understanding, which aligns well with the existing Basel II "use test."

Pillar 2: Single Supervisory Review

A single, coordinated process, covering all relevant jurisdictions. The concept behind Pillar 2 (supervisory review of Pillar 1 calculations and compliance, along with a review of banks' assessments of the role of capital in managing other risks) is sound. What would significantly improve it would be to make it a single assessment, binding on all supervisors who are involved with the bank. This does not, however, mean creating a single assessment that includes all of the varying requirements from every regulator.

Pillar 3: Enhancements to Disclosures

Enhancement in this case does not necessarily mean more disclosure— but getting greater harmonization of disclosures so that the market can make meaningful comparisons between banks (without compelling banks to disclose commercially sensitive information) would be a real improvement to Pillar 3.

Conclusion

Notwithstanding the issues regarding complexity and costs, Basel II has done much to improve communications between banks and regulators. The framework that Basel II puts in place allows for a more open and granular discussion between banks and their regulators. While there is still considerable room for improvement, it may be that this more open communication process around regulation and risk management will prove to be the most tangible benefit of the whole process.

Thanks

I would like to acknowledge the assistance and support I have received from colleagues past and present, in particular Colin Jennings (Lloyds TSB) and Jonathan Gray (Royal Bank of Scotland), for their comments on the draft, and David Schraa (International Institute of Finance) for input on the IIF's current work. As always, any errors or omissions are the responsibility of the author alone.

CHAPTER 12

Citigroup's Basel-Ready Tool: The Consolidated Credit Risk Model

Jennifer Courant, Bryce Ferguson, and Ákos Felső vályi

Citigroup

Introduction

As part of Citigroup's efforts to implement best practice risk-rating tools and prepare for Advanced Bank Status under the Basel II Accord, the Risk Rating Analytics Unit of Citigroup Risk Architecture introduced a new generation of credit risk models in 2002. By year-end 2004, the new credit risk model (CRM) application, known as the "Consolidated CRM" (hereafter, the CRM), had incorporated all 14 proprietary credit risk models deployed across Citigroup.

In this chapter, we describe the CRM in the context of the Basel II Accord and the credit risk management practices of Citigroup. The CRM has a double meaning in the chapter: it refers both to the mathematical statistical models used to calculate the "baseline" risk ratings of the customers and the software, which contains the risk-rating algorithm along with the entire database back-end. As a consequence, CRM is referred to as both plural and singular.

"A Consistent, Global Approach to Risk"

Citigroup's approach to credit risk measurement, which closely conforms to the principles of the Basel II Accord, was described in the article

"A Consistent, Global Approach to Risk" by Bryce Ferguson.[1] That article discussed many aspects of credit risk measurement tools and processes in use at Citigroup. This present article focuses on one aspect highlighted in that article: namely, the credit risk models and their context within the Basel II Accord effort. Before we talk about CRM specifically, let us review a few key components of the risk rating process at Citigroup, many of which were described in the earlier Ferguson article.

Citigroup is one of the largest global financial companies in the world with a unique institutional credit knowledge, experience, and unparalleled wealth of data. The risk-rating process at the institution relies on statistically based risk-rating models and sound judgment by local credit professionals. The risk ratings form the basis of all facets of portfolio management (approval, concentration limits, loss forecasting, loan-loss reserves, and economic capital). The risk-rating process is a framework which was developed with the goal of delivering consistent risk ratings across businesses, regions, and economic cycles.

Citigroup employs a risk rating scale of 1 to 10, where 1 is the best quality risk. Ratings from 1 to 7, which are applied to performing obligors and facilities, are further differentiated by +/− subgrades. The categories of 8, 9, and 10 are assigned to defaults of various definitions. The counterparty's (or obligor's) risk rating is a pure one-year probability of default. In 2000, Citigroup redefined its obligor risk ratings (ORRs) to explicitly map into specific ranges of one-year default probability. Facility risk ratings (FRRs) continued to be a measure of expected loss, as measured by the one-year probability of default of the obligor in combination with the loss-given default (LGD) of the facility.

The stand-alone credit risk models developed and enhanced throughout the 1990s were a key component of deriving the ORRs for many of Citigroup's corporate clients and established a consistent analytical framework within the rating process. These models were statistically developed and built primarily on internal data covering both private and public, rated and unrated companies in all regional markets, regardless of the existence of an efficient equity market. One of the key

---

[1] Bryce, F. February 2000. "A Consistent, Global Approach to Risk." *The Journal of Lending & Credit Risk Management*, pp. 20–24.

aspects of the Citigroup process is that the ratings derived from these statistical models are always reviewed by independent credit risk management as well as the relationship team in the field, which has specific knowledge of the markets and companies in question. Limited adjustments to the model's ratings are permitted via Citigroup's Risk Rating Policy (RRP), given appropriate rationale and documentation of such in all approval documents.

Both as a check on the consistency and accuracy of these final ratings, as well as an important input into future model enhancements, the Risk Architecture team performs annual validations of all ORRs against actual defaults: across the corporate banking group, within regions and by industry to determine the consistency and accuracy of the overall rating process.

Since the publication of the Ferguson article, Citigroup has implemented a number of projects with the goal of enhancing internal risk measurement and achieving Advanced Bank Status under Basel II. The most important of these include:

- introduction of the CRM;
- newly enhanced models for predicting the probability of significant credit deterioration;
- implementation of a global default data collection that supplements Citigroup's long-term LGD studies with detailed information on the facilities that default;
- development of a global database structure where databases on defaults (internal and external), LGD (internal), agency ratings, internal ratings, equity market information, bond spreads and financials, can all be sourced on a specific customer or portfolio segment; and
- introduction of hybrid probability of default (HPD) models for publicly traded corporates and financial institutions, that utilize both equity market information and firm financials.

This chapter will focus on the creation, structure and performance of the CRM, within the context of Basel II compliance.

The CRM and the Basel Accord

The 1988 Basel Capital Accord of the Bank determined the current amount of regulatory capital for international settlements, which is based primarily on the amounts of exposure to a few types of counterparties (such as sovereigns, corporates or banks). The current approach does not include any assessment of the riskiness of a given bank's portfolio. For instance, a bank that actively seeks out very low-risk customers may be required to hold the same amount of regulatory capital as a bank that deals with high-risk customers, assuming similar exposure amounts.

In June 1999, the Basel Committee on Banking Supervision announced a proposal to replace the 1988 Capital Accord with a more risk-sensitive framework. That framework is known as the Basel II Accord. A second proposal was released in January 2001 that incorporated comments on the original proposal. The proposal is based on three pillars—minimum capital requirements, supervisory review and market discipline—that would allow banks and regulators to evaluate various aspects of banking risk, including market, credit, and operational risk.

The new proposal was developed in response to a clear need for more risk sensitivity in the calculation of capital and, under the internal ratings-based (IRB) approach, which would allow banks to use internally derived risk measures, within certain limits, to set regulatory capital. It attempts to cover a variety of risk measures, including the risk ratings provided by a bank's own internal credit risk models.

The proposal formulates two approaches to credit risk: the standardized and the IRB approaches. The standard approach is very similar to the existing Accord, but the single risk weight is replaced with four. The IRB approach allows banks to use their internally built credit risk models, like the CRMs, in determining what amount of capital will need to be held. This approach is broken into two implementation forms: foundation and advanced. In the foundation approach, a bank will be able to use the output of its credit risk models (the rating, which is associated with a likelihood of default) and the banking supervisor will provide the other necessary parameters (LGD, exposure at default (EAD), and maturity) to calculate the capital requirement. In the IRB approach, a bank will use the output of its credit risk models and supply the other parameters as well.

The advanced approach provides significant benefits to banks that can prove the validity of their models and their risk management systems to their regulators, both in better measurement of the portfolio's risks and in better aligning regulatory capital with internal measurement of portfolio quality (either expected loss measures or economic capital measures).

The Consolidated CRM Framework

History of the CRM at Citigroup

Prior to the economic recession of the early 1990s, very few institutions used statistically based credit risk assessment. Instead, banks and rating agencies relied upon the expert judgment of credit officers and analysts in assessing individual credits. Following the real-estate collapse of the late 1980s and the US recession in the early 1990s, some banks sought to re-evaluate how they could measure and manage credit risk on a more consistent basis across their operations. At Citigroup, the recognition of a need for more consistent risk tools led to the development of the credit risk models, initially within the corporate and investment banking group.

The first CRM was introduced in 1990 and was used to assign risk ratings for North American corporates. It was a relatively simple model developed to replicate the S&P ratings for a sample of North American corporates. The CRMs rely on financial inputs (income statement and balance sheet), as well as some qualitative inputs. This is a necessity given the large number of privately held firms in the portfolio and the inefficient equity markets that exist in many regions where Citigroup has significant operations. In contrast, the newly developed Citigroup's HPD models are mainly based on market signals.

Over the next five years, CRMs were developed using more sophisticated statistical techniques and their coverage was expanded to other geographic regions. By 2000, there were 14 separate CRMs in use, some of which encompassed multiple industry modules or regional models, and the coverage had expanded to include commercial banks, as well as commercial and industrial firms, private banking and business and professional customers. With few exceptions, almost all of the models continued to be benchmarked to public agency ratings or internal ratings, given the relatively small number of defaults (and associated financials) among customers.

Models were distributed physically on diskettes, with heavy reliance on the users to apply the appropriate models and gain access to updates, as they were made available. Furthermore, the software required that the user closely follow instructions for saving the model inputs and outputs, and return this information to the Risk Architecture team upon request (more on this later).

Reference Dataset for Modeling

Clearly, the key input into any successful modeling effort is a significant amount of high-quality data about the customers. As part of credit model development at Citigroup, significant amounts of time are taken in order to design, clean and assemble the reference (i.e., development) dataset. Basel II also recognizes the importance of the data and thus puts much emphasis on appropriateness of the reference datasets for the portfolio to which the risk tools are applied. As information on a company's financial strength is one of the key pieces of data required, we capture the (annual) financial statements of the companies of interest. For public companies in some markets, these data can be purchased from a vendor or downloaded from websites (e.g., the SEC's EDGAR website for public US companies). Similarly, it is relatively easy to find reliable data on some types of defaults, such as bankruptcy filings in the United States or liquidations in the UK.

In other countries, or for private companies, these data are not readily available. This can prove to be an insurmountable challenge for building CRMs in some countries or regions. Fortunately, Citigroup's long-standing and broad geographic coverage has provided us with access to both large amounts of data (on public and private companies) and credit expertise across a wide population of countries, corporations and industries. Even with the recognized shortcomings of the first generation of stand-alone CRMs, Risk Architecture was able to collect the financials of thousands of companies globally, along with their respective ratings.

The hardest part of the data-gathering effort, however, is to identify and collect financial information on defaulted companies, for use in building models that predict default. Not only do companies in trouble often stop publishing or providing financials in a timely fashion, but there may be little incentive to run a credit risk model (and thus collect the financial data) on a failing company, particularly if the decision has been taken to leave the relationship. While Citigroup has over 30 years of loss data across the globe, it has been a difficult task to link those defaults to financial statements for use in modeling.

To help remedy the situation, Citigroup has been building financials databases and extensive default databases, covering customers and non-customers alike. To the extent that there are insufficient defaults among clients within a given industry, for instance, we can also utilize the external defaults in our database, if they reflect our internal data.

Access to these broader datasets has greatly enhanced our credit risk modeling abilities and allowed us to build models that directly predict default, rather than emulate an agency or internal rating.

Thus, our models rely on as much internal and external data as possible and practical. In order to bring all this data together into an easy-to-use database, we set up a global identification table, which links the various and numerous company identifiers of the different sources. The linkage is established and maintained along two dimensions: across all sources and over time (as our databases house historical data).

Data Cleaning

If the first challenge is finding the data, the second major challenge is in cleaning it. This is an indispensable, time-consuming, and often unappreciated part of modeling. No matter how much data we have, inconsistencies and inaccuracies in the reference dataset can jeopardize the quality of any modeling effort. Data quality is a concern whether we are working with our own internal data or a vendor's external data. Unlike market data, credit risk data (such as financial statements and defaults) is "low frequency." As a result, almost every item of data is valuable and a concerted effort is made to ensure that the data are accurate and as little as possible is discarded.

To speed up the process, many elements of the dataset will be checked extensively through automated processes, such as missing fields in a financial statement, or a mismatch between assets and liabilities. In the end, however, much of the data cleaning for model development continues to be heavily labor intensive. For instance, in modeling default, it is critical that there be good documentation on each default to prevent inclusion of defaults where the financials are strong but the statements were misleading due to fraud. What is also critical is that each step of the data cleaning is well documented to allow for replication, validation, and review.

Model Structure

The large amount of financial and rating data that the bank has actively collected and accumulated over the last 15 years, along with the extensive default database, allows researchers to build a variety of models that measure and predict credit risk. Regardless of the specific statistical technique utilized, we employ similar structures in all of our credit risk models. In general, the CRMs calculate obligor risk ratings by relying on three key categories of input:

- Financial ratios (e.g., the interest coverage ratio, the leverage ratio or the cash-flow-to-debt ratio);
- The size of the company; and
- Qualitative aspects of the company, such as management experience and risk controls.

During model development, many financial ratios are tested. Those that manifest both statistical strength and theoretical and business raison d'être qualify for inclusion. The raw financial items and the calculated financial ratios vary from region to region and from industry to industry due to local accounting rules, business practices, data availability and, most importantly, statistical significance. When modeling across groups of countries, for instance, we construct financial variables that take into consideration the local accounting regimes in order to maintain accounting neutrality.

A second key factor in determining the credit quality of a company is often related to its size, which we have found, in many industry segments, to be representative of factors that are correlated with credit quality (e.g., financial flexibility, diverse revenue streams, expansive customer base, and geographic reach). A variety of size measures are investigated and selected by a process similar to that used to choose the financial ratios.

To the extent that we have historical detail on more "qualitative" aspects of the firms, such as market position, quality of management, and infrastructure, these data elements allow the modeler to "fine-tune" the model. The contribution of the subjective qualitative factors is always limited in our algorithms.

Performance/Validation

The CRMs possess three important properties: consistency, accuracy, and verifiability. The creation and maintenance of the CRMs involve constant testing, analysis, critique (both by the members of Risk Architecture and risk management professionals in the business), validations (internal), audits (internal and regulatory), re-estimation, and redevelopment on a regular, policy-prescribed basis.

One of the key tests of the quality of the model is whether or not the default rates produced fall into the Citigroup-defined ranges of default probabilities (i.e., "policy bands") set up a priori. The model should manifest a positive relationship between increasing risk and the incidence of default. The default rates in the combined reference dataset should also show an excellent fit to the desired distribution. Exhibit 12.1 contains the counts numerically and Exhibit 12.2 displays them graphically. The default rates at full grades (from 1 to 7) all fall into the policy-mandated bands of probabilities.

The effectiveness of the algorithms can be presented by a cumulative accuracy profile, where we measure how quickly the algorithms capture defaults (see Exhibit 12.3). We sort the entire sample by the predicted probability (see the horizontal axis entitled "Percent of sample ordered by predicted probability of default") and, on the vertical axis, we tally the percent of defaults captured at every value along the ordered sample. The steeper the profile, the more effective the model is. We present the profile for the combined sample used in Exhibit 12.3. The chart shows two reference lines, which trace the profiles of the perfect model (which assigns

Rating (full grade)	1	2	3	4	5	6	7	Total
Number of non-defaults	182	4,142	6,831	16,147	16,217	5,953	1,601	51,072
Number of defaults	0	1	3	45	266	503	551	1,369
Default rate	0.00	0.02	0.04	0.28	1.61	7.79	25.60	2.61
Total	182	4,143	6,834	16,192	16,483	6,456	2,152	52,441

Exhibit 12.1 Default rates in the combined reference dataset of the CRMs

Source: Author's own.

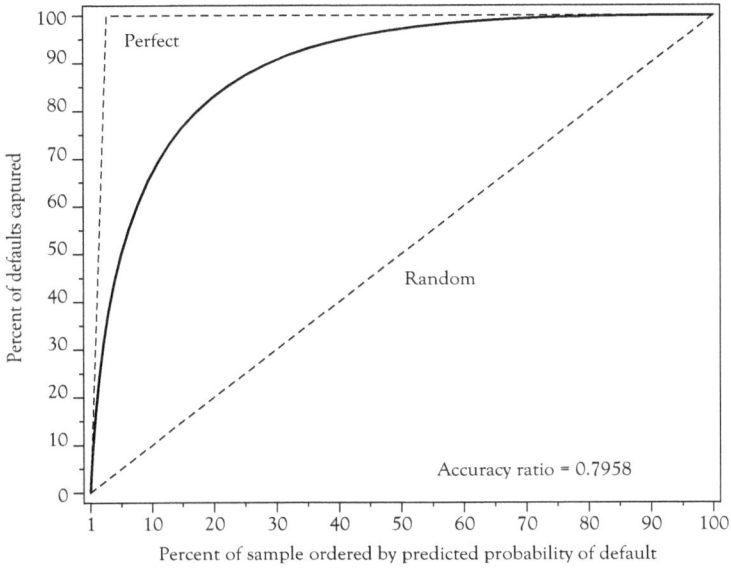

Exhibit 12.2 Default rates in the combined development sample

Source: Author's own.

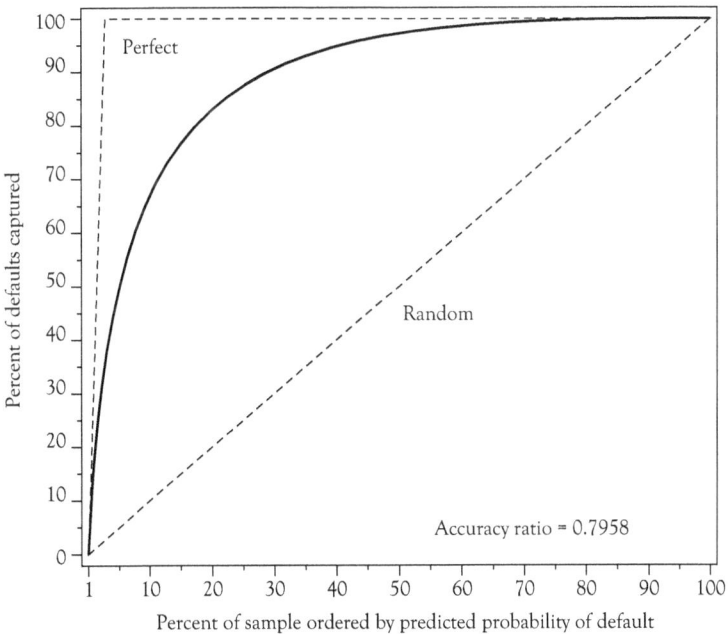

Exhibit 12.3 Combined cumulative accuracy profile of the CRMs

Source: Author's own.

the highest probabilities to the defaults, followed by lower probabilities to all non-defaults) and the random or non-informed model.

Software Solution

The predictive power of these models has been well established through years of development, testing, and application. From a practical perspective, however, delivering the CRMs across the globe in an efficient and user-friendly application may be even more critical in ensuring appropriate use of the CRMs. Prior to 2002, the models were delivered to the users as stand-alone desktop applications, although the desktop applications created numerous problems for Risk Architecture, the users, and internal security. First, it was virtually impossible to keep track of the software: who used it, who had it and who had copied it. This resulted in making updates to and discontinuance of expired versions of the software difficult to manage. Secondly, it did not allow users within a team to share information and, if someone left, there was no access to their cases. Thirdly, there was no means to confirm appropriate use of the models on an ongoing basis. Last but not least, data collection for validation and redevelopment had to be done on a manual basis, relying heavily on the cooperation of hundreds of users.

These weaknesses became increasingly evident with the growth in the number of models, the number of users and geographic breadth, as well as the increasingly restrictive security requirements. Due to both ongoing frustrations with the software, and in order to satisfy expected requirements under Basel II, Citigroup launched a new credit risk model application in 2002 across a Citigroup-wide global network. The software features of this second-generation tool, known as the Consolidated CRM, include:

- One database housing all the input and output data for all cases run through any of the CRMs from all over the globe;
- One application into which various credit risk algorithms are loaded. Currently, there are 19 CRMs loaded, which cover a large range of regions and industries;

- Unique user identifiers and individualized permissions for user access (a user located in Tanzania who works on the bank's corporate exposures would have access only to the models that are used on corporates in Tanzania while a super-user may have access to models for multiple countries or regions);
- Security and privacy requirements, which govern sharing and transferring of data, including a Chinese Wall to separate public and private data and users;
- A consistent data input platform, supporting high-quality data (input line items are defined in detail and some fields are provided by feeds from other internal systems);
- Unique customer identifiers that link to credit risk reporting systems, credit approvals, and other credit risk data that the bank captures;
- Automatic saves of the final calculation of a credit risk rating to the database, which is attached to the credit approval documentation. These "official" CRM records are permanently saved in the dataset, cannot be deleted and will eventually be fed into the credit risk reporting systems for comparison to final ratings;
- The non-official records are the so-called "draft" records and can contain certain scenarios of mergers, acquisitions or stress testing. Draft records can be altered and deleted; and
- Central updates to software and algorithms, ensuring use of approved and supported models.

Data Warehousing

An important requirement of Basel II revolves around data capture and data warehousing. The CRM software not only provides a tool to assign a risk rating to an obligor, but also serves as a data warehouse to store all risk ratings generated by the software, the underlying probabilities of default, as well as all financial and nonfinancial inputs into the calculations, providing a clean, reliable, ready-to-use financial and risk dataset for model validation and re-development. The CRM also makes possible data collection on prospective companies through input under special user IDs.

MH1>CRM Usage

The CRM and its database reside on a protected, dedicated server within the Citigroup network. All CRM users are connected to this single application, which, since 2002, has run 24 hours a day, 7 days a week. Some usage statistics are presented in Exhibit 12.4, showing the usage by hour using Greenwich Mean Time and, in Exhibit 12.5, tallying the day of the week when the CRM records are saved. These demonstrate the truly global usage of the application.

At the time of writing this chapter, the CRM database had 26,713 baseline company records with 91,330 records of yearly financials from 146 countries. See Exhibit 12.6 for the statistics of both types of company records (draft and baseline) individually and together. The monthly usage of the CRM has been steadily increasing since its introduction in June 2002 (see Exhibit 12.7). Currently, about 4,000 records are saved each month. The number of worldwide users is more than 2,000.

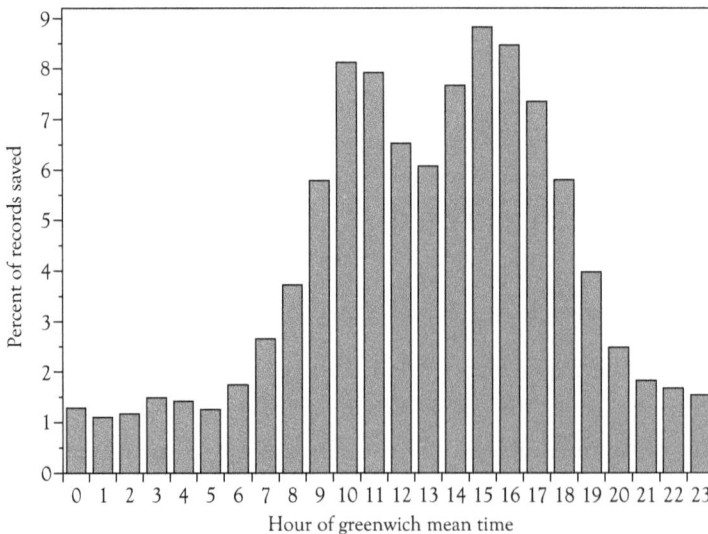

Exhibit 12.4 **CRM usage by hour of day (draft and baseline records)**

Source: Author's own.

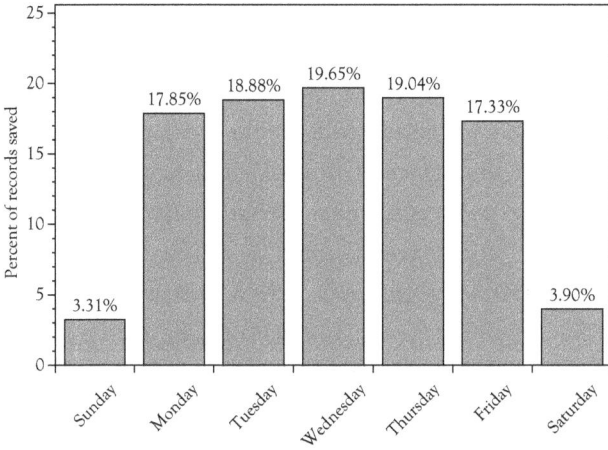

Exhibit 12.5 CRM usage by day of week GMT (draft and baseline records)

Source: Author's own.

	Draft records	Baseline records	All records (draft+baseline)
Number of countries	182	146	182
Number of CRM runs	121,874	26,713	148,587
Number of years with financials	455,371	91,330	546,701

Exhibit 12.6 Record-counts in the CRM database

Source: Author's own.

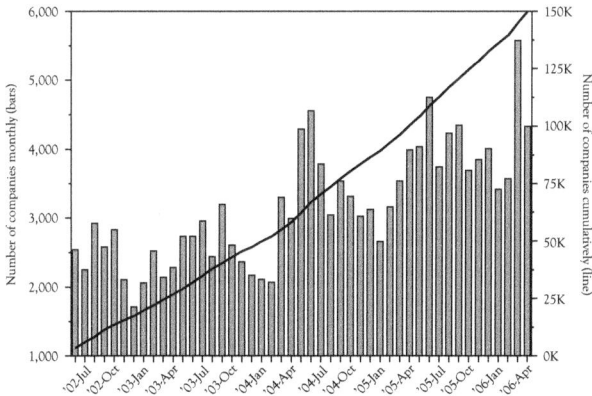

Exhibit 12.7 Number of company records saved (draft and baseline)

Source: Author's own.

As stated earlier, the risk rating of a company provided by the CRM is the baseline, or official, record, which serves as the baseline obligor rating in the risk rating process at Citigroup. Based on the credit professional's experience and any special knowledge of the company in question (which is not reflected in the financials), that risk rating might be adjusted within a narrow band to arrive at the final risk rating. About 45 percent of the baseline obligor ratings were accepted as the final ratings without any discretionary override. When applied, the adjustment is symmetric, since about the same number of ratings is increased as decreased by the adjustments (28 percent versus 27 percent).

The program automatically extracts the baseline records of official, reliable, financial data and loads them into a research dataset (reference dataset) maintained by risk architecture. This predominantly contains our internal data, which is augmented with relevant external data. All model validation, recalibration and development work utilizes this reference database. It provides a given CRM with data pertinent to the business and region the CRM covers. Moreover, it makes many specialized and innovative usages possible. For example, if a region does not have a rich enough sample in a certain industry, we can "borrow" similar companies from another, relevant region in order to enrich the development sample, or we can track and compare trends in certain financial ratios globally or locally.

Illustrative Analysis of the Reference Dataset

Currently, the reference dataset has financial data going as far back as 1996 (see the distribution in Exhibit 12.8), as many users have uploaded past financial statements into the new application. There are now more than 91,000 financial years, which are stated in 115 currencies. As the Consolidated CRM treats the financial ratios uniformly across the regions and the businesses, we can examine the generic behavior of a ratio in relationship with the risk rating. In the following example, we extract one of the common ratios of the rating algorithms: debt to capitalization. Although the exact definition of this ratio varies slightly from region to region and business to business, we observe that the overall behavior of the ratio is quite uniform. To illustrate this claim, we used the ratio from the most recent financial year for each company, excluded some extreme

Financial year	Frequency	Percent
1996 and before	174	0.19
1997	319	0.35
1998	1,735	1.90
1999	4,598	5.03
2000	9,725	10.65
2001	15,695	17.18
2002	20,605	22.56
2003	20,852	22.83
2004	13,875	15.19
2005	3,740	4.10
2006	12	0.01
Total	91,330	100.00

Exhibit 12.8 Number of records in the reference dataset

Source: Author's own.

values and examined its distribution by risk rating category. The distribution is provided in a tabular, numerical form shown as follows, showing the elementary statistics of mean, standard deviation, quartiles, and so on. (Exhibit 12.9) and in a graphical form (Exhibit 12.10).

For each risk rating category, Exhibit 12.10 represents the middle 50 percent of the distribution as a rectangle. The median values are connected by a tick polygon indicating the overall relationship of the ratio and risk rating. As shown in the graph, it is clear that as the value of debt to capitalization increases, the risk rating decreases across all the separate models. Debt to capitalization in our reference dataset is a truly "global financial ratio," which we achieved by:

- handling the raw financial data in a uniform manner in the development samples (which requires adjustments due to different accounting standards);
- defining the ratio such that it could be utilized in many regions and businesses; and
- instructing the users to supply the financial items of this ratio in a uniform and consistent manner.

Rating	Number of companies	Mean value	Standard deviation	Minimal value	Lower quartile	Median value	Upper quartile	Maximal value
1	62	0.11	0.25	0	0.00	0.01	0.13	1.74
2+	40	0.32	0.41	0	0.08	0.20	0.34	1.79
2	67	0.22	0.23	0	0.12	0.22	0.36	1.29
2-	76	0.28	0.26	0	0.10	0.24	0.37	1.66
3+	134	0.23	0.17	0	0.10	0.23	0.34	0.84
3	264	0.36	0.37	0	0.13	0.28	0.43	1.90
3-	409	0.28	0.27	0	0.08	0.25	0.42	1.76
4+	747	0.31	0.32	0	0.04	0.26	0.44	1.84
4	1,078	0.24	0.24	0	0.00	0.20	0.39	1.56
4-	1,761	0.21	0.22	0	0.00	0.14	0.37	1.56
5+	2,349	0.23	0.23	0	0.00	0.18	0.38	1.46
5	3,110	0.25	0.24	0	0.01	0.19	0.40	1.98
5-	3,628	0.30	0.25	0	0.06	0.28	0.48	1.52
6+	3,677	0.37	0.27	0	0.14	0.37	0.56	1.95
6	3,382	0.46	0.28	0	0.25	0.49	0.66	1.85
6-	2,119	0.55	0.31	0	0.35	0.59	0.77	1.89
7+	955	0.64	0.32	0	0.45	0.70	0.86	2.00
7	387	0.69	0.42	0	0.44	0.72	0.94	1.96
7-	423	1.00	0.47	0	0.77	1.04	1.25	2.00
Total	24,668	0.36	0.31	0	0.08	0.33	0.56	2.00

Exhibit 12.9 Distributions of debt to capitalization by risk rating in the reference dataset

Source: Author's own.

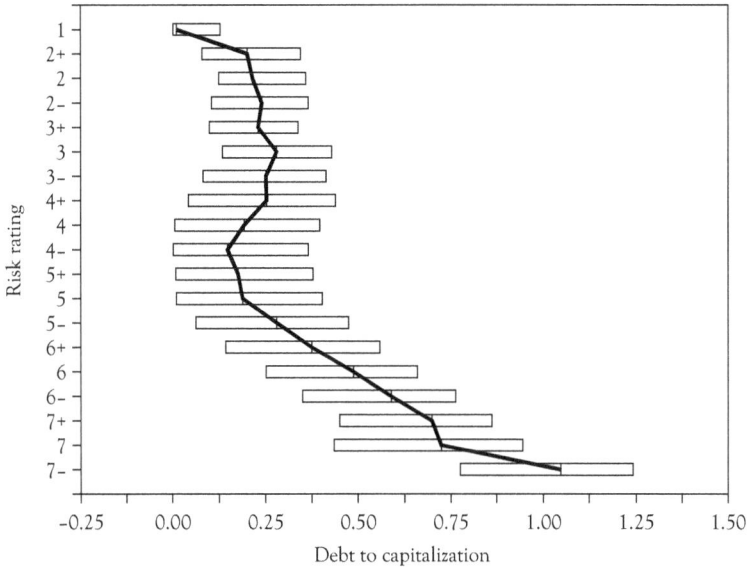

Exhibit 12.10 *Rating plot of debt to capitalization*

Source: Author's own.

Future Plans

The consolidated framework represents a high-quality credit risk rating tool, built upon years of experience with credit risk modeling and implementation, which also satisfies the anticipated requirements of the Basel II Accord. As part of our constant effort to improve our tool, we plan the following improvements over the next few years:

- massive risk rating option (i.e., risk rate all companies of a portfolio once);
- web-based delivery mechanism (faster and easier model updates and additions);
- enhanced stress-testing capability;
- expanded peer-comparison analysis;
- reporting risk rating along with early warning risk measures (both internal and external);
- providing short- and long-term risk assessment metrics;
- increased frequency of model validations and re-estimation; and
- improved user permission and security.

CHAPTER 13

Overcoming the Challenges in the Credit Derivatives Market

Pontus Eriksson

SunGard FRONT ARENA

A Bird's-Eye View of the Credit Derivatives Market

There are many obvious advantages to an expanding credit derivatives market. The main advantage is that financial institutions can meet investor demands, for example:

- investors can hedge credit risk in isolation from other risk types;
- banks can sell off credit risk without consent from the borrower; and
- banks can tailor and originate synthetic credit risk.

There are, however, opposite forces, which include increased operational risk, coupled with a heavier burden of capital allocation, something that could hamper the profits of a bank. While it is probably fair to say that the benefits currently outweigh the drawbacks, these issues are still worth monitoring, especially considering the effect they might have on the credit derivatives market in the future. As food for thought, consider this: the growth rate of the operational problems could well be higher than the gain. Only time will tell.

The rapid maturation of this marketplace has created a somewhat unique challenge for technology vendors to the financial community, as they have been forced to adapt at a rate that established, proven systems often have trouble coping with. Additionally, the credit markets contain nuances foreign to other capital markets, eliminating the ability to simply add a new "flavor" of existing instruments in an effort to expand a system's asset coverage.

An Expanding Market Approaching Maturity

What's Fuelling the Credit Derivatives Market Growth?

The credit derivatives market has emerged from humble beginnings to become an established asset class in recent years. Credit default swaps have overtaken their securitized counterparts in terms of volume traded and the credit derivatives market in general has seen a phenomenal growth that has outstripped all forecasts.

Compared to the interest and currency markets, which date back to the 1970s, the credit derivatives market is a relative newcomer, having only emerged and taken off in the early 1990s. The increase in corporate spreads liquidity and the development of standardized legal documentation have been vital ingredients in this growth. Larger and smaller defaults have not hindered growth but rather had the opposite effect as market players have increased their appetite to hedge credit risk.

By far the largest default was Enron in 2001. Enron was an important player in the market and traded large amounts of bankruptcy swaps with several counterparties. Its own bankruptcy triggered large mark-to-market losses at its counterparts. This was the first important milestone in the development of the credit derivatives market. The first tradable credit index emerged in 2002 and generated an increased liquidity in standardized sets of obligors as well as lower margins. The following year, tranched index products began to appear; substantially boosting the market for correlation trading. It was around this time that correlation began to be perceived as a commodity in its own right rather than a pricing variable.

Standardizations and Conventions—a Sign of Maturity

The market has gradually become more standardized over the last couple of years. In the early days, the market had no standard legal documentation, which clearly hampered its growth. The introduction of standardized International Swaps and Derivatives Association (ISDA) definitions during 1999 was a vital contributor to the market development we have seen so far. A few years later, the 2003 credit derivatives definitions were published and have, since then, been the standard.

The market has also adopted the convention to trade credit default swaps with four standardized maturities every year, a concept similar to the IMM dates used in the money market. These standardized maturities and payment dates have significantly reduced risk stemming from mismatches in maturities between contracts.

Other standards are the credit fixings, operated by Markit™ and Creditex™ together with a number of major dealers. The credit fixings are calculated for the three most liquid iTraxx™ indexes in the European marketplace. This benchmark value facilitates the determination of exercise values for credit derivative contracts by providing a transparent, readily available number to be used as a settlement rate. Without this benchmark, it would be necessary to call several active dealers for a quote in order to settle a contract; a complicated and time-consuming practice. Credit fixings can help market players to mark-to-market their positions and to perform fixings on cash flows such as constant maturity products referencing other CDS instruments.

Products referencing a credit fixing face a challenge relating to the vintage effect of indexes. The name composition of the index may change every six-month roll and off-the-run indexes might all be slightly different to the prevailing on-the-run index. The key issue here is, for a historically traded contract, to know against which index to make the fixing and what to use for future estimation of the index value.

In 2005, ISDA launched the Novation Protocol, governing the rules of assigning a trade, which most buy-side parties agreed to follow. The standardized novation protocol offers parties to ISDA's various master agreements a way to agree to a uniform process to obtain consents to transfer of interests in credit derivative transactions. Parties who adhere to the protocol commit to exchange a novation confirmation. The goal of the Novation Protocol is to assist in remedying backlogs in confirmations due to novated trades. Difficulties in novations processing have been a major cause for outstanding confirmations. However, the backlog of outstanding confirmations has, at the time of writing, been significantly reduced.

Current Challenges Facing the Credit Derivatives Market

While the credit markets have made great strides in reaching some form of consensus on

market conventions, standard pricing models and the like, the credit markets face their share of challenges to reach the same state of maturity as the equity or interest rate markets.

First, the user base that trades credit products is primarily limited to banks, insurance houses, buy-side institutions such as hedge funds and, to some extent, asset managers. In order to further increase its footprint, the credit market may need to attract the broader mass of both corporate and retail investors. Although some corporates participate in the credit market, they are few compared to the larger players and hardly add to the overall diversification. While retail customers have ready access to the interest rate and currency markets, they are barred from the credit market.

Secondly, credit derivatives are not yet traded electronically on exchanges. Electronic trading would boost efficiency and perhaps also liquidity, while helping the market cope with its massive straight-through processing needs. There has been a discussion about launching credit futures at exchanges, but at the time of writing this had not happened. Electronic trading sometimes refers to electronically automated trade matching, which is different from exchange trading. Automated trade matching provides a quick and easy way to affirm trade details electronically between counterparties. Where appropriate, it then automatically sends the affirmed trade to DTCC for legal execution. Obviously, this is a key tool in reducing the time needed to confirm disputed trades and significantly improves straight-through processing.

Thirdly, there is still a lack of standardized data in this market although much has been done recently. Both spread quotes and reference data need to be improved. An example of data shortage is the poor coverage of names outside Europe and North America, where bid/ask levels are missing and intra-day quotes are needed for trading.

In general, the pricing information for credit default swaps can be obtained from many different locations such as prime brokers, BloombergTM and MarkitTM. The prime broker data could be used for real-time trading, while MarkitTM is still mostly used for end-of-day mark-to-market. Regardless of source, the fact remains that readily available, near real-time credit data for a wide variety of issuers is not to be found. Whereas the equity markets have reached a level of maturity where liquid options markets exist for hundreds of issuers worldwide (not to mention the real-time quotes available for many thousands of equities worldwide), such timely and comprehensive data seem a long way off in the credit markets

As an example, a better quote on the volatility of a call on a firm's future assets (i.e., equity options) can be obtained compared to the probability of default for a firm (i.e., CDS premiums). This poses substantial challenges to traders, portfolio managers and risk professionals alike. As with other risk management analytics such as value-at-risk, the involved mathematics is seldom the problem. (Indeed, the credit markets have reached some consensus on the pricing of such complicated structures as synthetic CDO tranches reasonably quickly.) Rather, the difficulty in finding, managing, and maintaining credit data creates issues in the calculation and monitoring of a credit portfolio's exposures and risks. In fact, models often attempt to unify equity and credit data, in part to find trading and arbitrage opportunities within a firm's capital structure, and in part to allow the credit markets to utilize equity market data, which is so much more prevalent.

A fourth challenge is the timing of data available. Current vendors tend not to provide real-time data or even intra-day rates for many issuers. Whereas the interest rate swap markets have evolved to the point where reliable real-time rates that are based on dealer quotes are readily available, no such facility exists for credit data at present, save for in-house built data-aggregation tools that vary in quality as much as the institutions that built them. Only when this challenge is met will a true integrated real-time trading and desk-level risk environment be possible. Until that time, intra-day analysis will have to suffice.

Another challenge is the settlement issues that affect the entire credit market, partly due to increased volumes but also disputes about the reference obligations being used. The hedge fund market has also added to the settlement burden by assigning large portions of trades to third parties. In this unwinding process they sometimes obtain a better price compared to closing the trade, but the drawback to the market as a whole is an abundance of unconfirmed credit derivative trades that have been difficult to track because of the non-transparent assignment of trades. The number of outstanding unconfirmed CDS trades has, as previously mentioned, been significantly reduced, however. In 2006, outstanding, unconfirmed CDS trades are no longer considered a major problem, thanks to the rising prevalence of DTCC connections as well as the introduction of the novation protocol. The market is still far from reaching T+0, however.

Lastly, there has yet to occur a series of large-scale defaults in a short timeframe by which the market's real strengths and weaknesses can be assessed. Whereas the equity markets have had multiple crashes and other large-scale moves with which to fine-tune regulations and best practices, the credit markets have yet to experience any event that might introduce systematic risk. Other risks will probably surface in turbulent times.

Credit Trading Desk Challenges—and How to Overcome Them with Technology

There are plenty of hurdles facing participants in the credit derivatives market, but not all would apply to any one player. The challenges faced by a trading desk are different from those faced by a dealer or an individual trader. The common denominator is that many can be overcome with the help of technology.

There are a variety of challenges facing credit traders today. In this chapter, we have opted to focus on a few, but will not attempt to cover all of them. While there certainly are other problems in the credit market, the sheer prevalence of those mentioned in the following makes them impossible to ignore.

A natural starting point when discussing challenges is the basic requirements of any trading system infrastructure.

Basic Building Blocks of a Trading System

A key concern applicable to all systems is time-to-market, that is, the time it takes to implement a system and go live. Toolkit systems often take a long time to implement, making them unattractive to those who need fast time-to-market. On the other hand, a black-box system can be quick to implement but lack the necessary flexibility to adjust to the ever-changing credit landscape. Thus, a trading system should be implemented with the speed of a black-box system, yet have the flexibility of a toolkit.

A basic trading system environment should be based on the following four building blocks:

Ensuring flexible financial contract representation. Straightforward, solid representation of plain vanilla, commoditized, financial instruments is the foundation of any trading system as this is the bread and butter of most trading desks. A concise method for defining forthcoming financial contracts is also a necessity, however. The user should be able independently to define and handle new instruments as they emerge, without waiting for a new release from the system vendor. This can be called a universal contract definition concept. Needless to say, flexibility is of utmost importance here, as it must be possible to accommodate even the most obscure structure invented by the market.

Fostering complete lifecycle management. Every trade has its own lifecycle from inception to settlement. All external activities affecting a trade, such as fixings or call events, must be handled during the trade lifecycle. A system must also be able to process trades automatically between front office and back office, also known as straight-through processing (STP).

Establishing infrastructure and risk management tools for financial attributes. Every trading system needs to warehouse financial market data and provide a risk view against market variables. Each financial attribute should be treated as an independent building block that can be used to assemble risk views by any dimension. This ensures maximum flexibility, as risk figures can be sliced and diced freely according to each user's preferences.

Creating consistent and flexible pricing frameworks. A trading system must be able to price financial contracts for trading and mark-to-market purposes. Financial product innovation has generated a need for more complicated pricing routines. Every financial contract is composed of one or more cash flows, synthetic or otherwise, and every cash flow is contingent. This contingency could either be a call event, a default event, a corporate action or something along those lines. The challenge is to relate pricing frameworks to these contingency effects, where similar pricing issues are handled in the same framework. If a new formula has to be introduced for each instrument type this will quickly make the system difficult to maintain and extend.

Specific Demands and Challenges for a Credit Trading System

While these matters apply to trading systems in general, there are additional issues that a credit trading system must address, or that firms involved in the credit markets must consider. The following issues are the most important ones:

- trade capture;
- trade processing;
- access to market data;
- handling complex datasets;
- pricing framework;
- position keeping and risk management;
- extension capabilities; and
- cross-asset coverage.

Trade Capture—the Constant Introduction of New Credit Products

New credit derivative structures are constantly hitting the market. In the steady stream of new structured credit products, a clear pattern can be detected: as the products emerge, they almost immediately become securitized. They are soon followed by innovation in credit derivatives, after which an index may be introduced. Liquidity increases and the new products are commoditized almost before anyone knows what happened.

An aggressive quest for yields is the primary driver of the steady flow of new products, but more defensive structures such as constant proportion portfolio insurance (CPPI) products are gaining in popularity as well. Technology vendors and trading desks must be able to book, trade, price, and risk-manage these new products with a short time-to-market. To illustrate the demands placed on trading desks, a few new products are discussed in this chapter.

The credit-linked CPPI approach has become popular as a way to create principal-protected, credit-linked notes. CPPI notes use the form of a dynamic asset allocation to protect principal yet provides the potential for upside in returns. In some countries, CPPI-linked contracts have been issued to the retail network. This is an interesting development and a new area for structured credit. The management of these products can be complicated as the portfolio needs rebalancing depending on credit performance. For this reason, the need for a solid technical infrastructure is even more pronounced with these types of products.[1]

The development of credit contracts on the ABS market has opened up the trading of retail credit risk to investors and provided new opportunities. This vast area is particularly interesting as the market is now trading both credit derivatives on individual, asset-backed securities under

---

[1] A CPPI note is basically constructed as a zero-coupon bond paying par at maturity, although other variations exist. This note references a portfolio of credits. In this portfolio, the investor shifts asset allocation between risk-free asset and risky assets over the investment horizon. At any point, the investor should have enough money to buy a risk-free bond that at maturity will pay par. This amount of money is called the "bond floor" and is the part of the contract that is called the insurance. In fact, this amount is not guaranteed (due to gap risk) and thus is no perfect insurance. The difference between the portfolio value and the bond floor is called the "cushion." The cushion is invested in risky assets and this investment will vary over time as the credits change in value (default losses and spread-widening). This cushion is invested using leverage called the "gearing factor." The gearing factor remains constant over time and this fact gives rise to the term "constant proportion." When spreads change or default losses occur, the portfolio needs to be rebalanced according to the bond floor, the cushion and the gearing factor. Because of this, rebalancing the overall portfolio performance is path-dependent (in contrast to a static hedge). Therefore, Monte Carlo simulation is needed to perfectly price these structures.

the "pay-as-you-go" ISDA definition, as well as credit derivatives on the standardized ABX index. Tranches have been traded on these indexes and the development of the credit derivatives market referencing asset-backed securities indexes is very similar to the development of the iTraxx index made up of corporate names.

Other important new products are the credit derivatives on European leveraged loans now traded by market participants other than banks. The development of the leveraged loan market has in general increased, creating a greater interest in trading derivatives on this underlying asset class. The emergence of collateralized loan obligations referencing loan CDS and standardized loan indexes is a natural development step to come.

Streamlined Trade Processing

The ability to easily capture a trade and its instrument-specific nuances (restructuring clauses, etc.) and to have automated processes that send appropriate information to downstream systems is of utmost importance. A streamlined workflow and consequent error reduction saves everyone money in the long run. Hedge fund managers especially benefit from streamlined workflows as they often run a leaner ship than sell-side institutions. A portfolio manager's time is best spent reading balance sheets and analyzing markets as opposed to checking that a trade's restructuring clause has been properly handled at execution.

Any system that does not cater to easy data access leaves itself open to lengthy and expensive interfacing tasks as conditions change.

Automated Access to Market Data

True, available market data remains a challenge. While a trading system infrastructure should be capable of linking to whatever market data provider the client wants, an out-of-the-box interface for both market data and static data such as Reference Entity Data (RED™), standardized indexes and their tranches should exist. It should be possible to upload standard market data in the form of spreads, tranche quotes and recovery rates for all issuers, currencies, seniorities, and restructurings that the system supports. Both of these datasets should be easily accessible within the system.

A more subtle issue to consider is how to manage points along the credit curve where no spread quote exists. A trading environment should interpolate between adjacent existing points automatically.

Handling Complex Datasets

The credit market is, in many cases, similar to the interest rate market, but when it comes to amounts of market data, the credit market is much more complex and vast. Take, for example, spread data that is available for all traded issuers, currencies, seniorities, and restructuring methods. Add to that bid/ask levels and intra-day quotes and you end up with an enormous amount of data to capture. Consider as an example the credit correlation business. If you are a portfolio manager trading index tranches, then maintained, base-correlation structures are needed. There will be one base-correlation curve for each maturity, each series, each version, and each index. The number will easily exceed 30 curves and, while this may not sound too difficult, when more indexes emerge (such as indexes on asset-backed products) and more series are added it will quickly be a large amount of data. It might not be a problem from a sheer memory perspective, but other intricate problems may arise such as mapping correlation curves to trades and consistently changing illiquid correlation curves according to their liquid counterpart.

Keeping and maintaining this data obviously places tough demands on the trading infrastructure. Small trading desks can be engaged in complex credit derivatives trading and could require a trading system to keep this amount of data. The amount of credit data does not pertain to the size of the trading operation but rather to its complexity of the products traded. It is fair to say that many software vendors struggle to cope with large amounts of data. Just keeping the data might be easy; the ability to bundle and unbundle the data and view risk against the "packages" is the real challenge.

Spread Curve Engine: The Lifeblood of Any Credit Trading System

Building and managing an informative credit curve environment takes more than keeping credit spread data in an Excel file and plotting credit curves from publicly available data from sources such as Markit. Administering a credit curve environment is about constructing credit curves for pricing of CDS, bonds, indexes, index tranches, bespoke portfolios and even CDS on asset-backed securities.

Credit spreads need to be managed by issuer, currency, seniority and restructuring. Recovery rates should be explicitly maintained and the time buckets for spreads should be flexible. It should be possible either to follow the CDS roll-date convention or for each user to define them. The spread engine itself should allow the use of either credit default swaps or bonds as the benchmark for calibrating default probabilities. Credit curve data should be stored, edited and displayed in a variety of formats, such as par rates, forward rates, default probabilities, survival probabilities or hazard rates.

A Complete Pricing Framework

Many banks struggle to price a wide range of credit products consistently. A flexible and powerful credit-pricing engine is fundamental as it allows truly consistent valuation across diverse credit instruments, ranging from structured corporate bonds to more advanced default swaps.

While there is no shortage of academic pricing models, it is important to consider the availability and quality of input data, as illustrated in the following.

Sparse Data and Advanced Pricing Models

During the last decade, several contributions to credit derivatives pricing have been proposed in articles and textbooks. Academic research is booming, which has some important consequences. Many of the pricing models clearly illustrate the behavior of credit risk and in many ways are tractable models. A major problem, however, is that they require market data to be calibrated and these data are difficult to find. In a way, the complexity of the models contrasts with the sparseness of available data needed for calibration and pricing. Some quants phrase this as "garbage in, garbage out," referring to the fact that no matter how sophisticated the model is and how well it adheres to real credit risk behavior, its accuracy depends on the quality of the input data. Even though research is good in the long run, the credit market suffers from this phenomenon and the main problem is that market participants may rely too much on these models.

Reduced-form models typically work with risk-neutral default probabilities calibrated from market prices. It is also tempting to take historical default probabilities and plug them into the pricing routine instead of carrying out a calibration. This is not easy as historical default rates and risk-neutral default rates do not represent the same thing. There is a difference in the risk premium as well as liquidity. It is no secret that models built on readily available market data are gaining popularity. One good example of this is the Libor Market Model, which uses liquid standardized caps and swaptions as benchmark volatility data that are observables in the market. At the very outset of model creation, one of course has to assess what assumptions to use to explain the behavior of risk but, more importantly, to base the model on market observables with high quality.

The scarceness of quality data also leads to higher focus on obtaining data from adjacent areas such as the fixed income or the equity market. Some proposed models use equity information to calibrate default probabilities used to price credit derivatives as the data are more readily available. The equity market is, after all, further advanced than the credit market.

For trading system vendors as well as purchasers it is important to be aware of this. The models sought by most credit market players are those that are tractable, pragmatic and standardized. Finding the right models to implement is, therefore, a balancing act for both system vendors as well as trading desks.

Examples of Pricing Challenges

Having discussed the relationship between pricing models and data, there are some specific pricing challenges concerning index and synthetic CDOs that deserve some extra attention.

Correlation dependence is crucial for multi-name referencing instruments, such as tranches or bespoke portfolio trades, valued with copula methods in conjunction with either Monte Carlo simulation or semi-analytic formulas. Correlations used in the market should be easily summoned to use as base, compound or full matrix correlations. It should also be possible to use each of them for different purposes, as each has pros and cons. Base correlations can be used to price a wide variety of portfolio products, including standardized index tranches. For more bespoke portfolios, base correlations can be maintained and calibrated to standard market data using standardized benchmark index tranches. As the base correlations are calibrated from standardized market data (i.e., index tranches), they are typically used to price standardized tranches. First-to-default baskets, on the other hand, are typically priced with a full matrix correlation, especially if the number of issuers in the basket is few.

One important area of development is how best to price off-the-run index tranches and bespoke portfolios where the basket composition is similar to the on-the-run index. A key question is how to price and mark-to-market an off-the-run index tranche. Taking the base correlation curve for the on-the-run tranche might not be feasible as there may have been defaults or a name in the index may change due to liquidity, changing the composition of the index. In this case, many market players adjust the base correlation according to a specified formula to allow the use of a liquid, on-the-run, index-base correlation curve to price older tranches. This adjustment mechanism is substantial and places increasing demands on the trading system needs as more participants in the credit market face this effect.

Several banks and hedge funds trade bespoke portfolios that may be composed of existing indexes or handpicked portfolios to fit an investor's individual needs. Pricing these portfolio trades is complicated as it is difficult to obtain the correct correlation figure. If the portfolio is composed of two or more existing indexes, the corresponding base correlations can be weighted according to the trader's preference. Although far from straightforward, this can be achieved. A trading system must have the ability to map several base correlations to one portfolio and to view sensitivities against these.

As the credit option market is gaining ground, it is likely that more desks will start to trade these products more regularly. A trading system must offer intuitive and powerful tools to build and manage advanced volatility structures to price a variety of credit options, ranging from standard index swaptions to more complex ones. The requirements are similar to those of the interest rate derivatives area, although the credit option market is much less developed and, therefore, the trading system requirements for credit options are less pronounced.

Position Keeping and Risk Management

A trading system should offer fully integrated market and credit risk management across asset classes, in as close to real time as market data allow. Position keeping, including realized and unrealized profit and loss calculations, should be available across asset classes. The system should be able to calculate sensitivities toward all asset classes and find hedge suggestions within and outside the pure credit world.

As mentioned before, any trading systems should calculate sensitivities to market rates. The credit markets, however, require several credit-specific analytics such as credit delta, credit gamma, credit vega, correlation delta, jump-to-default risk, recovery risk, and restructuring risk, some of which have little to no counterpart in the equity or rates markets. Such analytics require that a system natively understands the nuances of credit-specific instruments. The next step is the ability to display and aggregate these figures according to individual preference. Sorting and aggregating analytics by a wide range of attributes, including issuer, rating, sector, country, currency, counterparty, guarantor or any other important attribute, is very important. If these are available as dynamic rather than static reports, they add to the overall value.

While very few trading systems come with a transparent, drill-down functionality allowing the trader to view graphically the calculation trace and intermediary results, there are some that do. This powerful tool makes it easier to find direct errors or unexplained inconsistencies.

Effortless Extension and Customization

Markets evolve faster than systems vendors can keep up with the changes. Hence the extensibility and ability to customize a solution to fit future needs is a key requirement today among banks, hedge funds and other players in the credit market. Very few trading organizations, however, live by this rule and therefore have difficulties adapting their trading environment to new needs. In part, this is due to the rapid pace at which the credit markets have matured, leading to systems' obsolescence at an alarming rate. New products keep hitting the market and new risk measures must continuously be implemented. The ability to swiftly account for this is a key differentiator.

For instance, a trading desk might need to engineer new products by combining elements from core products or specify them from scratch. The importance of being able to extend the data model, customize the deal capture GUI and link proprietary valuation models to cater for a new product cannot be over-emphasized.

A Cross-Asset Infrastructure

Native credit support is critical, but far from the only aspect worth considering. A major competitive advantage can be gained by implementing a single solution across all asset classes for deal capture, pricing, position management, deal processing, and consolidated risk management. The rates, credit, FX, and equity markets are becoming more rather than less connected. As a result, a "siloed" systems approach runs the risk of handcuffing a firm's traders and portfolio managers. With native support for credit derivatives alongside all other asset classes, it is easy to seek opportunities, create exotic products and hedge away risk across markets.

As an illustration, consider the convergence of the equity and credit markets as described as follows.

The Convergence of the Equity and Credit Markets

Cross-asset trading is not a new phenomenon. Traders have built hybrid products for decades, mixing, for example, FX risks with interest rate exposures or equity components. Since around 2002, more and more of them have also become acutely aware of the need to manage those risks separately and specifically. It is not surprising that the markets have also brought credit and equity components together in products such as convertible bonds and equity default swaps. The tight link between the credit and fixed-income markets is less subtle, as traders have been trading asset swaps especially in the eurozone. In retrospect, the early credit derivatives market was actually developed from the fixed-income market, where bond and floating rate note (FRN) spreads were used to price credit default swaps.

Whenever asset classes are bridged in a hybrid product or in one portfolio, different pricing models tend to come together. As long as the risks are easily deconstructed, this does not cause a great challenge. FX optionality in a FRN can easily be laid off in the FX option markets. The pricing of the FX, interest rate and credit components can easily be separated and therefore the hybrid can easily be managed.

The emergence of credit derivatives has, however, raised some new questions in this respect. The questions arise from the similarity of the risks traded with those traded in the equity markets. Credit spreads mainly reflect expectations on the likelihood of the obligor defaulting on its commitments. The stock price of the same obligor reflects expectations of future dividend streams, earnings and growth of shareholder's equity. Healthy future dividends often occur only when a company's overall health indicates a reduced risk of default. As one would expect, a negative correlation exists between share price and credit spread.

The similarities between the two asset classes could make an outsider believe that there should be strong similarities in the models used to price risks in the two asset classes. Nothing seems to be further from the truth, nor do the models typically used refer to the other risk type. It is surprising that the pricing models tend to be different for different asset classes. Considering single-name risks, discounted expected cash flows, based on some fundamental analysis, are standard in the equity markets. Reduced-form models, based on market spreads, are the name of the game in the credit markets.

Doing so, however, comes with a set of challenges. First, the typical, reduced-form model and the firm-value model, (such as the CreditGrades™ model) point to different asset classes. Depending on which model a trader chooses to value his trades, they will show sensitivities either to the stock price or the credit spread. Even if a trader is not faced with two sets of sensitivities across his portfolio, aggregating them to give total exposure for the book is not straightforward. It requires bringing them onto the same denominator.

A second trading challenge is price-related. Two models, with different characteristics and different input parameters, lead to different prices for the same risk. The scale of the difference implies that the equity and credit markets have significantly different opinions about the price over a certain period.

How can a trader make use of this information about such a discrepancy? Arbitraging the market is technically only possible if you are guaranteed default. At the point of default, the credit and equity markets have to come together. Before that point, however, there is no guarantee of price convergence between the two markets in the same legal entity.

Herein lies the third challenge. In order to be able to benefit from the information, the trader must have access to the information. In practice, this is not always as obvious as that may sound. Traders typically use pricing tools that have either been written specifically for them by in-house developers or built by a third-party software vendor. How well they are suited to provide this type of value to the trader depends on the setup to price and calibrate using both models, mapping flexibility to deal with more than one model and workflow structured to simulate under either model.

Clearly, the linking of different asset classes via pricing models and hybrid products creates some challenges and, potentially, confusion with some market players. Those people who see the value offered by this phenomenon, however, and can use it to their benefit stand to gain significantly. The technology infrastructure will be a key contributing factor behind success or failure.

The Challenges—a Summary

In this chapter, we elected to highlight two separate categories of problems: general challenges and trading desk-related challenges. The general challenges affect the majority of the participants in the credit derivatives space. The credit market's ability to expand will be hampered until these challenges have been remedied:

- a limited user base;
- not yet traded electronically on exchanges;
- a lack of standardized data;
- a lack of real-time or even intra-day data;

- settlement issues—a challenge that the market has now remedied to some extent; and
- there has yet to occur a series of large-scale defaults to test the market.

Other challenges are specific to credit trading desks and their technology. In our experience, it is common to encounter certain obstacles, certainly when entering the credit derivatives market or when being a part of it. It is possible to avoid the most common pitfalls by introducing a solid structure in the following areas of a trading system:

- trade capture;
- trade processing;
- access to market data;
- representation of financial data;
- pricing framework;
- position keeping and risk management;
- extension capabilities; and
- cross-asset coverage.

Authors Biography

About the Editor

Dennis Cox is CEO of Risk Reward Limited, a strategy and risk consultancy for the financial services industry, as well as being a CEO or director of a number of other companies. He was formerly Director, Risk Management, at HSBC Operational Risk Consultancy and Director, Risk Management at Prudential Portfolio Managers Limited, having spent 12 years in practice with Arthur Young and BDO Binder Hamlyn. A fellow of the Institute of Chartered Accountants in England and Wales (ICAEW) and also of the Chartered Securities and Investments Institute (CISI), among a range of external interests, he was a Council member of the ICAEW, together with being Chairman of the Risk Forum for the CISI. Dennis also represented the public interest in the regulation of the Institute of Actuaries for financial service matters.

About the Contributors

Asif Ahmed was Director in the ALM Group at Citigroup. He was advising Citigroup's clients on risk management since 1999. His breadth of experience ranges from structuring optimal yield-enhancing strategies for the securities portfolio to recommending optimal financing structure for the balance sheet, all within the relevant IFRS and regulatory constraints. Since 2003, Asif has been focusing on ALM issues for banks and corporate pension funds. Prior to working for structured products at Citigroup, Asif was working in derivatives sales for Bear Stearns. Asif trained as a chartered accountant, has an MBA from London Business School and a BSc in Management Science from London School of Economics.

Roger Bach, after graduating from Leeds University, spent 10 years at Ernst & Young, where he was a Senior Manager in the Financial Services Group. He then joined the Pershing division of DLJ where he spent the next 13 years as Managing Director and Chief Administrative Officer, responsible for finance, compliance and risk. He then became the CEO at Henyep Investment (UK) Limited, a commodities and foreign exchange broker in London. .

David Blackmore, ACIB, MSI, and MIMgt, joined MHA in 2005 as a senior executive, following a 34-year career in banking in the City of London, including 18 with HSBC (Midland Bank). He has also held a number of high profile MLRO and compliance officer roles with foreign bank subsidiaries and branches operating in the UK. David is an Associate of the Institute of Internal Auditors—UK, and has served for several years on their banking and finance special interest group. He holds a BA Politics degree from Leicester University.

David Breden was Managing Director of HSBC Operational Risk Consultancy and the architect of OpRisk Modeller, a scenario-based commercial risk mapping tool developed by HSBC to meet the needs of the Basel II AMA quantification requirements. Previously he worked for NatWest for over 20 years in both England and Spain and developed and implemented an operational risk management system for the Spanish retail network. He has been involved in operational risk management since 1995 and is a Fellow of the Institute of Operational Risk.

Aaron Brown was an Executive Director in risk methodology at Morgan Stanley and the author of *The Poker Face of Wall Street* (Wiley 2006). He has worked on Wall Street for 25 years as a quant, trader, portfolio manager, head of mortgage securities and risk manager. He holds degrees in Applied Mathematics (Harvard) and Finance and Statistics (University of Chicago). He is a regular columnist for *Wilmott* quantitative finance magazine, serves on the editorial board of the Global Association of Risk Professionals and has been elected to the National Book Critics Circle.

Stuart Burns was Head of Economic Capital and Model Risk Management at Standard Chartered Bank. He is responsible for overseeing risk management in over 50 countries in the Asia Pacific Region, South Asia, the Middle East, Africa, the UK, and the Americas. His main responsibilities include coordination of stress testing across portfolios and risk types, as well as leading the group's model validation team. Stuart joined Standard Chartered in November 2004 from RBS Financial Markets, where he was responsible for developing the credit models for Basel II.

Angela Caldara formerly working in the finance area of VTB Bank Europe plc, involved in the project regarding the implementation of the new Midas Plus software with particular emphasis on product accounting and all aspects of reporting requirements. She previously worked for Unicredito Italiano in the finance area, where her responsibilities included all aspects of taxation. She was involved also in project management: for example, Y2K and the introduction of the euro. Angela previously worked for Lloyd's of London, where her responsibilities included the registration of Lloyd's brokers when Lloyd's of London was self-regulated. She is a chartered accountant, a chartered secretary and a member of the Chartered Insurance Institute.

Craig Cohon has worked with a dozen Fortune 100 companies. Prior to this, Craig had a 14-year executive-level career at The Coca-Cola Company. He was the first employee to live in Russia and started their operations in the Soviet Union in 1990 and finished his first career by serving as Deputy Division President for the Northwest Europe Division, a US$2bn operating unit. In 1993, he received an Honorary Doctorate of Economics from Moscow International University. In 2000, the World Economic Forum named him "A Global Leader for Tomorrow." In 2003, he was asked by the UN to participate in a high-level commission on International Development. He has been featured in the *FT*, *News Night*, the *New Statesman*, *National Post* in Canada and the *Wall Street Journal*. You can reach him at craig@craigcohon.com

Jennifer Courant was the Managing Director and Head of Credit Risk Model Development of Citigroup Risk Architecture. She has responsibility for the lifecycle development of the credit risk models used by Citigroup to generate probability of default estimates for its wholesale customers, including the analytical framework, systems architecture and model support for 3,000 global users. Jennifer joined Citigroup in 1997 in New York. Prior to joining Citigroup, Jennifer was a real estate economist at AEW Capital Management, Boston, MA. She has a BS in Economics from Saint Vincent College and has completed coursework toward a PhD in Economics at Boston College.

Errol Danziger, BA, LLB, LLM, is the Principal of Danziger Structured Finance, which researches, develops and markets innovative structured financial solutions for investment banks, major corporates and high networth individuals. He is a barrister and a former Big Four tax partner, and he publishes widely and lectures to professionals and executives on tax, derivatives, and financial structuring and planning.

Thomas Day was Senior Vice President of Product and Engineering for SunGard's BancWare business unit, responsible for product management, financial engineering, direction and strategy for the company's risk management solutions. At BancWare since 2005, Thomas has over 15 years of banking experience, including seven with the Federal Reserve System. Prior to joining SunGard, Thomas was Senior Vice President of Risk and Strategy at Amsouth Bancorporation. He has worked for the Office of the Comptroller of the Currency, SouthTrust Bank and Barnett Bank, and as a coordinator for national level market and liquidity risk supervision for the Federal Reserve Board of Governors.

Pontus Eriksson has worked in several positions within SunGard over the past eight years including development, project management, and product management. He is currently global product manager for credit and interest rates at SunGard FRONT ARENA. Pontus has a Masters in Engineering Physics from the Royal Institute of Technology in Stockholm.

Ákos *Felső* **vályi** was a Managing Director at Citigroup. He is heading an area dedicated to analyzing and modeling the global credit losses at Citigroup. He joined Citigroup in 1987, working in the Credit Card Division and building statistical models for direct marketing. He has been in risk management since 1991 in various capacities. He holds an MS in Applied Mathematics from Eötvös Loránd University, Hungary.

Bryce Ferguson was a Managing Director and Head of the Credit Risk Analytics Unit of Citigroup Risk Architecture. She is responsible for

rating policies and approval of rating processes, calculation of loss-given default and exposure at default, and development of statistical models used to assign risk ratings, provide early warnings and derive credit risk capital. These responsibilities cover Citigroup's wholesale credit portfolio. Bryce joined Citibank in 1977 as an economist and covered the restructurings of sovereign and private sector debt of several major Latin American countries. During the late 1980s and 1990s,
Bryce worked as a consultant to various businesses in Citicorp, including the Office of the Chairman. Bryce has a BA in History/Economics from Grinnell College and completed coursework toward a PhD in International Finance and Trade at New York University.

Rod Hardcastle was Head of Credit Risk Regulation in the Wholesale and International Banking Division of LloydsTSB Bank plc. Over the course of a 17-year career as banker and banking consultant, he has worked in New Zealand, Canada, the United States, Continental Europe, and the UK for a variety of banks in roles spanning retail and wholesale banking, and covering strategy, operations, relationship management and, particularly, credit risk and Basel II. Rod holds a Bachelor of Business Studies (Banking and Finance) and a Postgraduate Diploma in Banking from Massey University, New Zealand and an MBA from the Cranfield University School of Management, Cranfield, UK.

Markus Krebsz is a freelance management consultant. He is currently acting as Subject Matter Expert for Rating Agency and Securitisation, focusing on covered bonds, MBS, ABS, synthetic structures, Basel II and regulatory reporting. At the time of writing his chapter for the book, he worked in Fitch Ratings' corporate and infrastructure securitisation team. Prior to joining Fitch in 2004, Markus worked for over 10 years for German banks in retail and corporate banking, project management, software development and risk management. He is a member (MSI) of the Securities and Investment Institute, of the Professional Risk Managers' International Association (PRMIA) and of the Chartered Institute of Bankers.

Dilip Krishna was Director of the Enterprise Risk Management practice (Americas) at NCR Teradata. He held the role of Chief Architect of the Basel II program at a major Canadian bank and has had several implementations of securities trading solutions and Internet-based trading platforms. He has also consulted on risk management with several North American financial corporations. Dilip has authored numerous articles on risk management and implementations and has also spoken on the topic in diverse settings. He holds CFA and FRM designations as well as degrees from the Ohio State University and the Indian Institute of Technology.

Michael Mainelli leads Z/Yen, the City of London's leading think-tank which counts every global investment bank as a client. Michael started as a research scientist, then became a partner in a leading accountancy firm directing consultancy work. He is a qualified accountant and computer specialist with a Government degree from Harvard, mathematics and engineering at Trinity College Dublin and a PhD from the London School of Economics. Michael is Mercers' School Memorial Professor of Commerce at Gresham College. Michael advises and writes widely on compliance, risk and regulation. Michael's humorous risk/reward management novel, *Clean Business Cuisine: Now and Z/Yen*, was published in 2000.

Frank H. Moxon, CF, FSI, FIMM, FEI, has over 17 years' experience as a corporate financier. Formerly head of corporate finance at Williams de Broî, he now heads up the natural resources team at Evolution Securities. To date he has successfully completed more than 115 corporate finance transactions raising over US$1.3bn in new funds. Among other things, he is a Fellow of the Securities and Investment Institute, Chairman of its Corporate Finance Forum and a Fellow of the Energy Institute.

Ralph Nash joined Barclays in November 2006 as the Operational Risk Director in Business Banking Risk. Prior to this, Ralph was the Director of Group Operational Risk at AXA UK and the Head of Group Enterprise Risk Methodology and Policy at RBS. He also has earned experience at the Bank for International Settlements, where he worked on the operational risk components of Basel II, the Bank of England and the House of Commons. Ralph holds an MA in Geography from Cambridge University.

Krishnan Ramadurai was a managing director in Fitch Ratings' Financial Institutions department, where he is responsible for special projects for Europe, the Middle East, and Africa. His duties include analyzing, monitoring, and publishing research on several subjects spanning the new Basel II framework, credit derivatives, IFRS, and operational risk. Before joining Fitch in 2001, Krishnan worked for HSBC for 12 years. He held a variety of jobs in operations, corporate banking, credit risk and training in India, the Middle East and the UK. A graduate from Xaviers Institute of Management, India, Krishnan holds an Economics Masters from Madras Christian College University.

Diccon Smeeton was currently responsible for European Hedge Fund Risk at ABN AMRO in London. Following a career as a hotel manager in East Africa, he returned to the UK and spent some years employed as a Counterparty Credit Analyst at Kleinwort Benson in London, prior to moving to Lehman Brothers, as a Hedge Fund Credit Analyst. He then moved to Deutsche Bank, where he spent time in both the London and New York offices, specializing in Hedge Fund Risk. He joined ABN AMRO in 2004.

Anthony Smith, FCII, APFS, FCoI, Chartered Insurance Practitioner, is a Director of AJS Consultancy Services providing compliance consulting to product providers and retail intermediaries. He is the organizer of the Annual European Financial Directives Conference and regular conference speaker. Anthony is a board member of the Association of Professional Compliance Consultants (APCC), a trade body representing over 100 consultancy firms with the explicit purpose of raising standards in compliance consultancy. He has worked in financial services since 1989 as a compliance manager of financial promotions and complaints handling and Pensions Review Manager for the only large network not to be fined by PIA for pensions review failures.

Nina Sodha currently works as a London-based Vice President within the Strategy, Planning and Analysis team of a major international investment bank. Her role primarily covers offshoring within the research and finance functions, assisting existing and new migrations to India. Prior to this, she worked at Abbey as a Strategy Manager and worked on corporate-wide projects such as offshoring, product development and business strategy. Her career started at PricewaterhouseCoopers within financial services audit followed by consulting. She has written numerous articles on offshoring within industry journals and publications. She has also coordinated a report for the ICAEW in 2004 on outsourcing and offshoring and organized a conference on the same topic featuring prominent speakers. Nina has a BSc in Economics from LSE and an MBA. She is also a qualified Chartered Accountant and Certified Management Consultant.

Paul Sweeting graduated from the University of Bristol with a degree in Economics before qualifying as a Fellow of the Institute of Actuaries and subsequently gaining a master's degree in Actuarial Science. Paul has since held a number of roles in both consultancy and fund management, and was a Director at Fidelity Investments, based in its Portfolio Strategies Group. Here, he designs a variety of innovative solutions for institutional and retail investors. Paul is also a CFA charterholder, a regular contributor to the pensions and investment press, and has produced a number of papers on pensions and investment topics.

Gary van Vuuren is a Senior Director in the Financial Institutions Special Projects Group of Fitch Ratings. As a quantitative analyst he holds responsibility for overseeing quantitative aspects of projects which require mathematical or statistical input. Gary began his career in nuclear physics at South Africa's Atomic Energy Corporation before moving on to market risk at ABSA Bank, Johannesburg, Old Mutual Asset Managers in Cape Town and Standard Bank in London. He was head of the Quantitative Analysis Group at Ernst & Young before he moved to Fitch in 2006. He is a GARP-accredited Financial Risk Manager.

Index

OTHER TITLES IN OUR FINANCE AND FINANCIAL MANAGEMENT COLLECTION

John A. Doukas, Old Dominion University, Editor

- *Rethinking Risk Management: Critically Examining Old Ideas and New Concepts* by Rick Nason
- *Towards a Safer World of Banking: Bank Regulation After the Subprime Crisis* by T.T. Ram Mohan
- *Escape from the Central Bank Trap: How to Escape From the $20 Trillion Monetary Expansion Unharmed* by Daniel Lacalle
- *Tips & Tricks for Excel-Based Financial Modeling: A Must for Engineers & Financial Analysts, Volume I* by M. A. Mian
- *Tips & Tricks for Excel-Based Financial Modeling: A Must for Engineers & Financial Analysts, Volume II* by M. A. Mian
- *The Anti-Bubbles: Opportunities Heading into Lehman Squared and Gold's Perfect Storm* by Diego Parrilla
- *Risk and Win!: A Simple Guide to Managing Risks in Small and Medium-Sized Organizations* by John Harvey Murray
- *Essentials of Enterprise Risk Management: Practical Concepts of ERM for General Managers* by Rick Nason and Leslie Fleming

Announcing the Business Expert Press Digital Library

Concise e-books business students need for classroom and research

This book can also be purchased in an e-book collection by your library as

- a one-time purchase,
- that is owned forever,
- allows for simultaneous readers,
- has no restrictions on printing, and
- can be downloaded as PDFs from within the library community.

Our digital library collections are a great solution to beat the rising cost of textbooks. E-books can be loaded into their course management systems or onto students' e-book readers.
The **Business Expert Press** digital libraries are very affordable, with no obligation to buy in future years. For more information, please visit **www.businessexpertpress.com/librarians**. To set up a trial in the United States, please email **sales@businessexpertpress.com**.

www.ingramcontent.com/pod-product-compliance
Lightning Source LLC
Chambersburg PA
CBHW071627200326
41519CB00012BA/2195